Therapeutic Communities in Corrections

Therapeutic Communities in Corrections

Edited by

Hans Toch

Foreword by
Allen Breed

PRAEGER SPECIAL STUDIES • PRAEGER SCIENTIFIC

Library of Congress Cataloging in Publication Data

Main entry under title:

Therapeutic communities in corrections.

   Includes index.
   1. Prisoners--Psychiatric care. 2. Therapeutic
community. I. Toch, Hans.
RC451.4.P68T43   362.2   80-12158
ISBN 0-03-052746-5
ISBN 0-03-052741-4 (pbk.)

Published in 1980 by Praeger Publishers
CBS Educational and Professional Publishing
A Division of CBS, Inc.
521 Fifth Avenue, New York, New York 10017 U.S.A.

© 1980 by Praeger Publishers

0123456789   038   987654321

Printed in the United States of America

FOR MAX AND FRITZ,
from the rest of us

Attending to what another person tells us and being able to hear what is in his heart as well as on his lips is an exceptional skill, growing rarer by the day . . . the same goes for addressing another person and being able to tell him—frankly, simply, and without humiliating him—what we think of his predicament and of his options to extricate himself from it. It was a tragic folly in the past to try to confine this sort of human helpfulness with the bounds of accredited creeds, and to restrict the right to dispense it to clerics; and it is a tragic folly now to try to confine it within the bounds of accredited cures, and to restrict the right to dispense it to clinicians.

Thomas S. Szasz

FOREWORD

My interest in the therapeutic community began early in my own correctional career. As a novice to corrections I was initiated into the soul and the substance of institutional life—a contained environment within which the keeper and the kept find themselves dealing with the same problems and issues, from surprisingly similar perspectives. Unfortunately, the approaches of these segments to their shared fate are frequently in opposition, because their respective systems for exercising power do not touch, or encourage coexistence.

No one can work in an institution—correctional or otherwise—without sensing the spontaneous and informal organization of inmates which develops to deal with the power of their opposite numbers in the formal organization, i.e., guards, social workers, doctors, administrators, teachers and the like. The critical issue becomes, How can those who are the keepers use these natural forces and organize them in ways that will help to create a healthy, humane, fair and just living experience for inmates? Obviously, the answer is participation—participation by both inmates and staff in the development of a sense of community and collective common good.

Experience teaches us that determined people of good will can organize themselves into small social networks, communes, neighborhoods, etc. to do things cooperatively. It is the quality of that cooperative effort and partici- pative opportunity that forms the basis of what has come to be known as the therapeutic community. Whether the setting is a hospital, factory or correctional institution, the needs and general processes are basically the same.

I am deeply grateful to the persons who have contributed to this publication. They have, in their collective effort, put into writing and on record the essence and the structure of a way for each of us to work creatively with one another, regardless of our status or position in life. It is with considerable pride that NIC helped, along with others, to stage the encounter that culminated in this book.

Practioneers and laypersons will find the work interesting and useful in understanding one of the most significant practices made available to the medical and helping professions this century.

Allen Breed

PREFACE

This book is unusual enough to call for a brief explanation, especially since no one—least of all, I—has shaped or created these pages. The project grew sequentially, through a set of stages. To describe the book is to relate its history.

If this history started somewhere, it was over a plate of pastrami shared with Stephen Chinlund, who chairs New York's Correction Commission. Chairman Chinlund had over time shaped an idea for prison reform (the Network Project, described in Chapter 7) and was about to implement it. Since this process involved creating therapeutic communities in several prisons, we talked of the benefit of gaining input from Maxwell Jones, the father of the therapeutic community (TC) concept. From this notion it was an inviting step to consider polling a second seminal thinker (Fritz Redl) and talking with pioneers known for their application of Jones's concept to correctional settings (Dennie Briggs, Elliott Barker, Doug Grant).

One trouble—and one virtue—of thinking big is that it leads to thinking bigger. In this case, the roster of our hypothetical consultants expanded to include a key representative of the federal prison system (Bob Levinson), prominent state officials (Jack Birnbaum, Edward Elwin, Marguerite Saunders, and Jack Wright), executives from a therapeutic community in New York (Mitchell Rosenthal and George DeLeon), staff members associated with the incipient New York program (Cheryl Clark and John Devlin), and a Department of Justice observer (Ann Schmidt).

For me this ideal conclave would have remained a dream. But Chinlund is not a dreamer, and neither is the director of the National Institute of Corrections (NIC), Allen Breed. Thanks to a grant from the NIC, and to the effort of the Corrections commission staff, our dream became a two-day conference on therapeutic communities in corrections, at the Institute of Man and Sciences in Rensselaerville in December 1978.

The Rensselaerville workshop dealt with implementation details of the Network Program, but most of the talk revolved around themes related to the TC concept and issues related to the running of therapeutic communities in prisons. It seemed to us that this sort of content would be of interest to a larger audience, if we could capture and preserve the dialogue and communicate it in a lively fashion.

Thus was born this monograph—or rather, the idea for Part 3 of this monograph. The rest (Parts 1 and 2) evolved as an effort to build a foundation for the topic, through systematic statements about issues dealt with at our conference. To broaden further the base of expertise that underlies this thinking, we not only included chapters by our principal participants (Barker, Briggs, Chinlund, Grant, Jones, and Levinson), but added two contributions by the creators of therapeutic community enterprises whose special features struck us as important. One of these contributions is by Robert Scott and describes a program run with minimal resources in state institutions; another chapter is by Peter Scharf and details a theory-based inmate-and-staff-run community created in a women's prison. (There are more experiences we could have included; among these are the work of Robert Carkhuff and Martin Groder, which we shall refer to later). In the appendix of this book we provide a consumer view, the testimony of a prison superintendent. Higher-level consumers are featured elsewhere in this volume.

I have listed some debts to Allen Breed and to Stephen Chinlund, who are mainly responsible for this book. Chinlund's informal role was that of my editorial conscience; my other supervisor was Robert Levinson, who has a penchant for language. My erstwhile secretary Barbara Meilinger transcribed the conference; no one else could have done it. Doug Grant helped me think, and Max and Fritz inspired us to think harder.

CONTENTS

PART I

THEORETICAL ISSUES

THE THERAPEUTIC COMMUNITY AS COMMUNITY

Hans Toch

The term "therapeutic community" is not self-defining. The word "therapeutic" comes from the Greek word "theraps," which means "attendant," and is used to describe the ministrations of physicians. "Community" is more helpful: the Latin root, according to Webster, connotes a "unified body of individuals." Social science usage of "community" is of distinguished vintage, and resembles the dictionary definition because it is inherited from the German translation (Gemeinschaft); the concept highlights the grouping of committed members who are intimately acquainted with each other and warmly share common interests.

In our next chapter, Fritz Redl addresses the difficulties one runs into in adopting the word "therapeutic." We shall see that these problems derive only partly from the narrow, disease-related, ancestry of the term, and are more powerfully related to the no-holds-barred connotations we inherit when we abandon the "theraps" of the Greeks and vest our "therapeutic" impact in the person's social environment, as we do in therapeutic communities.

Before we turn to an examination of the TC process (in Chapter 3), we must round out our concept by viewing the word "community" in the context in which we use it.

COMMUNITY, THE NOT-TO-BE-RECAPTURED PAST

"Community" (Gemeinschaft), as opposed to "the community" (Gesellschaft), brings up memories suffused with simplicity and nostalgia. Sociologists considering contemporary urban life see a morass of problems produced by forces beyond the control of community members; they see a world filled with hierarchical bureaucracies that nominally exist to perform "functions" such as educating people and keeping them in line, but which get in each other's way, become unresponsive to their clients, and are pawns of larger-world pressures and/or selfish elites. "The community" summarizes the impersonal social order into which modernization has thrown us, which separates and alienates us from ourselves and each other. "The community" is a subject social scientists continuously deplore while they assiduously study and classify it.

By contrast, "community" is the social science version of the ghost of Christmas past. It is the (largely mythical) form of organization appropriate to an idealized preindustrial age, in which people's needs were modest enough that they could satisfy them through friendly barter; in which services could be exchanged informally and cooperatively; a world in which we knew and loved each other, and shared (rather than pretended to share) the same values.[1]

For many sociologists, "the community" is not only the locus of social problems—of poverty, crime, and mental disorders—it is the cause or breeding ground of these problems. The proliferation of impersonal modern institutions and of uprooted and reshuffled groups creates "social disorganization" and "normlessness" that makes it difficult to pursue goals, and turns fringe citizens inevitably to suicide, drugs, violence, psychosis, divorce, stealing, rioting, and discriminating against each other. Just as inevitably, our institutional responses to such social problems become ritualized, inhumane, unfeeling, and self-perpetuating, and cause more problems than they solve.

An enticing hypothetical answer involves reversing the clock of evolution to the bucolic village, the communitarian tribe, the extended family we stubbornly and fondly imagine must have existed. On a large scale, this nostalgic prescription is difficult to advance, because, undoing the industrial revolution would depopulate assembly lines, leaving us without amenities. Further, we suspect that "restored" communities would invariably reinvent divisions.of labor, government, police forces, armies, schools, hospitals and jails, social disorganization, normlessness, alienation, discrimination, war, suicide, crime, and mental disorders.

No such criticisms can be leveled at localized or partial creations of community. No matter what anyone argues in the abstract, history teaches us that determined groups of people *can* organize a commune or a neighborhood, run a family network or a cooperative nursery, humanize a factory, democratize a school, and turn a hospital ward into a "therapeutic community."

SKEPTICAL DENIALS AND MESSIANIC CLAIMS

Persons who restore community in a localized or partial fashion disprove (by exception) the dehumanizing impact of their host institutions or organizations. For this reason, some people define away community experiments when they occur in settings such as factories, schools, slums, and mental hospitals. Community developers are "utopians," or they have been "duped"; reform becomes "cosmetic"; client participation is a "sham," and collaboration "sweeps conflicts under the rug." Where reform occurs in closed institutions, the pitch of its critics becomes strident. Prisons "by their nature" are dehumanizing. A prison reformer is *at best* a fool. At worst, he serves the oppressor by engendering pliability in the oppressed.

The same social diagnosis leads community builders to adopt messianic self-images, to see themselves as turners of tides. A cooperative farm, progressive classroom, democratized ward, or peer-run drug program becomes the outpost of salvation and the harbinger of a revolution essential for the survival of the race. Schools destroy youth; hospitals promote poisons; cities kill the spirit; and prisons (needless to say) are concentration camps; only the elect community members, and their successors, are saved from the destructive fate that engulfs the rest of us.

This view is dangerous, because it exaggerates the difference between "community" and "the community" and hardens the borders between the two, thus making transitional movement difficult. The view glorifies the process of community building. In this way it prevents self-appraisal and—' in the long run—promotes disillusionment. Community building carries risks and requires delicacy or orchestration; intimacy *does* breed contempt; trust creates vulnerability; openness invades privacy; group sanction is painful; lack of structure is anarchy; contempt for expertise glorifies ignorance. There are virtues to community, but there are difficulties too, and these must be recognized to be neutralized.

COMPONENTS OF COMMUNITY

It is possibly a paradox, but the assets of community are *simultaneously* its liabilities.[2] This holds not only for differences between extreme and moderate features (the Svengali versus the charismatic leader, democracy-turned-anarchy, the norm that enslaves) but also for identical events, because community members differ in their perceptions of the community's features and in their vulnerabilities to their impact. One person's informality may become another's chaos; the beliefs of one may be another's dogma; and one member's samaritan may be another's busybody.

There is no consensus about what the essential features of the stripped-down community are—as opposed to the optional features of deluxe communities. If we extrapolate from the standard sociological image, a spare-parts inventory of community components could comprise:

1. Face-to-faceness.   While communities are larger than small groups, they are small enough that no one is a stranger to anyone else. This means

that community members will recognize each other and will know a fair amount about each other. It does *not* mean that intimacy must be homogeneously spread over the group; a largish community can expect ingroups and outgroups, cliques and friendship patterns—some members will be more "face to face" than others.

2. Immediacy. A community is a microcosm—it is a small, salient world. The members of a community are aware of and conversant with what happens inside it, but only remotely aware of, or concerned with, what happens outside it. The same point holds for behavior. Community members tend to do anything that matters to them *within* the community, and members of some communities never set foot in the outside world.

3. Relatedness & 4. Commitment. Relatedness and commitment are phenomena that can be placed together under the heading "personal investments." These two are psychological cousins, because both link the member to the community. In a true community, all members function as "significant others" for each other, and each member is attached to the community—meaning that each member cares about his or her membership. The closeness of ties among community members creates interdependence and makes acceptance and rejection powerful influences. The member's investment in the community as a whole gives each member a stake to defend, which makes him or her an unpaid salesperson.

5. Shared assets. The community shares ownership of tangible or intangible commodities that "belong" to everyone, in the sense that everyone uses them or can "draw" on them. Such assets can be in the form of space (the "common" of the village or "common room" of the institution), larders of necessities, or human services or resources. Communitarianism is sometimes extreme (including, for example, sex) and can define the community for the outsider, who views communities from a competitive free-enterprise perspective.

6. Collaborative activity. Some communities are self-sufficient. In most communities, members are responsible for various maintenance tasks, including menial and survival-related work. Such labor is shared among subgroups of community members, who function collaboratively and whose output entitles them to the product of other members' labor. These group relationships are not just economic, but involve deliberations, decisions, conflict, and arbitration. In every case, work in a community has a component of group dynamics.

7. Self-governance. Even where communities have relatively formalized structures, they feature rank-and-file participation (such as town halls or community meetings) that deals with decisions affecting the community. Such decisions not only relate to goals or policies for the group as a whole, but include decisions determining the fate of individual members, whose careers tend to be discussed in personalized terms. Every member has a say

in what happens to the community, and the community has a say in what happens to members. There is thus no dichotomy between state and citizen.

8. A microculture. Every community evolves shared assumptions, beliefs, and premises; behavioral goals, standards, and values; and shorthand forms of communication (ways of talking or special language). This culture (including truths that are self-evident, judgments of good or bad, customs, and communication patterns) is usually *unselfconscious* though some of it is explicit and may even be incorporated into written documents. The culture is an evolving product, and only some of its features are predetermined by the founders of the community or by the screening process for new members.

9. Solidarity. In a community, one member's business is every member's business, and there is no demarcation between public and private. One reason for this feature is that the welfare of communities depends on the deportment of members, who can strengthen or attenuate the culture. Another reason is that interpersonal ties make members sensitive to each other's needs, and give them a feeling of responsibility for each other's problems. The adage "Ask not for whom the bell tolls" has little significance where the referent is humanity as a whole, but gains meaning in community settings.

10. Egalitarianism. Where status is assigned a role in the community, status does not determine the way members relate to each other. Membership takes precedence over status, face-to-faceness supercedes formality, structure subserves function. A community uses ceremony, but does not stand on it.

The components I have listed are not exhaustive, nor are they uniformly applicable. They are in practice apt to overlap, and one needs to decide which components are to carry the highest priority. But these components do help us define the concept "community," generally without the modifier "therapeutic community" to distract us.

THE MINISTERING CASTE

Hypothetically, a therapeutic community could consist of therapy clients, with an outside "theraps" who worked with members individually or in groups. Such an arrangement has sometimes been presupposed in "community mental health" or "social psychiatry" models. It has not been popular. Communities do not take to helpful "outsiders"; they have limited trust in them and feel inadequately understood by them. Communities also like to "take care of their own" through intracommunity supports. Most crucial, group cultures may incorporate what outsiders view as "symptoms";

at the very least, there is a risk here that an outsider may tamper with the culture while ministering to the psyche.

A compromise formula involves the "insider/outsider" model, in which a group of therapsae has membership in a community for *some* purposes and does not for others. Such is the theory of communitized wards in mental hospitals. Ward residents are defined as community members because (1) they are limited to each other's company, and cannot escape to the "outside"; (2) they have many problems in common, including those of cohabitation, and hence have common interests; (3) they are permitted to make decisions about themselves and to work at tasks; (4) they do a great deal of meeting and talking; (5) they can manage few status distinctions (having no status); (6) they become familiar with each other's personal lives and presumed pathology.

Members of the theraps caste are "outsiders" because they live elsewhere, belong to outside social circles, and get paid. Their "membership" consists of (1) deemphasized intracaste role differences; (2) participation in community activities on a verbal level; (3) the sharing of knowledge about community members, with some willingness to disclose facts about themselves (by no means to the same extent that patients do); (4) involvement in group dynamics; (5) involvement in relationships with other staff members and with ward members; and (6) endorsement of the community culture—particularly elements that are imported by the staff to begin with.

If we accept our spare-parts listing, these are programs that—however worthy they may be—are "therapeutic quasi communities," because they miss some of the ingredients of true community.[3] We suspect that there are also programs that are "quasi-therapeutic communities" or "quasi-therapeutic quasi communities," but this is not our concern. What does matter, besides any compromises or cut corners we conclude exist in community-building, is that such communities are *synthetic*, meaning that they are artificially created.

Communitized wards are traditional wards democratized. This flies in the face of the romantic premise, which supports spontaneous community arising fruit-fly-fashion in protest against dehumanizing institutions. Such a process has *presumably* occurred in history with the advent of religious sects and some utopian communities—and such is the self-image of some commune residents today. Such, however, is not the sequence we observe when people react against institutions, *nor* when communities are built.

Antiinstitutional responses in hospitals and prisons are most often solitary and defensive. Inmates build immunity against institutional encroachment by insulating themselves emotionally and physically, which protects them not only against pains of institutionalization, but against involvements with each other. Occasional reactions take the form of contracultures, with chips on their shoulders or (more frequently) with a penchant for violence and illegal trafficking. Such groupings make up an "underworld" that resists change-relevant norms.[4]

Communities in real life tend to have "founding fathers" who are extrinsic to the community and who "organize" members by catalyzing the process of community formation. Community building as social science falls under the heading of "organizational development" (OD) or "community development" (CD). While it is arguable that the overall aim of OD and CD is general social reform (neutralizing evils of "the community"), the strategy involves converging aims of social institutions and their memberships rather than undermining societal objectives. A community organized in this fashion—including a "therapeutic community"—is an effort to humanize an institution by making it more responsive to the needs of its membership. In accomplishing this task, community builders help institutions to "reach" people via communities and to realize institutional goals. A therapeutic community ward in a mental hospital is not a revolution against hospitals, but a vehicle to link the patients' needs to more progressive goals of the hospital. The same point holds for the creation of therapeutic communities in prisons.

Our concern in later chapters will be with the way in which progressive correctional goals (resocialization and reintegration) can be accomplished through community building. Our concern in the remainder of this chapter is with the way in which prison communities (therapeutic or quasi-therapeutic) can respond to inmate needs.

THE COMMUNITY AS A STAFF-INMATE OASIS

A basic dictum in social psychology is that inhumane institutions are not only morally indefensible but ineffective. An alienated worker will stay home as frequently as possible and will work slowly and ineffectively. The same holds true for the alienated student, the patient who is therapy-resistant and manifests secondary symptomatology, and the slum inhabitant who lurks sullenly on street corners or turns to drugs and crime.

Prisons are destructive warehouses—not by design, but because people treated as commodities become recalcitrant, and have their less-than-effective personal reactions magnified. This does not mean that inmates become more antisocial, though those whose antisocial traits are dominant may react as caricatures of themselves. Vulnerable inmates become more vulnerable, and sick inmates get sicker. The average inmate gears down—he "does time" like the disaffected worker or turned-off student, but more dramatically—because he has less to lose and less to gain. Prison factories become breeding grounds for lethargy, and prison classrooms spawn zombies and disrupters. Involved inmates are typically self-made, and their involvement occurs despite prison, or to defy it.

Progressive prison staff members suffer a fate similar to that of progressive managers in factories, good teachers in bad schools, or idealistic psychiatrists in asylums. The "burn-out" process for such staff consists of psychological retreat and a cynical view of their role, a view aimed at survival. Staff members who escape this do so by creating humane subenvironments in inhumane institutions, where institutional structures permit it. Some of these special places arise because staff members locate inmates whose problems in surviving are serious enough to call for settings with intensive supports. Others are created by staff members who care and who arrange milieus in which they can work. Whatever their origins, these enclaves attract like-minded officials and responsive clients, and may acquire attributes of community. In the best of these niches, staff members perform meaningful functions and clients become committed and involved. These niches are prototypes of thereapeutic communities.

CLIMBING THE MASLOWIAN HIERARCHY

The involvement of staff members in niche building satisfies staff needs for achievement and self-actualization. A different process is needed, though, for the clients to become involved. Typically, inmates are seduced into niches by rewards such as escaping from stressful pressures of the larger milieu, entering a more manageable world of more congenial peers, encountering a caring staff, and acquiring supports for survival.

Such incentives draw inmates to physical membership. Enticing them into community means bringing community components to life. That entails creating a group process; inventing routines that make up a significant world; cementing relationships, both among inmates and between inmates and staff members; building commitment, loyalty, and a sense of group identity; creating a turf and a sense of ownership; finding activities for collaborative enterprise; maximizing participation in decisions; buttressing emerging norms and cementing a sense of mission; encouraging problem sharing and mutual concern; and exploring each member's potential (especially for leadership and significant contributions to the group) so as to exploit it to the maximum.

These strategies work if they are gradually and carefully orchestrated. Maslow is of help to us here, because he warned us to be attuned to people's needs. Maslow assumed that people will "quest for community," but he knew that they would demand safety first. In Maslow's terms, people seek each other and will search for meaning, once they feel sure of themselves.[5] Even the most creative of us take wing from sure footing. The community catalyzer must provide an accepting, reliable, and supportive milieu (an oasis) before asking clients to take risks.

Maslow's second point covers the next stages of this process: where a protective setting reduces the preemptiveness of survival concerns, one liberates higher human needs, which one must expect to harness. These higher needs include needs for companionship, for recognition, and for creative outlets. Effective community building ties its strategies to these developing needs as they become liberated and available. The chapters that follow (especially Chapters 3 through 9) provide varying prescriptions for accomplishing this task. Each emphasizes key components of community building, and together they provide a testimonial to the feasibility of the model.

IMPACT TOWARD CHANGE

A White House official recently surveyed his domain, and concluded that "we've had too much of a democracy around here, and not enough of an organization." Community "democratizes" and dilutes organization by increasing the contribution of people who are low in status and by collectivizing decisions made along chains of command. Communities affect organizations externally as well, because organizational traffic is intercepted at community borders, and because rules change as one moves from the community to the organization and back. A Martian landing in the midst of a community and asking to be taken to the leader is apt to get a response very different from the one the Martian would receive next door, where the same request would produce a sergeant, foreman, head nurse, or chief accountant.[6]

A community has an impact not only on organizational and social patterns, but the person who becomes a member of a community *must* change his or her orientation and behavior patterns as a corollary of membership. Given the community components we have listed, it is nonsense to argue that the impact of a community need not be toward change in its members, just as it is silly to assume that such impact must outlive the person's membership, if and when he or she leaves.

Community impact is responsive to strategy, and does not just automatically occur to the same degree. Strategy starts with the management of the member's transition into the community. Even the most adventurous among us are creatures of habit. We bring our past with us as we move through various settings, and we try to replicate our favorite strategies for coping. The extent to which we succeed depends on the magnitude of the transition we experience. In extreme cases—as with some inmates who enter prison after living in rural settings—the carry-over is grossly insufficient, and the inmate is "stressed." Where differences are inconsequential—as with a gang member entering a gang-dominated institution—adjustment to prison means "business as usual." In abrupt and inconsequential transitions, new options for coping are never explored, and personal change is minimal.

A environment that induces change must invalidate prior adjustment modes, but it cannot leave the person resourceless. This means that the environment must make available and must reinforce new habits, skills, and modes of communication. An "orientation" phase must feature clarity and specificity of expectation, behavior models and group support, and plausible arguments for conformity.

A second strategic concern is phasing: complex change is incremental, and disillusionment occurs when change is insensitively accelerated. We also expect boredom or resentment where readiness for change is ignored. Most communities have developed a sequence that takes aspiring members from a novitiate state—which begins with orientation—through specific stages of membership. Passage from one state to the next is premised on the acquisition of a set of habits, which is tested by community representatives.

Behavior required of community members varies from community to community, but invariably includes two aspects of collectivization.[7] One is receptivity to community impact, and the other is participation. On the average, the community member must expand the arena of what has heretofore been viewed as private—this means there is little behavior left that is still the member's own business and no one else's. The borders between private and public are invaded in other settings, but the one invaded usually remains passive. The schizophrenic's delusions and the offender's offenses are scrutinized, diagnosed, and subjected to frontal attack, but such incursions are acquiescently experienced. In communities, the socialized member invites, values, and engages the attention of others in relation to his or her affairs. The member not only grants the legitimacy of community concern, but demonstrates receptivity through change. A member of the community lets his or her conduct be monitored and reinforced in areas that are of relevance to the community.

The other side of the coin is that members are expected to become involved with the lives of fellow members. This entails assuming more responsibility for the fate of others than most people are accustomed to; it also involves abandoning or subordinating competing interests. For the idiosyncratic or subjective deviant (such as the schizophrenic), this may mean being extricated from self-centered symptomatology by the need to participate in decisions and activities involving others. For the antisocial deviate (the predatory offender), it means redirecting energy and concern from the next "score" to community-related obligations and projects.

The extent to which these sorts of behavioral change are long-term (one use of the word "therapeutic") hinges on their relevance to post-community adjustment. A setting can be exemplarily successful in producing new behavior, but, given sufficient discontinuity, the behavior may decay when supports, norms, and rewards are withdrawn and the member feels that the behavior favored in the community now looks silly. This is particularly likely where premembership habits are still alive. These may be revived when the exmember is again exposed to free-world reinforcers—the temptations, pressures, and norms that produced and sustained the person's symptoms or offensive conduct in the past.

EXPORTING COMMUNITY

Most members of hospital and prison TCs are delighted to "graduate," because leaving the TC means an end to their confinement. This fact is usually far more salient to individuals leaving a TC than is the loss of the community's social supports and of the various ties that have linked them to the fellow members who congratulate them as they exit. Members also often leave with confident smiles, assured of their ability to deal with life, because of their progress in the community from self-centered recruits to contributing members.

Progress in community settings is often equated with individual growth, despite the fact that with every change experienced by a community member, reciprocal changes take place in the group that relates to the member. As the person enters a new stage, so do his or her peers; as the person assumes responsibility, opportunities to exercise it are furnished. An individual's self-mastery may be tangible, but the arena in which it is exercised is equally tangible. A community cannot glorify unqualified autonomy, because it socializes its members for a world of interdependence.

In some contexts, community and societal socialization may coincide. Students of Chinese mental hospitals have noted this parallel in the People's Republic of China (PRC). Lee C. Lee has written that "the Chinese view society as a large family, wherein each individual plays an important part in its maintenance. . . . Each individual . . . has the social responsibility of serving and cooperating with other members toward shared goals. The individual's sense of self is intertwined within these interpersonal relationships and only has meaning in relation to other members of the group. Thus, the human relationships of belonging, caring and helping are all integrally a part of one's sense of self.[8] Not surprisingly, in the PRC the borders between therapeutic communities and their outside world are highly permeable, which means that a member's network of family, friends, and associates is routinely used as a treatment adjunct. This practice culminates in the discharge procedure, where a neighborhood briefing session marks the member's transition from the intramural community to the societal one.[9]

In the context of the United States, lesser and more localized means must be considered for extending community into society. Some of these strategies will be discussed in chapters that follow. These include transferring the member to a free-world TC, mobilizing the family as a substitute support system, and using the TC graduate as a human services paraprofessional. The use of halfway houses or intensive parole experiences may be added to this roster when we think of prison TC alumnae.

The most exciting options are those that involve the advanced community member as a community-building, therapeutic resource or an agent for change, rather than simply embedding him or her in a supportive milieu, which may be the path chosen for the member whose separation from the TC occurs at an earlier developmental phase. In some sophisticated models—particularly in the mental health area—communities evolve from supportive to participatory systems as the average member matures.[10] Other TCs, such as Asklepieion (see Chapter 3) have emigrated from prisons to the streets. When we "export" community, we multiply modalities for achieving not only personal change but also institutional reform. This holds true particularly where graduates of therapeutic communities create settings that involve new members and where they act in concert to expand participatory roles in society at large.

PRISON AS A BASE FOR COMMUNITIES

It is easier to build community in prisons than in other organizational settings, despite the gulf between inmates and staff, and despite the presumed mission of prisons—or rather their goal by default—of punishing. There are positive and negative incentives for creating TCs in prison. On the positive side:

1. Inmates are a "captive" clientele living in a small enclosed world, with limited involvement in the larger society. Prisoners are confined to prison not only physically but psychologically. Their sanity hinges on reducing emotional ties with outsiders, whose fate they cannot affect. The prison's inside world simultaneously acquires great importance, with various details of the physical and personal environment coming to matter more than they would in the outside world.

2. Prisons are uncomfortable, but the more progressive and less crowded prisons respond to basic inmate needs, including the need for adequate food, clothing, medical services, and other necessities. Whatever prisoners must be concerned about to survive in prison, they need not worry about the struggle for survival (except as concerns safety from attack by other inmates).

3. Prison is a "controlled" environment. This means not only that it is tightly supervised, but also that the environment is subject to arrangement and rearrangement, including determining where people are when, who they are with, and what they do. Milieu alteration—engineering of the social environment—is comparatively easy in prisons.

On the negative side:

1. While prison inhabitants insulate themselves, they are also interdependent. For most inmates, a guard, cell neighbor, or fellow worker can spell the difference between suffering and having peace of mind. Guards are similarly dependent on their changes for congenial or uneventful work shifts; one obstreperous inmate can make an officer's life miserable. Suppressing the recognition of this type of interdependence makes facing and solving prison problems difficult.

2. Prison is an institution in search of meaning. Officers gain limited satisfaction from counting, escorting, and assorted demeaning tasks. Inmates who "play the system" improve their individual fates, but may not like what they do. Game playing tends to cement cynicism, and rewards the nonmeritorious for their nonmeritorious-ness. There is, in most institutions, no way in which inmates or low-echelon staff members can as groups affect the prison environment.

3. Machismo is fashionable in prison, but even "tough" prisoners are vulnerable. Being sent to prison is a dramatic index of failure, and failure is an incentive to learning.

These features are preconditions of the therapeutic community, in that they make recruiting community members and building community easier or more inviting.

CLOSED SYSTEMS AND OPEN SYSTEMS

In Chapter 3, Maxwell Jones contrasts the hierarchical, self-perpetuating world of the "closed" system with the community as "open system." Open systems, as they are defined by Jones, Argyris, and others, are organizational settings in which people can affect each other and learn from each other, and can thus change the organizations of which they form a part. In theory, open systems are the enemies of closed systems, and vice versa. This means that a closed system often becomes "defensive" if one tries to open it; it also means that open systems pose threats to closed systems, by setting antibureaucratic precedents.

This scenario is real, but there are realities even more tangible, and at times more pressing. Among these realities, one we have already noted is that closed systems are usually less than effective and less than fulfilling, which creates tension. We have also pointed out (with reference to prisons) that some closed systems have organizational attributes that are potentially useable. This does not mean that closed systems usually invite opening, but that it is easier to open a closed system than it is to organize a nonsystem. OD practitioners may be highly paid by members of closed systems to harass and harangue them; CD organizers, by contrast, must fight fear, apathy, and hostility to gain access to potential clients.

Another feature that mitigates against contrast between "open" and "closed" is that large systems are seldom monolithic. Prison programs may not exist if they defy prison rules or ignore central office priority listings, but they are otherwise seldom vetoed or mandated by system headquarters. When they are, debate about whether to institute programs more often focuses on budgets and on personnel dislocations than it does on matters of philosophy or content.

Most therapeutic communities in prison have been founded by prison "insiders," although there are notable exceptions (for an example, see Chapter 10). This does not mean that such programs are inbred; most typically, the "insider" has his views strongly influenced by a catalytic "outsider," but the "insider" usually carries the ball. Programs can be initiated by high-level staff members (as in those described in Chapter 9), but this is not essential. What is desirable is that the high-level staff be "sold" on the program or view it as an asset. If this does not occur, a program may survive its inception, because programs that have won places on an organization's chart are seldom routinely abolished, but such a program remains vulnerable. It can be abolished if it attracts negative publicity, or if its resources are coveted when money gets tight. Such a program also has limited claim to support or protection if and when crises develop. Administrators approached at such times can legitimately ask why they have not been consulted previously. This points up the mistake of not including higher-level staff members in the philosophy of participatory organization, which is as substantial an error as the standard OD practice of centering on management to the exclusion of workers and clients.

Vulnerability can relate to self-defined autonomy, which makes communities oblivious or unresponsive to their contexts. A community culture can emphasize confidentiality (see Chapter 11), to the point of illegality, and may invite its abolition. A community must have integrity, but it cannot define this commodity at others' expense. The integrity of a subculture must end where the integrity of the larger culture starts, as one's right to place one's fist anywhere ends where another person's nose begins. A host agency must view the community as a *relevant* transplant, not as a foreign body or cancerous growth.

A progressive federal prison (Fort Worth) has shut down a therapeutic community whose members—in line with the premises of their culture—destroyed a cache of drugs imported by a unit member, to dramatize their disapproval of his conduct. This action was deemed necessary, but violated a provision of the criminal code relating to disposal of evidence. Martin Groder's Asklepieion, an inmate-run community at Marion (see Chapter 3), could have been the pride of the prison system, but invited self-destruction through a de facto secession from its context. A community must be insulated to gain immunity from pressures (see Chapters 6 and 14). It must simultaneously be law-abiding and respectful of the sensibilities and norms of nonmembers.

OPEN SYSTEMS AND OPEN-CLOSED SYSTEMS

One theme of the sociological literature we have not yet touched on is the assumption that "community" is feeling-centered, while "the community" prizes rationality. Tönnies, the German Gemeinschaft theorist, carried this point to extremes. He suggested that community has a feminine orientation and that urban society expresses male values. The essence of community, in this general view, is its irrationality. The distinguishing feature of community becomes the attachment of its members to the group and each other. One assumes that community culture reflects personal needs while societal culture serves rationally defined ends, and that communities follow charismatic leaders, whose mandate comes from heaven.

This perspective matters; because communities are intimate enough forms of human organization to *permit* irrationality to surface, and because *some* communities—including some therapeutic communities—are emotionally charged, feeling-oriented, centered on relatedness, and committed to expressing feelings. Occasional communities may provide forums for the projection of early-childhood traumas and replicate the transference phenomenon of analysis. Such communities clearly need professional involvement to provide reality-testing safeguards.

Communities incur risks because of their potential for irrationality. An open system maximizes group development and individual growth (see Chapter 3). This requires free exploration, openness to information, and clear-headed digestion of what is learned. An open system closes to the extent to which faith, dogma, and invested belief replace tentativeness, self-criticism, and discipline. Whereas closedness in "the community" means ritual and bureaucratization, closedness in "community" implies the advent of fanaticism. A community loses its open-system quality when it becomes a social movement, even if it remains egalitarian and democratically organized.

The mixture of closed and open ingredients in communities must be orchestrated to ensure internal and external effectiveness.[11] Communities need loyalty, dedication, and commitment, but they must avoid chauvinism, smugness, and zealotry. They need identity and definition, but not dogma and parochialism. They need leadership, not Leaders.[12] A community must have permeable borders; it must absorb from the world at large what is valuable and will promote growth. It must avoid pride and exclusivity so as not to lose its capacity to survive.

"THERAPEUTIC" WITH A SMALL *t* AND "COMMUNITY" WITH A SMALL *c*

Chapters 2 and 3 suggest that "therapy" and "social learning" can be read interchangeably, which is an assumption that is consonant with the broad-spectrum view of psychotherapy prevalent today.[13] This perspective changes our conception of helper and helped by widening the range of the former and assigning a more active role to the latter. It attenuates the borders between the therapy process and the process of change elsewhere in the world.

We have heretofore avoided the issue of what is therapeutic by centering on the question, What is community? Answering the latter helps in dealing with the former, but the two concerns must never be equated. Some communities are not therapeutic—some are destructive, as is much formal therapy.

There are enterprises inside prisons that have *some* of the features of community but can be *eminently* therapeutic for inmates, staff, or both. Among such programs is a well-known experiment in training correctional officers and inmates in peer counseling techniques, a program conducted under the auspices of Robert Carkhuff in the Federal Correctional Institution at Lompoc,[14] and in other prisons. The training has as its premise that vital but elementary human services (exploration, understanding, action) can be rendered by empathetic individuals anywhere in an organization, and that relevant skills can be communicated through short-term training. The result of such an intervention potentially enriches the prison with personnel and prisoners who are capable of delivering human services to inmates (and, presumably, staff members) who may be experiencing personal crises or are otherwise in need of noncasual responses.

Whereas communities are localized, other strategies saturate the organization, at its assembly-line level, with informal talent. Such strategies can change the climate flexibly, upgrade personnel and enrich jobs, inspire inmates to consider careers in the human services, build staff-inmate and inmate-inmate bridges, and provide social support to people in need.

I cite this example to make a case against an all-or-none view of what is desirable. A prison can be a sterile or destructive environment: a place for marking time, suffering, for noncoping under stress. An *ideal* response to this challenge calls for building growth-promoting communities in prison, but a *necessary* response entails the exploration of *all* options for humanizing and enriching the milieu.

NOTES

1. Robert Nesbit, who notes that "the most fundamental and far-reaching of sociology's unit-ideas is community," points out that "the ties of community—real or *imagined*, traditional

or *contrived*—come to form the image of the good society." (*The sociological tradition.* New York: Basic Books, 1966. P. 47. Emphasis added.)

Nostalgia for community rooted in myth of community is a leitmotif not only of sociology, but also of other social sciences. This includes the Jeffersonian tradition in politics and the Marxist view in economics. The idealized rural past is (paradoxically) a key theme in *industrial* psychology. Loren Baritz makes this point in relation to Elton Mayo, the father of the field. He notes that Mayo "pictured a happy preindustrial America and argued that individual isolation, rootlessness, the 'lonely crowd' as characteristic social manifestations were caused by industrialism. The intense physical and social isolation of frontier and backwoods existence were left out of his picture. So were the pathetic, socially isolated lives of alienated farmers and laborers, of free and indentured whites of the lower classes, and of parts of the conveniently forgotten slave population. . . . [Mayo] went on to say that in this simple and good preindustrial America, when standards were supposedly clear and obligations and privileges supposedly defined, 'the individual lived a full communal life and knew that his services were a necessary social function'." (*The servants of power: a history of the use of social science in American industry.* New York: Wiley, Science Edition, 1960. Pp. 110–11.)

2. Assets and liabilities of communities are partly a matter of fashion. Jacqueline Scherer points this out when she writes that "ironically, a century ago intellectuals despaired of the tyranny of communities because they feared the suppression of individuality and personal desires. But today communal man has an attractive image: he is not competitive, selfish and driven, but is dedicated, committed, and, most important, 'belongs'." (*Contemporary community: sociological illusion or reality?* London: Tavistock, 1972. P. 1.)

3. Seymour Sarasen—one of the most eloquent champions of community building—has voiced powerfully documented reservations about the "ministering" structure of programs that deliver human services. Sarasen contends that liberalized treatment settings do not foster a sense of community, and are ultimately as alienating as more traditional social milieus.

One point Sarasen makes is that the separateness of special settings may be psychologically more salient than the reforms engendered in such settings. He tells us that "the special class teacher, the regular class teacher, the retarded pupil, the nonretarded pupils, the principal, the parents—one of the major effects of the special class on each is to accentuate their sense of apartness and aloneness. Far from feeling a part of a mutually dependent and interactive community of people, they are aware that they are isolated from each other, despite their presence in the same building. And yet it all seems so 'natural' that it rarely occurs to ask if the price being paid is not too high." (*The psychological sense of community: prospects for a community psychology.* San Francisco: Jossey-Bass, 1974. P. 167.)

4. Goffman, E. *Asylums: essays on the social situation of mental patients and other inmates.* New York: Doubleday (Anchor), 1961.

5. Maslow, A. H. *Motivation and personality.* New York: Harper, 1954.

6. A third role of communities in organizational change is described by Scherer, who sees them as raising *moral* questions that are bypassed by technologically oriented organizations. "Communal man," writes Scherer, "is able to bring into focus those issues that have escaped the attention of specialists: he can insist through the social structures of community that additional factors enter debate, creating a platform for raising new terms and suggesting viable alternatives to standardized systems and programs. . . . Only when man is viewed as a whole being do the disharmonies and discontinuities of life become visible. . . . The unique characteristic of communities is that members can express common concern over values, beliefs, and goals, thereby becoming a potential force to stimulate change." (op. cit. Pp. 126–27.)

7. Meticulous psychometric studies and field observations by a group of Yale researchers have established that value changes among patients in a TC occur early in the patients' careers. The Yale group reports that "major themes are associated with group membership, openness in discussing problems, accepting responsibility for one's self and other patients, and active confrontation of problems." See, Almond, R., Keniston, K. and Boltax, S. Patient value change in milieu therapy. *Archives of General Psychiatry* (1969) 20:339–51, p. 340.

8. Lee, L. C. Mental health: A people's project. *APA Monitor* (American Psychological Association), September-October 1979, p. 20.

9. Ibid. P. 21.

10. Fairweather, G. W., Sanders, D. H. Cressler, D. L. and Maynard, H. *Community life for the mentally ill: an alternative to institutional care.* Chicago: Aldine, 1969; Atthowe, J. W., Jr. Behavioral innovation and persistence. *American Psychologist* (1973) 28:34–41; McDonough, J. M. The Veterans Administration and community mental health: new approaches in psychiatric rehabilitation. *Community Mental Health Journal* (1969) 5:275–79.

11. The open-closed dilemma is highlighted by Scherer, who observes that "proponents of the moral collectivity seek the disadvantages of exclusiveness, parochialism, and intolerance and the advantages of 'togetherness'. Rarely can they achieve both, for they seek openness and closure at the same time." (Op. cit. P. 6.)

According to Nesbit, "the problem, as Rousseau posed it so momentously, was 'to find a form of association which will defend and protect with the whole common force the person and goods of each associate, and in which each, while uniting himself with all, may still obey himself alone, and remain as free as before'." (Nesbit. Op. cit. P. 49; from Rousseau's *Social Contract*, Chapter 1.)

12. A charismatic leader is often mentioned as a feature of the therapeutic community. Almond *et al* contend that TC charismatic leaders are not born, but are made, in the sense that they assume a role demanded the the TC itself. Almond *et al* write: "Initially, we tended to view the leader's charisma as a personality characteristic, facilitating staff acceptance of values and therapeutic style. We then observed in this and other similar settings locally and elsewhere that the charisma of the unit director may be strongly role-related. Several individuals who replaced leaders of such settings commented that they felt an intense pressure to behave in ways that were uncharacteristic for them but consistent with charismatic expectations of staff and patients." Almond, R., Keniston, K. and Boltax, S. The value system of a milieu therapy unit. *Archives of General Psychiatry* (1968) 19:545–61, p. 557.

13. Harper, R. A. *The new psychotherapies.* Englewood Cliffs, N.J.: Prentice-Hall (Spectrum), 1975. Albert Bandura has suggested that "the day may not be far off when psychological disorders will be treated not in hospitals or mental hygiene clinics but in comprehensive 'learning centers,' when clients will be considered not patients suffering from hidden psychic pathologies but responsible people who participate actively in developing their own potentialities." (*Scientific American* 1967) 216:86.

14. Mosford, R. H., Moss, C. S., eds. *The crumbling walls: treatment and counseling of prisoners.* Urbana, Ill.: University of Illinois Press, 1975.

2

THE CONCEPT OF "THERAPEUTIC MILIEU"

Fritz Redl

The worst trap that explorers of the milieu idea sometimes seem to be goaded into is the ubiquitous use of the term "therapeutic," if it is coupled as an adjective, with "milieu" as a noun. I have described the seven most common meanings squeezed into this word in scientific writings and scientific discussions elsewhere,[1] but I must at least point at this possible confusion before we go on. Whenever people demand that a really good "therapeutic milieu" have this or that quality to it, they may refer to any one—or a combination of—the following issues:

1. Therapeutic—meaning: *don't put poison in their soup.*
    Example—Demand for absence of crude forms of punishment in a place that calls itself a "residential treatment center."
2. Therapeutic—meaning: *you still have to feed them,* even though that has little to do directly with a specific operation you are planning to perform.
    Example—Youngsters need an activity program, so if you keep them for a while you'd better see that they get it, even if your specific theory of psychiatry thinks nothing of the direct implication of play life and activity diet in terms of therapy as such.
3. Therapeutic—meaning: *developmental phase appropriateness and cultural background awareness.*
    Example—It would not be therapeutic to keep adolescents in an infantilizing "little boy and girl" atmosphere; or: a fine lady fussing over a little boy's hair grooming might convey "warmth" to a neglected middle-class child, but would simply be viewed as a

This chapter comprises most of the paper that appeared under the same heading in the *American Journal of Orthopsychiatry* (1959), Vol. 29:721–36. The material is reprinted by permission.

hostile pest by a young toughie from the other side of the tracks.

4. Therapeutic—meaning: *clinically elastic.*

Example—The fact that rules and regulations were too rigid to fit particular disturbance patterns or needs of patients, I have heard referred to as "untherapeutic," and with all due respect to numbers and group psychology, there is a point where the inability to make exceptions becomes "untherapeutic" too.

5. Therapeutic—meaning: *encompassing fringe-area treatment goals.*

Example—Johnny is here for treatment of his kleptomania. His therapist works hard on that in individual therapy. Johnny also has a severe deficiency in school learning, and is clumsy in his play life with contemporaries. Even while the therapist is not yet in a position to pull any of these factors in, some other aspect of the milieu to which Johnny is exposed must give him experiences in this direction. Or else, the place is not "therapeutic enough" for him.

6. Therapeutic—in terms of *"the milieu and I."*

Example—Some types of cases with deficient superego formation can be lured into identification with value issues only through the detour of an identification with the group code within which they live. For those cases the "therapist" is only one of the therapeutic agents. The "institutional atmosphere" that makes the child want to identify with what it stands for is another, *on equal rights.* In this case, this part of the "milieu" is expected to become a direct partner in treatment of the specific disturbance for which the child was brought in.

7. Therapeutic—in terms of *re-education for life.*

Example—Especially for larger institutions the demand is often made that the institutions should not only provide people who treat the patient, but that they should also have features in them which come as close to "real life outside" as is possible, or else they wouldn't be "therapeutic enough." Thus, all those features that would seem to be needed for a very sick person are considered as rather countertherapeutic and bad, though unfortunately still necessary, while all semblance to open community life is considered a therapeutic ingredient in its own right. How far one and the same institution can cater to illness and at the same time lure into normality is then often a case for debate.

Enough of this dissection of an adjective. I hope I am understood correctly: Any one of these meanings of the term "therapeutic" is a justified issue in its own right. Any one of them may, in a given case, assume priority importance or may fade out in relevance to the zero point. All I am trying to convey is the importance of remembering who is talking about what—and about which patients—when we use the term in a scientific free-for-all. So far I haven't been too impressed with our ability to do so.

By the way, even in all those seven cases the term "therapeutic" may still be used in a double frame of reference: (a) Was it therapeutic for a given patient—if so, how do you know? (b) Is this expected to be potentially "therapeutic"—meaning beneficial for the treatment goal—from what I know about the basic nature of the issue under debate? These two frames of reference need to be kept asunder too.

A "MILIEU": WHAT'S IN IT?

Obviously I am not going to use the term in the nearly global meaning which its theft from the French language originally insinuated. For practical reasons, I am going to talk here only of one sort of milieu concept: of a "milieu" artificially created for the purpose of the treatment of a group of youngsters. Within this confine you can make it somewhat wider if you want, and think of the "Children's Psychiatric Unit" on the fourth, eight, or ninth floor of a large hospital, or you may hold before your eyes, while I am speaking, a small residential treatment home for children that is not part of a large unit. Of course, I know that the similarity of what I am talking about to other types of setups may be quite great, but I can't cover them all. Hence, anything else you hold before your eyes while I talk, you do strictly at your own risk.

So, here we are on the doorstep of that treatment home or at the keyhole of that hospital ward. And now you ask me: If you could plan things the way you wanted to, which are the most important "items" in your milieu that will sooner or later become terribly relevant for better or for worse? The choice is hard, and only such a tough proposition gets me over the guilt feeling for oversimplifying and listing items out of context.

1. *The social structure.* This is some term, and I have yet to see the psychiatrist that isn't stunned for a moment at its momentum—many would run and hire a sociologist on the spot. Being short on time, I have no choice, but let me hurry and add: this term in itself is as extendible and collapsible as a balloon. It doesn't mean much without specifications. So, let me just list a few of the things I have in mind:

a) A hospital ward is more like a *harem society than a family*, no matter how motherly or fatherly the particular nurses and doctors may feel toward their youngsters. The place I run at the moment is purposely shaped as much as possible after the model of an American camp, which is the only pattern I could find which children would be familiar with, where a lot of adults walk through children's lives in older brother and parentlike roles without pretending it to be an equivalent to family life.

b) The *role distribution* of the adult figures can be of terrific importance for the amount of clarity with which children perceive what it is all about. Outspokenly or not, sooner or later they must become clear about just who can or cannot be expected to decide what; otherwise, how would one know when one is getting the run-around?

c) The *pecking order* of any outfit does not long remain a secret to an open door neighborhood-wise toughie, no matter how dumb he may be otherwise. He also smells the outspoken "pecking order" among the adults who take care of him, no matter how carefully disguised it may be under professional role titles or Civil Service Classification codes.

d) The *communication network* of any given institution is an integral part of its "social structure." Just who can be approached about listening to what, is quite a task to learn; and to figure out the real communication lines that are open and those which are secretly clogged in the adult communication network is usually an unsoluble task except for the suspicious outside researcher.

I mentioned only four illustrations of all the things I want included under "social structure." There are many more, and I have no quarrel with the rich inventory many social scientists have invented for this. The quarrel I have goes all against oversimplification, and if you tell me social structure is only what goes into a power line drawing or a sociogram, or the social structure is the only important variable in "milieu" that psychiatrists have neglected in the past, then you have me in a mood to fight. By the way—if I list "social structure" as one of the important milieu variables, I'd better add in a hurry: a mere listing or description of the social structure extant on a given ward is of no interest to me at all if it doesn't go further than that. From a clinical angle, the excitement begins *after* the sociologist tells me what social structure I have before me. Then I really want to know: What does it do to my therapeutic goals? What does it imply for my choice in techniques? In which phase of the therapy of my children is it an asset, and in which other phase does it turn into a serious block? To use just one example for the clinical question to be added to the social scientist's answer: The kind of ward I run—harem society style—makes individual attachments of child to worker difficult to achieve; on the other hand, it pleasantly dilutes too excited libidinous attachment-needs into more harmless distribution over a larger number of live props. Question: Is that good or bad, and for whom during what phase of their treatment?

2. *The value system that oozes out of our pores.* Some people subsume that under social structure. I think I have reasons to want a separate place for it here, but let's not waste time on the question why. The fact is, the youngsters not only respond to what we say or put in mimeographed writing; they smell our value-feelings even when we don't notice our own body odor any more. I am not sure how, and I can't wait until I find out. But

I do need to find out which value items are there to smell. Does the arrangement of my furniture call me a liar while I make a speech about how much at home I want them to feel, or does that gleam in a counselor's eye tell the child: "You are still wanted," even though he means it if he says he won't let you cut up the tablecloth? By the way, in some value studies I have missed one angle many times: the *clinical convictions* of what is professionally correct handling, which sometimes even questionnaire-clumsy workers on a low salary level may develop, and which become a motivating source for their behavior in its own right, besides their own personal moral convictions or their power drives.

3. *Routines, rituals, and behavioral regulations.* The sequence of events and the conditions under which people undergo certain repetitive maneuvers in their life space can have a strong impact on whether they can keep themselves under control, or whether their impulse-control balance breaks down. Since Bruno Bettelheim's classic description of the events inside a child while he seems engaged in the process of getting up or getting himself to sleep, no more words should have to be said about this. And yet, many "therapeutic milieu" discussions still waste their time on arguments between those who like regularity and those who think the existence of a rule makes life an unimaginative drudge. All groups also have a certain "ritual" by which a member gets back into the graces of the group if he has sinned, and others which the group has to go through when an individual has deviated. Which of those ceremonial rites are going on among my boys, thinly disguised behind squabbles and fights, and which of them do adult staff people indulge in, under the even thinner disguise of a discussion on punishment and on the setting of limits? Again—the mere discovery of phenomena fitting into this category is not what I am after. We are still far from having good research data on the *clinical relevance* of whatever specific practice may be in vogue in a specific place.

4. *The impact of the group process.* We had better pause after pronouncing this weighty phrase—it is about as heavy and full of dodges as the phrase "social structure," as previously pointed out. And since this one milieu aspect might well keep us here for a week, let me sink as low as simple word-listing at this point. Items that I think should go somewhere under this name: over-all group atmosphere, processes like scapegoating, mascot-cultivation, subclique formation, group psychological role suction,[2] experiences of exposure to group psychological intoxication, dependency on contagion clusters, leadership tensions, etc. Whatever you have learned from social psychology, group psychology and group dynamics had better be written in right here. The point of all this: These phenomena are *not* just interesting things that happen among patients or staff, to be viewed with a clinical grin, a sociological hurrah, or with the curiosity stare of an anthropological slumming party. These processes are forces to which my child patient is

exposed, as real as the oedipus complex of his therapist, the food he eats and the toys he plays with. The forces producing such impacts may be hard to see, or even to make visible through x-ray tricks. They are there and as much of his "surroundings" as the unbreakable room in which he screams off his tantrum.

5. *The trait clusters that other people whirl around within a five-yard stretch.* I first wanted to call this item "the other people as persons," but I know this would only call forth a long harangue about feelings, attitudes—Isn't it people anyway, who make up a group?—etc. From bitter discussion experience, I am trying to duck these questions by this somewhat off-the-beat phrase. What I have in mind is this: My youngsters live as part of a group, true enough. But they are also individuals. And Bobby who shares a room with John is within striking distance of whatever personal peculiarities John may happen to throw at others. In short, we expect some children to show "shock" at certain colors on a Rorschach card. We expect children to be lured into excited creativity at the mere vision of some fascinating project outline or plane model seductively placed before this eyes. Well, the boy with whom Bobby shares his room is worse than a Rorschach or a plane model. Not only does his presence and the visualization of his personality do something to Bobby, for John not only *has* character traits and neurotic syndromes; he swings them around his body like a wet bathing towel, and it is going to hit whoever gets in its path, innocent or not. In short, personality traits remain psychological entities for the psychologist who watches them in the youngsters. They are *real things that hit and scratch* if you get in their way, for the roommate and all the other people on the ward.

We have learned to respect the impact of certain extremes in pathologies upon each other, but we are still far from inspecting our milieus carefully enough for what they contain in "trait clusters" that children swing around their heads within a five-yard range. Let me add: not all traits and syndromes are "swung"; some stay put and can only be seen or smelled, so they become visible or a nuisance only to the one who shares the same room. Also: we are far from knowing what this all amounts to clinically. For the question of just what "milieu ingredients" my ward contains, in terms of existent trait clusters of the people who live in it, is still far removed from the question of just which *should* coexist with each other, and which others should be carefully kept asunder.

6. *The staff, their attitudes and feelings—but please let's not call it all "transference."* This one I can be short about, for clinicians all know about it; sociologists will grant it to you, though they may question how heavily it counts. In fact, the attitudes and feelings of staff have been drummed up for so long now as "the" most important aspect of a milieu, often even as the only important one, that I am not afraid this item will be forgotten. No argument needed, it is self-evident. Only two issues I would like to battle

around: One, while attitudes and feelings are very important indeed, they are not always all that counts, and sometimes other milieu items may gang up on them so much they may obliterate their impact. My other battle cry: Attitudes and feelings of staff are manifold, and spring from many different sources. Let's limit the term "transference" to those for which it was originally invented. If Nurse's Aide A gets too hostile to Bob because he bit him too hard, let's not throw all of that into the same terminological pot. By the way, if I grant "attitudes and feelings of staff" a place on my list of "powerful milieu ingredients," I mean the attitudes and feelings that really fill the place, that are lived—not those that are only mentioned in research interviews and on questionnaires.

7. *Behavior received.* I tried many other terms, but it won't work. There just isn't one that fits. In a sentence I would say: what people really *do* to each other counts as much as how they feel. This forces me into a two-hour argument in which I have to justify why it isn't unpsychiatric to say such a thing. For, isn't it the underlying feelings that "really" count? That depends on which side of the fence your "really" is. The very fact that you use such a term already means you know there is another side to it, only you don't want to take it as seriously as yours. In short, there are situations where the "underlying feeling" with which the adult punishes a child counts so much that the rather silly form of punishment that was chosen is negligible. But I could quote you hundreds of other examples where this is not the case. No matter what wonderful motive—if you expose child A to an isolation with more panic in it than he can stand, the effect will be obvious. Your excuse that you "meant well and love the boy" may be as futile as that of the mother who would give the child an overdose of arsenic, not knowing its effect.

This item of *behaviors received in a day's time* by each child should make a really interesting line to assess. We would have to look about at "behaviors received" from other boys as well as from staff, and see what the implications of those behaviors received are, even after deducting from them the mitigating influences of "attitudes that really were aiming at the opposite." The same, by the way, should also be taken into consideration for staff to be hired. I have run into people who really love "crazy youngsters" and are quite willing to sacrifice a lot. Only they simply cannot stand more than half a pound of spittle in their face a day, professional attitude or no.

In order to make such an assessment, the clinician would of course be interested especially in the *forms* that are being used by staff for intervention—limit-setting—expression of acceptance and love, etc. The totality of prevalence of certain forms of "behavior received" is not a negligible characteristic of the milieu in which a child patient has to live.

8. *Activity structure and nature of constituent performances.* Part of the impact a hospital or treatment home has on a child lies in the things he is allowed or requested *to do.* Any given activity that is halfway shapeful

enough to be described has a certain amount of structure to it—some games, for instance, have a body of rules; demand the splitting up into two opposing sides or staying in a circle; and have certain assessments of roles for the players, at least for the duration. At the same time, they make youngsters "do certain things" while the game lasts. Paul Gump introduced the term "constituent performances" into our Detroit Game Study, and referred by this term to the performances required within the course of a game as basic. Thus, running and tagging are constituent performances of a tag game, guessing word meaning is a constituent performance in many a charade, etc. We have plenty of evidence by now that—other things being equal—the very exposure of children to a given game, with its structure and demand for certain constituent performances, may have terrific clinical impact on the events at least of that day. Wherever we miscalculate the overwhelming effect which the seductive aspect of certain games may have (flashlight hide-and-seek in the dark just before bedtime) we may ask for trouble, while many a seemingly risky game can safely be played if enough ego-supportive controls are built right into it (the safety zone to which you can withdraw without having to admit you get tired or scared, etc.). In short, while I would hardly relegate the total treatment job of severely distrubed children in a mental hospital ward to that factor alone, I certainly would want to figure on it as seriously as I would calculate the mental hygiene aspects of other factors more traditionally envisioned as being of clinical concern. What I say here about games goes for many other activities patients engage in—arts and crafts, woodwork, outings, overnight trips, cookouts, discussion groups, musical evenings, etc. Which of these things takes place, where, with which feeling tone, and with what structural and activity ingredients is as characteristic of a given "milieu" as the staff that is hired.

9. *Space, equipment, time and props.* What an assortment of names, but I know as yet of no collective noun that would cover them all equally well. Since I have made such a fuss about this for years, I may try to be shorter about it than seems reasonable. Remember what a bunch of boys do when running through a viaduct with an echo effect? Remember what may happen to a small group who are supposed to discuss plans for their next Scout meeting, who have to hold this discussion unexpectedly, in a huge gym with lots of stuff around, instead of in their usual clubroom? Remember what will happen to a baseball that is put on the table prematurely while they are still supposed to sit quietly and listen, and remember what happens to many a well-intended moral lecture to a group of sloppy campers, if you timed it so badly that the swimming bell started ringing before you had finished? Do I still have to prove why I think that what an outfit does with arrangements of time expectations and time distribution, what prop-exposure the youngsters are expected to stand or avoid, what space arrangements are like, and what equipment does to the goals you have set

for yourself, should be listed along with the important "properties" of a place where clinical work with children takes place? So far I have found that in hospitals this item tends to be left out of milieu discussions by psychiatrists and sociologists alike; only the nurses and attendants have learned by bitter experience that it may pay to lend an ear to it.

10. *The seepage from the world outside.* One of the hardest "milieu aspects" to assess in a short visit to any institution is the amount of "impact from the larger universe and the surrounding world" that actually seeps through its walls and finds its way into the lives of the patients. No outfit is airtight, no matter how many keys and taboos are in use. In our own little children's ward-world, for instance, there are the following "seepage ingredients from the world outside" that are as much a part of our "milieu," as it hits the boys, as anything else: Adult visitors and the "past case history" flavor they leave behind. Child visitors and the "sociological body odor" of the old neighborhood, or the new one which they exude. Excursions which we arrange, old haunts from prehospital days, which we happen to drive through unintentionally on our way to our destination. Plenty of purposely pulled-in outside world through movies, television, pictures, and stories we may tell them. And, of course, school is a full-view window hopefully opened wide for many vistas to be seen through it—if we only could get our children to look.

There is the "hospital impact" of the large building that hits them whenever they leave the ward floor in transit, the physically sick patients they meet on the elevator who stir the question up again in their own mind: "Why am I here?" There are the stories other boys tell, the staff tells, the imputed secrets we may be hiding from them whenever we seem eager to divert attention to something else. As soon as the children move into the open cottage, the word "seepage" isn't quite as correct any more. Suffice it to say: the type and amount of "outside world" particles that are allowed in or even eagerly pulled in constitute a most important part of the lives of the captive population of an institutional setting, and want to be given attention to in an appraisal of just what a given "milieu" holds.

11. *The system of umpiring services and traffic regulations between environment and child.* Those among you who have a sharp nose for methodological speculations may want to object and insist that I am jumping category dimensions in tagging on this item and the next one on my list. I don't want to quarrel about this now. For even though you may be right, it is too late today to start a new chapter, so please let me get away with tagging these two items on here. In some ways they still belong, for whether there are any umpiring services built into an institution, and what they are like, is certainly an important "milieu property" in my estimation.

What I have in mind here has been described in more detail in a previous paper.[3] In short, it runs somewhat like this: Some "milieu impacts" hit the children directly; nobody needs to interpret or translate. Others hit the child all right, but to have their proper impact someone has to do some explaining. It makes a great difference whether a child who is running away unhappy, after a cruel razzing received from a thoughtless group, is left to deal with this all by himself; or whether the institution provides interpretational or first-aid services for the muddled feelings at the time. Some of our children, for instance, might translate such an experience, which was not intended by the institution, into additional resentment against the world. With sympathy in the predicament offered by a friendly adult who tags along and comforts, this same experience may well be decontaminated or even turned into the opposite.

A similar item is the one I had in mind in using the phrase "traffic regulations." Much give-and-take can follow naturally among the inhabitants of a given place. Depending on the amount of their disturbance, though, some social interactions which normal life leaves to the children's own resources require traffic supervision by an adult. I would like to know whether a given milieu has foreseen this and can guarantee the provision of some help in the bartering custom among the youngsters, or whether that new youngster will be mercilessly exposed to the wildest blackmail with no help from anyone, the moment he enters the doors to my ward. In short, it is like asking what medical first-aid facilities are in a town before one moves into it. Whether this belongs to the concept of what makes up a "town," or whether it should be listed under a separate heading I leave for a later chance to thrash out. All I want to point at now is that the nature of and existence or nonexistence of umpiring services and social traffic regulations is as "real" a property of a setup as its walls, kitchen equipment and clinical beliefs.

12. *The thermostat for the regulation of clinical resilience.* If it is cold in an old cabin somewhere in the midst of "primitive nature," the trouble is obvious: either there isn't any fire going, or something is wrong with the stove and the whole heating system, so it doesn't give off enough heat. If I freeze in a building artificially equipped with all the modern conveniences, such a conclusion might be off the beam. The trouble may simply be that the thermostat isn't working right. This, like the previous item, is a property of a given milieu rather than a "milieu ingredient" in the stricter sense of the word. However, it is of such utmost clinical relevance that it has to go in here somewhere. In fact, I have hardly ever participated in a discussion on the milieu concept without having this item come up somehow or other.

The term under which it is more often referred to is actually that of "flexibility," which most milieu therapy enthusiasts praise as "good" while the bad men in the picture are the ones that think "rigidity" is a virtue. I have more reasons to be tired of this either/or issue than I can list in the remaining time. It seems to me that the "resilience" concept fits better what most of us have so long tried to shoot at with the flexibility label. A milieu certainly needs to be (sensitive to the changing needs of the patients during different phases of the treatment process) it needs to "tighten up"—lower the behavioral ceiling when impulse-panic looms on the horizon; and it may have to lift it when self-imposed internal pressures mount. Also, it needs to limit spontaneity and autonomy of the individual patients in early phases of intensive disorder and rampant pathology; it needs to throw in a challenge toward autonomy and even the risking of mistakes, when the patient goes through the later phases of recovery. Especially when severely disturbed children are in the process of going through an intensive phase of "improvement," the resilience of a milieu to make way for its implications is as important as its ability to "shrink back" during a regressive phase.

JUST HOW DOES THE MILIEU DO IT?

Listing these 12 variables of important milieu aspects which can be differentiated as explorable issues in their own right is only part of the story. I hold no brief for this list, and I am well aware of its methodological complications and deficiencies. The major value of listing them at all lies in the insistence that *there are so many of them* and that they *can be separately studied and explored.* This should at least help us to secure ourselves against falling in love with any one of them to the exclusion of the others, and of forcing any discipline that wants to tackle the job, whether it be psychiatry, sociology or what not, to look beyond its traditional scope and directly into the face of uncompromisingly multifaceted facts.

Since the major sense in all this milieu noise is primarily the impact of these variables on the treatment process of the children we are trying to cure, the question of the clinical assessment of the relevance of each of these items is next on the docket of urgent jobs. This one we shall have to skip for today, but time may allow us to point at the other question leading into the most important core of the problem: If we assume that any one of these milieu ingredients, or whatever you want to call them, may have positive or negative impacts on our therapeutic work—how do they do it? Just what goes on when we claim that any one of those milieu givens "did something to our youngsters"? This gets us into one of the most noteworthy gaps in all our theory of personality, and frankly, I don't think even our most up-to-date models are quite up to it. True enough, we have learned a few things about just how pathology is influenced in the process of a specific form of psychiatric interview, and we know a little about influence of human over human, here or there. We are not so well off when we come to the impact of more abstract sounding entities, such as "group structure." We have even more trouble to figure out just how space, time and props are supposed to do their job, whenever we claim that they have the power to throw an otherwise well-planned therapeutic experience out of gear.

One phase of this problem sounds familiar—when psychiatry first began to take the impact of "culture" seriously, we were confronted with a similar puzzler: just where, within the individual, is what going on at the moment when we say a "cultural" factor had some influence on a given behavior of a person?

This problem is far from solved. I think it might help, though, to introduce a thought that might lead to greater specificity in observation and ultimately to more "usuable" forms of data collection. Frankly, I have never seen the "milieu" at work. My children are never hit by "the milieu" as such. It always hits them in a specific form and at a given time and place. I think the researchers who play with the concept of a "setting" have a technical advantage over us in this field. Of course, the setting alone doesn't interest me either. For what it all hinges on is just what *experience* a given setting produces or makes possible within my child patient and what this child patient does with it.

Rather than study the "milieu" per se, and then the "reactions of the children," how about making it a four-step plan? Let's keep the "milieu" as the over-all concept on the fringe; its basic ingredients come close to my youngsters only insofar as they are contained in a given setting. For example, my children on the ward can be found engaged in getting up, eating a meal or snacks; they can be found roaming around the playroom, or in a station wagon, with all their overnight gear, on the way to their camping site. They can be found in their arts and crafts room, or schoolroom, engaged in very specific activities. Enough of illustrations—the point is, in all those settings the whole assortment of milieu aspects hits them in very *specific forms*: There is an outspoken behavioral expectation floating through that arts and crafts room at any time. There are spatial characteristics, tools, and props. There is the potential reaction of the other child or adult, the feeling tone of the group toward the whole situation as such; there is the impact of people's goal values and attitudes as well as that of the behavior of the child's neighbor who clobbers him right now with his newly made viking sword. In short: *I may be able to isolate observations of milieu ingredients as they "hit" the child in a specific setting during a specific activity.* On such a narrowed-down level of observation, I may also be able to trace the actual *experience* which such a concrete situation in a given setting produced in the child; and if I know what the child *did with the experience*, it may make sense, since I have both ends of the line before me. The youngster's reaction to his experience—the nature of the ingredients of the "setting" on both ends of the line, plus plenty of good hunches on the child's experience while exposed to its impact.

It seems to me that much more work needs to be done with the concept of "setting" so as to make it clinically more meaningful, and that sharper observational techniques, capable of catching "implied milieu impact" as well as "child's coping with" the experience produced by the setting, need to be developed. This, however, leads into a theme to be discussed in other sessions of our Annual Meeting.

One more word before closing. It is time that we take Erik Erikson's warning more seriously than we have done so far—and I mention him as symbolizing a point of view that many of us have been increasingly impressed by. If I may try to say what I think he would warn us about after all this discussion of "milieu impacts" on therapy of children, it would run somewhat like this: Why are you still talking most of the time as though "milieu" or "environment" were some sort of rigid structure, and the individuals were good for nothing but to "react" to it?

How does some of that "environment" you talk about come into being, after all? Couldn't we reverse the story just as well, and ask: "What do your child patients do to their milieu?"—not only: "What does the milieu do to them?" Mine, by the way, are doing plenty to it, and I have little doubt but that many of the items which we describe as though they were fixtures on the environmental scene are actually products of the attitudes and actions of the very people who, after they have produced them, are also exposed to their impact in turn.

I, for one, would want to exclaim loudly what I didn't dare whisper too much at the start of my paper, or I would have scared you off too soon. I would like to find out not only what milieu is and how it operates, but also how we can describe it, how we influence it, and by what actions of all involved it is, in turn, created or molded. At the moment I am convinced of only one thing for sure—we all have quite a way to go to achieve either of those tasks.

NOTES

1. "The Meaning of 'Therapeutic Milieu,'" in *Symposium on Preventive and Social Psychiatry, 15–17 April 1957*, Walter Reed Army Institute of Research (Washington, D.C.: Government Printing Office, 1958).

2. Some more detailed description of this appears in *Group Processes: Transactions of the Fourth (1957) Conference*, Bertram Schaffner, Ed. (New York: Josiah Macy, Jr. Foundation, 959).

3. *Strategy and Techniques of the Life Space Interview*, Am. J. Orthopsychiatry, 29:1–19, 1959.

3

DESIRABLE FEATURES OF A THERAPEUTIC COMMUNITY IN A PRISON

Maxwell Jones

Below outlines a list of principles essential in putting together a therapeutic community in a prison setting:

1. Clients and staff members must be motivated. In practice this means that they must volunteer to work as a problem-solving group.

2. Confidentiality within the therapeutic community must be respected.

3. Prison authorities must delegate responsibility and authority to the therapeutic community.

4. The therapeutic community (TC) leader, or his or her equivalent, must have access to the prison authorities at all times.

5. Traditional prison rules must be modified to accommodate an atypical social system, which is what a therapeutic community is.

6. The inevitable crises at the interface between the two systems must, when possible, lead to learning as a social process for both parties.

7. At this interface a facilitator is desirable who is acceptable to people in both systems.

8. Clients should have as much responsibility and authority as they are competent to manage.

9. Decision making by consensus should be a goal from the start.

10. There should be an inverse relationship between the growth potential of the clients and the degree of staff intervention and role modeling that is practiced.

11. The clients should nominate their own leaders (a client committee).

12. This committee should represent culture carriers for their peer group.

13. Discipline and other important decisions can, through time, be delegated to this committee.

14. With rapid turnover of clients, the staff members have to be prepared to recycle basic principles as required.

15. This oscillatory process has peaks when clients assume considerable responsibility and the staff becomes largely supervisory, and times when this process is reversed.

16. Growth in the direction of social maturity is an immediate goal for the staff and ultimately for the clients too.

17. Follow-through of clients on leaving the TC, in terms of social support and housing, a sufficient peer-group identity, job security, and satisfaction, is the ultimate goal of a TC.

18. The concept of "treatment" is an existential one in which the individual and the group seek a feeling of purpose in relation to society. The process is one of two-way communication of content and feeling, listening, interaction, and problem solving, leading to learning.

19. Treatment and training overlap, so that one can talk of treating staff and training clients as well as vice versa.

20. Twenty prisoners or less is a manageable size; but larger numbers can be broken down to create units of optimal size.

21. These principles are applied in the daily community meeting of inmates and staff followed by process review involving all staff members and the inmate committee.

It may take months before a culture-carrying group of inmates has emerged who can interpret the principles of a therapeutic community to new prison referrals. Staff members act as role models and help inmates to learn the fundamentals of group dynamics, problem solving, and decision making by consensus. As the trust level improves, so does the quality of communication of content and feeling. The aim is learning as a social process, with inmates playing responsible roles in relation to their peers, improving each individual's self-image, and so on.

A concrete example of procedure is our current routine at the Maricopa County Jail at Durango, Phoenix, Arizona, where we have a brief daily staff meeting (15 minutes) to go over events since the previous day's community meeting, followed by a preview (15 minutes) with inputs by four elected members of the inmate committee, resulting in a tentative agenda for the community meeting of inmates and staff, which lasts about 50 minutes. This meeting aims at information sharing, interaction, listening, and problem solving.

Immediately following the community meeting we have a review lasting as long as the community meeting itself. The four members of the inmate committee attend, along with all staff members, and relive the community meeting from start to finish. This is a difficult exercise because we inevitably criticize our individual performances: Did we listen, respond sensitively to verbal and nonverbal cues, ignore painful inputs and psychotic thinking? Did the staff tend to dominate the meeting and fail to reinforce positive inmate remarks? Were we irrelevant at times, did we use reminiscence as a defense or fail to develop an important or threatening theme? A daily exercise of this kind sharpens the skills of both inmates and staff and enhances the process of growth.

Much can depend on the orientation, experience, and skills of the TC leader or leaders. His or her previous training and experience must inevitably have an impact on the ideology that emerges. However, the general principles of a democratic egalitarian society will produce very similar social organizations as demonstrated by diverse TC experiments in various settings.[1] Recently confusion has been caused by Synanon and other drug-abuse programs that, starting a decade after the original therapeutic community movement, also used the term therapeutic community. This latter development is fundamentally different from the earlier one and uses confrontation, punishment, and persuasion along with transactional analysis, in a very forceful way and in a relatively authoritarian social organization. These and other differences between the two models have been described elsewhere[2] and will be returned to later in this chapter.

THE MEDICAL (CLOSED) AND THERAPEUTIC (OPEN) SYSTEM

My own interest and involvement date from 1940,[3] although we have used the term therapeutic community only since 1947. For four decades, we have enjoyed increasing support and help from the behavioral science field, and have become more and more estranged from the doctor-dominated medical world, as may be inferred from the roster of "principles" I have listed.

The two systems, the medical and the therapeutic-community, are almost diametrically opposed; the former is relatively authoritarian or closed, and the latter essentially democratic or "open."

It is possible, however, to move from a previously closed system or organization to a more open one. In practice, change in the direction of an open system implies certain stages, processes, or (again) principles. Let me list a few of these:

1. *Two-way communication,* which in this context means the sharing of valid information

2. The establishment of *primary goals,* which usually involves discussion and interaction

3. *Problems* usually arise, which may manifest themselves as *symptoms,* such as absenteeism, poor morale, or hatred of authority. (This means the system is unfrozen.)

4. *Identification of problems* through interaction and analysis of content and feeling

5. *Establishment of priorities* must occur. Areas to be emphasized might include lack of open communication, fear of authority, and other concerns

6. Long-term or short-term planning, which involves regularly scheduled *meetings*

7. Skilled psychodynamically trained resource personnel either from within the system or by contract with an outside *consultant or facilitator*

8. Interaction, discussion of relevant topics, and *problem solving* by the appropriate representatives of the social system at risk

9. Social learning, which implies a *change in individuals' attitudes and beliefs* in relation to the topic under discussion and the internalization of this information so that it modifies personality

10. Such a process of learning is an essential preliminary to reaching group consensus. *Consensus implies compromise* and a willingness for internal commitment to a group goal, which seldom is *exactly* what any one individual would choose

11. The above goes beyond *shared decision making*, which may involve no internal commitment and may simply call for a show of hands

12. *Internal commitment* means the course of action or choice that has been internalized by each member so that she or he experiences a high degree of ownership and has a feeling of responsibility about the choice and its implications. It means that individuals have reached the point where they are acting on the choice because it fulfills their own needs and sense of responsibility, as well as those of the system

13. *Implementation* is the action phase, which results from all the foregoing considerations

14. *Evaluation* is the process by which an attempt is made to assess the degree of success in meeting the organization's goals as originally planned.

The term organization development (OD) is often used to describe the process outlined above. There are at least two commonly used definitions of OD: an effort planned, organization-wide, and managed from the top to increase organization effectiveness and health through planned interventions in the organization's "processes," using behavioral-science knowledge; and a complex educational strategy intended to change the beliefs, attitudes, values, and structure of organizations.[4]

INTRODUCING THE THERAPEUTIC COMMUNITY INTO PRISONS

My colleagues and I have demonstrated the advantages of an open as opposed to a closed system in psychiatry on many occasions,[5] but the fact remains that the interest in therapeutic communities seems to have passed its peak, although there is a growing interest in this field in the prison service.

The resistance to the concept of therapeutic communities is very understandable. We are exposed to relatively authoritarian systems all our lives—at home, in colleges and other schools, and at work. The values of money, authority, and status are taken for granted. To reverse this trend in the direction of shared responsibility and decision making, open communication, and learning as a social process challenges the status quo. Take doctors as an example: their authority is seldom questioned except by their peers. We all fear death and need the support and skill of the medical profession to allay (partly) these fears. Add to this relatively unchallenged position of authority the fact that a doctor's training includes little or no exposure to learning theory, communication theory, or systems theory, and the resistance to change becomes even more understandable. The elitism of the medical profession makes democratic practices such as shared decision making with less extensively trained professionals (nurses, social workers, and others) far from appealing. Moving up in the hierarchy to hospital administrators and boards of management makes democratization of the whole bureaucracy seem even less possible. The same difficulties are apparent in the prison system, magnified by the need for security.

Bureaucracy has spread like a cancer in prisons and medical care systems, but even this would be "treatable" if the basic principles of organizational development were understood and practiced. At the very least, delegation of responsibility and authority to functional units in prisons or hospitals would allow a therapeutic community to emerge.

This was the case in a significant development in penal institutions associated with the name of Martin Groder, a psychiatrist. He was working at the maximum-security federal prison at Marion, Illinois, from 1968 to 1974, and developed a form of therapeutic community which was named Asklepieion after the temple of the Greek god of healing. Groder had been influenced by his contacts in California with Synanon (Chuck Dederich) and by Eric Berne's transactional analysis. He managed to convince the authorities to sanction an inmate group of some twenty-five volunteers who would evolve their own treatment program. The prison officers were not involved in forming the group, which was attended by Groder and two mental health staff members. To start with, the inmates, who lived in a separate unit in the prison hospital, were given lectures on TA and began to use Synanon confrontation groups. These special "games" could be invoked at any time of day or night by any member of the group. The focus of the interactions was always on one member, who was intensely confronted by his peers concerning his behavior and performance in the group. Twice a week, regularly scheduled games were held, which concerned everyone in the group. Jobs around the unit were allocated according to merit—the unsavory chores (such as toilet cleaning) amounted to punishment, except in the case of the newcomer, who always started at the lowest level of jobs. The basic rules, prohibiting physical violence or threats of violence, gambling, drugs, or homosexual behavior, were rigidly enforced, and an offender was automatically extruded from the group.

The prison itself housed approximately 700 felons who were thought to represent the most dangerous element in the U.S. prison system. Fighting, gambling and drug trafficking were common occurrences in the prison as a whole, but Asklepieion was a group of inmates who without interference by law enforcement officers were establishing and maintaining their own rules and their therapeutic culture. The principles of the peer group therapeutic culture, established twenty years earlier in London by the original therapeutic community, were rediscovered. Therapeutic responsibility and discipline at Marion were shared by the community as a whole. The peer group was deemed all-important and confidentiality was strictly adhered to. Inputs from any treatment modality were discussed by the group and adopted in accordance with their relevance to the group. Gestalt therapy, primal therapy, behavior modification, and other techniques made their contributions to the overall therapeutic culture. With such an open system, social learning was reinforced. Thus, the Synanon game was modified at Marion and is less "violent" than at Synanon, because Marion inmates believe that confrontation without caring is unproductive. In this context a "violent" verbal attack on a peer is immediately reacted to by the group and the angry peer is confronted. Although the unit at Marion is now closed, several models of this kind have been developed in prisons throughout the United States. The principles of Asklepieion differ significantly from the therapeutic community principles already outlined mainly in the use of forceful persuasion as eptiomized by Synanon-type games. Other differences include a more psychotherapeutic approach to problem solving, greater use of trained professional staff members who act as role models for the inmates, decision making by consensus, and learning as a social process leading to personality growth. At this stage in our evolution, both models deserve careful consideration, and it is probable that Asklepieion method may have advantages for certain "hardened" clients and the model I espouse may suit better the more sensitive, short-term inmates.

The only hope for the future as I see it is the establishment of viable models of a therapeutic community that can be demonstrated and experienced at first hand and used as a training base.

The wider educational and cultural factors must take precedence over improved correctional services. Preventive social action, like preventive medicine, is much more promising as long-term measures than as immediate first aid measures. But even here there are promising developments, such as the Therapeutic Community Act of 1978, a bill introduced by Senator DeConcini, 95th Congress S. 3227; and the plan to establish four separate therapeutic communities in the prison system of New York State.

We have described the principles of the therapeutic community which originated in 1947 as applied to hospitals, prisons, and other social organizations, and have contrasted this original therapeutic community with the therapeutic communities developed afterwards based on the Synanon model and later modified in prisons under the name of Asklepieion. The development of the original therapeutic community as a reaction to the traditional authoritarian hierarchical hospital social organization is discussed briefly.

NOTES

1. Rossi, J., & Filstead, W., eds. *The therapeutic community*. New York: Behavioral Publications, 1973.

2. Jones, M. Therapeutic communities old and new. *American Journal of Drug and Alcohol Abuse*, in press for vol. 6, 2 (1979).

3. Jones, M. *Social psychiatry: a study of therapeutic communities.* London: Tavistock Publications, 1952. Also published as *The therapeutic community: a new treatment method in psychiatry.* New York: Basic Books, 1953.

4. Argyris, C. *Intervention theory and method.* Reading, Mass.: Addison-Wesley, 1970; French, W. L. & Bell, C. H. *Organization development: behavioral science interventions for organization improvement.* Englewood Cliffs, N.J.: Prentice-Hall, 1978.

5. Jones, M. *Social psychiatry: in the community, in hospitals, and in prisons.* Springfield, Ill.: Charles C. Thomas, 1962; Jones, M. *Beyond the therapeutic community: social learning and social psychiatry.* New Haven, Conn.: Yale University Press, 1968: Jones, M. *Social psychiatry in practice.* Middlesex, England: Penguin Books, 1968; Jones, M. *Maturation of the therapeutic community.* New York: Human Sciences Press, 1976.

4

FROM "LIVING LEARNING" TO "LEARNING TO LIVE": AN EXTENSION OF SOCIAL THERAPY

J. Douglas Grant

Maxwell Jones has advocated the use of all social forces, not just the doctor-patient relationship in therapy. He stressed democratization and the participation of all in a process of social learning—learning from our efforts at living together. The core concept was *living learning*.

An an application of this concept, we have worked for 30 years to explore living learning that occurs when clients and front-line staff participate in social research.[1] Our efforts involve democratizing the process of organization development (see Chapter 3). While we have not eliminated emotional learning of the sort found in classic therapeutic communities, we have extended the concept of living learning to the acquisition of knowledge about contextual forces that affect problems of personal and organizational development. We see this as a merging of mental health and education through participation in applied social research.[2]

HOW FAR CAN ONE GO WITH A GOOD CONCEPT?

There is growing concern these days with problems of the future and building participation into strategies for solving these problems. This chapter will suggest the possibility of extending the notion of social therapy to cover people learning to address the use of ecological forces of the present, extrapolating such learning to the force fields of the future.

A United Nations spokesperson recently concluded that

> Futurists express different views on the issues of who ought to control the new technologies. Almost all believe that individuals should become more involved in the planning process, if only to avoid the past mistakes of poorly guided government planners. But politicians, futurists and others

who try to generate greater community action often encounter marked apathy, and occasionally deep pessimism, about personal and common futures. Also, as technologies grow in complexity, decisions on how to employ them fall more and more to specialists familiar to all the issues.

In the long run, though, the possibility of totalitarianism will disappear only if both intellectual expertise and popular sentiment contribute to decisions. The two-way flow of information needed to make this hope a reality would insure that the liberties guaranteed by democracy will remain intact in a technological world.[3]

This statement may appear to take us afield from issues of therapeutic communities, but I shall try to draw briefly some links to it in the next few pages.

DEMOCRATIZATION, MENTAL HEALTH, AND THE FUTURES PROBLEM

Democratization is a necessary but not sufficient condition for the occurrence of change. From the point of view of the individual, and that of society, *informed* constituencies are called for, because the ability to use knowledge to alter one's environment reduces anxiety.[4] Exchanging a state of powerlessness in the face of an overwhelming environment for competence (even partial competence) in dealing with the ineptness and inequities of that environment is conducive to improved mental health. The merging of learning with participation in program development is a way to build an informed constituency for participation in the present and for determining alternative futures. It is also therapeutic.

Why is this so? In thinking about what makes therapy effective, we once concluded that it helps to maximize a challenging uncomfortableness without producing rigidifying panic.[5] Participation in program development creates the challenging uncomfortableness of having to study a problem. As coping competence is developed through effective problem solving, anxiety and rigidifying panic are reduced. It is quite plausible that much of our ineptness about the present is related to a rigidifying panic about the future—that as a consequence we have an ostrich-like approach to problems of survival. It follows that the therapeutic model of introducing knowledge and participation in handling daily living crises can be applied to larger present-day problems and to issues of alternative futures. The acquiring of knowledge through participation in the study of alternative futures can lead to anxiety reduction, which can do away with our panic about the present and foster both the challenge and the uncomfortableness necessary for us to move through the present to the future. This boils down to a model that enhances mental health as it provides the competence and strategies that enable citizens to participate in social experimentation and planning.[6]

HOW DO WE DO IT?

The merging of education with participation in program development is really a living-learning, problem-centered method of education that starts where the learner is and can extend his or her horizons of knowledge. This expanding knowledge can be presented over three dimensions: community forces constituting the present, determinants of alternative futures, and technologies to influence potential alternative futures. This approach calls for reorganizing and categorizing knowledge. In studying a social-action problem, you introduce the relevant needs, objectives, obstacles, and strategies over the force field in which the problem operates. It is this force field and the understanding of it that open up the opportunity for using actual experiences and problems faced by the student. The force field extends plausibly from more intimate to more comprehensive sets of forces. Further, the force field can be projected from the present into alternative futures.

An example of such an expanding horizon is the problem of secondary school climate improvement. Students studying the problem of improving their school's climate have to address the dynamics of the school board, local and state funding, and other legislative opportunities and constraints. This leads to concerns with issues of inflation and employment issues, which lead to consideration of international impacts on U.S. policy and programs.

These interacting forces can be studied as interacting learning projects shared among the students. Small teams of students can study different facets, with the composite being shared through "social trends and issues" seminars in which specific force field analyses precede specific program development projects.

Studying problems of present and future program development fosters expansion of the knowledge of kinds of strategies from micro to macro strategies, and places the learner's private problems into relevant social context in which they can be addressed.

EDUCATION FOR AND THROUGH PARTICIPATION

To become an effective participant in program development requires, in addition to knowledge, specific competencies. What must one be able to do?

1. One must be able to determine where one wants to go. One must be able to state one's goals, and state them within a frame of reference about the nature of mental health. One must be able to state the things that will need to be accomplished (specific objectives) if one is to reach one's goal.
2. One must be able to obtain information to clarify the nature of a problem. This can include obtaining and using material developed by others as well as collecting systematic information of one's own.

3. One must be able to develop plausible interventions to cope with the problem as one has defined it and come up with appropriate strategies for handling anticipated obstacles.

4. One must be able to evaluate the effectiveness of one's interventions. This assumes that one has stated observable events that are expected to follow, based on the assumptions one has made about why one's intervention ought to work.

5. One must throughout this have some sense of the tentative nature of truth. One must be able to treat data as offering or failing to offer support for specific hypotheses about the nature of the world and of people, not as absolute truth that forecloses other options. This stance may be taken for granted among people at large.

6. I would add one more thing. Program developers not only need to develop their competence in institutional change—they also need to contribute to the development of these competencies in their clients and peers. There is no room for a new elite who would rearrange an agency (or the world) to make everyone more mentally healthy. Whether a new elite is preferable to the old elite is besides the point. A person's concern should be with assisting others to develop the competence to cope with the world on their own.

The learning experience offered clients in this type of program is based on two principles: knowledge is acquired through *using* knowledge; and learning is facilitated by maximizing learners' participation in developing their own learning programs and in providing knowledge to themselves and to others. This differs in several important ways from traditional education, and the structure for such learning evolved out of a project-learning model developed for mental health workers,[7] rather than from the classroom. The model features:

1. A learning contract: The learner shares his or her educational objectives, plans for reaching them, and how reaching them will be evaluated, in the form of a learning contract negotiated with persons in charge of the learning experience. If a formal accrediting institution is available, it must award agreed-upon credits, a degree, or both when the learner has reached the learning objectives outlined in this contract.

2. Program development projects: Carrying out specific projects is the essential mechanism for learning through using knowledge. The learners, individually or in teams, take problems facing settings in which they live or work, and study ways to bring about needed change and development within these settings. The learners acquire knowledge related to their learning objectives from their work on these projects. The project plan includes a statement of the learning objectives to be reached through carrying it out.

3. The role of the staff: Staff members serve as a resource to the learners by introducing whatever knowledge they need to plan and carry out their projects. They serve as a continuing resource to the learner, in both development of the learning contract and evaluation of the success with which the learner reaches his or her educational goals, which include products that reflect the knowledge he or she has acquired.

WHO IS COMPETENT TO PARTICIPATE?

What evidence do we have that lower-echelon staff and consumers of institutional services—students, patients, clients, teachers, policemen, mental health workers (populations that from an elitist model of research utilization and change are considered obstacles to change)—can be converted from perceived liabilities to effective assets in the process of social change?

One such line of evidence comes from the new careers movement, which has documented the capacity for learning and involvement in planned change of persons with little formal education or training, although research activity was not the main concern of services developed in New Careers programs.[8]

We have other evidence, however, because since 1964 we have worked with all sorts of non-college graduates in developing their competencies in social action research. The earliest of these studies was done with offenders who had committed felonies and were confined in California state prisons. It was intended to train them for roles as program development assistants in criminal justice agencies.[9] Overlapping this work with offenders, we also worked with police officers, developing them as students of the problems of their own agency.[10] We began with 7 officers we rated as having peer leadership abilities, whom we selected from a pool of 60 officers who had had a high incidence of citizen-officer conflict. With our support, the officers developed and administered a critical incident questionnaire that demonstrated awesome variance among officers and staff members in the ways they approached appropriately coping with potentially explosive conflict situations. These findings led to modifications in recruit and field officer training.

Our first group of officers later worked with a second group of 18 officers. Out of their joint work have come programs for the management of landlord-tenant conflict, for family crisis intervention, and for a new and unique officer review panel. An officer who has been involved in a large number of conflicts with citizens is contacted by peers and offered the opportunity of participating with them in a review of his or her ways of handling potential conflict situations.

In addition to the intervention itself, the officers, with our support, devised methods of coding incident reports, and from these enabled their department to obtain computer printouts that aid in selecting panel participants, provide information for the review panel, and give periodic performance evaluation. Since the inception of the review panel, the number of citizen-officer confrontations for the police department has been reduced by more than half, as has the number of internal affairs complaints and disciplinary actions taken. The reduction for 160 panel participants has been significantly higher than the reduction for the total department. Lower-echelon staff members in this agency, with a minimal amount of technical support, have brought about changes that affect that agency's dealings with its clients.

More germane to our concern has been work in which we have assisted the staff of new career community mental health projects in studying their own programs. What we have done is to render technical assistance to each project's own planning, program development, and evaluation effort. We work with the project's staff (in some cases mental health professionals, in some cases local community people) to get clear statements of project goals and objectives, with a view of where they stand in relation to those objectives, what obstacles they will have to face in moving from where they are to their objectives, and what strategies they must use to cope with these obstacles. This self-study process has used indigenous staff members, often non-college graduates, as principal on-site researchers.

There has been much objection to this kind of research. A three-fold premise voiced frequently by planning and evaluation experts is that a local researcher, indigenous to the program and the community, but not a research expert, first, would not know enough and, second, would not be accepted by people locally, because she or he would be seen as working for someone other than the local program. It is assumed, in addition, that a local researcher who did prove useful would be taken away from the evaluation operation and put in a position more "valuable" to the local program.

This set of hypotheses has been refuted. The projects have taken part in self-study, and the researcher roles have been seen as relevant by the local project staff. Another outcome strongly supporting the value of local participation in research is the correlation obtained between the extent to which the staff participated in program development study and the extent to which the program reached its stated objectives. Bench marks were determined for objectives. Rank order correlations between the number of such bench marks that were reached and an independent assessment of the effectiveness of programs in using program development correlated in the 60s. Further, initial ratings of the potential of each program do not correlate as well with its achievement, and participation does not correlate with the original ratings. In other words, this is not a case in which programs seen initially as potentially effective are good at reaching their objectives and at taking part in program development study. In addition, participation was not related to the original estimates of program effectiveness.

Project directors who at first resisted program development study now state that it has made their work more organized and more effective, that it has given them a framework for anticipating problems and handling problems, allocating staff time and effort, developing further proposals, and working with other resources. They also state that it has improved the mental health of the director and the staff.

I have described these programs in detail, because in each case change has been initiated and implemented by lower-echelon staff, consumers within an agency, or both. The same point holds of Fairweather's work with hospitalized diagnosed schizophrenics, who demonstrated considerable skill at self-governance and program innovation both within an institution and in a postinstitution setting.[11] Similarly, Schensul, who directs a research program within a community mental health setting at the Illinois State Psychiatric Institute, has demonstrated the capacity of a local constituency (largely Latino) to participate in community action research.[12] Sanford has reported that undergraduate college students are being effective researchers of their own education programs,[13] and Guttentag has documented local community participation in action research regarding community control of local schools in Harlem.[14] The Palo Alto school system in California has grouped teachers, students, and community representatives as a team to engage in social intervention.[15] In fact, there are growing numbers of secondary and elementary school community-based programs that are demonstrating the capacity of non-college graduates to engage in efforts toward community and institutional study and change.[16]

REENTRY AND CREATING SUPPORTIVE SETTINGS

Within confinement institutions, a therapeutic community setting provides a strong supportive base for building program development participation. We paradoxically run into our major problems in postinstitutionalization settings, where we encounter a plethora of concerns about ownership of turf. We join the struggles of employee participation and we inherit the struggles of labor and management over decision-making control. We also inherit the country-wide concern with empire building and empire protection. Program development has inherent in it the merging of forces from agencies dealing with areas such as mental health, secondary and postsecondary education, delinquency prevention, substance abuse prevention, and social welfare. In relation to such mergings, we find appreciable rhetoric and even supportive legislation, but we note that the power to resist shared development has remained strong.

A potential for turning a liability into an asset in strategies for building supportive settings is the growing concern of agencies, unions, and professional associations with the burn-out phenomenon.[17] Like decreasing employment, the burn-out phenomenon on the surface invites rigidifying defensive stands. However, the burn-out phenomenon can be addressed through employee participation, very much including the merging of personal development with program development, because the burn-out phenomenon is tied to the meaninglessness of lower-echelon (and, sometimes, higher-level) jobs.

Linkages between participatory program development efforts in confinement institutions and such efforts among nonconfined employees and clients can be promoted through the reentry responsibilities that both groups have. With the use, of work and education release, it would be possible to establish linkages prior to formal reentry, including knowledge of roles to be played and jobs to be filled in community-based program development for the exconfined trainee. This offers the chance of merging the support and knowledge of confinement programs with the strength and opportunities of community-based participatory efforts. In such ventures, one is not limited to full-time program development roles. It is possible that employee participation can be built into established jobs, within both public and private organizations, where one spends several hours a week as part of one's regular job engaged in development efforts to improve the organization.

ADDRESSING THE FUTURE

If we substitute scenarios of alternative futures for present program development, we can apply the merging of learning and program development principles to the study of futures. Again, one must be concerned with what is needed to bring into being alternative futures—with the objectives, the obstacles, and the strategies for meeting these obstacles. One can substitute the extended vision of a scenario for the goal of the immediate program. Program development then becomes the issue of how to get from the present through the projected force fields over time to the envisioned future.

BUILDING NORMS

Charles Silberman, in his recent publication *Criminal Violence, Criminal Justice*, concludes that "the development of more effective social controls in poor communities can provide a far larger payoff in reducing crime and improved order than can the development of more effective methods of policing, more efficient courts, and improved correctional programs. There is truth, in addition to rhetorical exaggeration, in E. H. Sutherland's dictum: "When the mores are adequate, laws are unnecessary; when the mores are inadequate, the laws are ineffective. It is not a question of either/or; both laws and mores are needed. The point is that they are complementary. The stronger the mores, the more effective the laws tend to be—it is possible to enfuse poverty stricken neighborhoods with a sense of community and purpose, and thus to develop the internal controls that help redress (or prevent) crime."[18]

Providing opportunities for reentering offenders to participate in community-based programming provides a strategy for the use of the product of the problem (offenders) in coping with the problem (crime) through their assistance in building a community having purpose and offering mores for internal control. We have a right to expect a merging of the development of the offenders' personal mores with their participation in development of community mores.

NOTES

1. Grant, J. D. The use of correctional institutions as self-study communities in social research. *British Journal of Delinquency* (1957) 7:301–7.

2. Grant, J. D. Management of conflict within correctional institutions. In *Medical care of prisoners and detainees*. London: Ciba Foundation Symposium 16 (1973):183–92.

3. Hamil, R. The fate of democracy in a technological world. *The futurist* (1979) 13:115.

4. Bell, C. S. A sane economy for a sane people. In *Mental health today and tomorrow*. San Rafael, Cal.: Social Action Research Center, 1974.

5. Grant, J. D., & Grant, M. Q. A group dynamics approach to the treatment of nonconformists in the Navy. *Annals of the American Academy of Political and Social Science* (1959) 322:126–35. Reprinted in Riessman, F., Cohen, J., & Pearl, A., eds. *Mental health of the poor*. New York: Free Press, 1964.

6. *Work in America*. Report of a Special Task Force to the Secretary of Health, Education and Welfare. Cambridge: MIT Press, 1973.

7. Grant, J. D. Staff and consumer participation in institution change: a merging of mental health and education. In *Mental health today and tomorrow*. San Rafael, Cal.: Social Action Research Center, 1974.

8. Grant, J. D., & Grant, J. Evaluation of new careers programs. In Struening, E. L., & Guttentag, M., eds. *Handbook of evaluation research*. Beverly Hills: Sage, 1975.

9. Grant, J. D., & Grant, J. Contagion as a principle in behavior change. In Rickard, H. C., ed. *Unique programs in behavior readjustment*. Elmsford, N.Y.: Pergamon, 1971.

10. Toch, H., Grant, J. D., & Galvin, R. T. *Agents of change: a study in police reform*. New York: John Wiley and Sons, 1975.

11. Fairweather, G. *Community life for the mentally ill*. Chicago: Aldine, 1969.

12. Schensul, S. L. The contributions of anthropology to education and service delivery in mental health. In *Mental health today and tomorrow*. San Rafael, Cal.: Social Action Research Center, 1974.

13. Sanford, N. Research with students as action and education. *American Psychologist* (1969) 25:544–46.

14. Guttentag, M. Children in Harlem's community controlled schools. *Journal of Social Issues* (1972) 28, No. 4:1–20.

15. Stromquist, N. and Johnson, R. Who participates? A field study of participation in planning in a school district. ED 131-605, Eric System, 1977.

16. *Youth participation*. Report of the National Commission on Resources for Youth to the Office of Youth Development, Department of Health, Education and Welfare, 1975.

17. Maslach, C. Client role in staff burn-out. *Journal of Social Issues* (1978) 34:111–23.

18. Silberman, C. E. *Criminal violence, criminal justice*. New York: Random House, 1978.

5

TC OR NOT TC? THAT IS THE QUESTION

Robert B. Levinson

Many of the procedures implemented in institutions are established essentially for the benefit of the managers. This point holds regardless of the identity of the clients in whose interest the arrangements presumably have been made, be they graduate students or prison inmates.

Management procedures are usually justified because of their humaneness—regardless of whether they are effective or efficient. It is serendipitous when the needs are met of both management and residents, *and* the endeavor turns out to be beneficial at the .05 level or better. Fortunately, such a case can be made for therapeutic communities.

WHY TCs ARE NOT OMNIPRESENT

As with most treatment approaches, therapeutic communities (TCs) help some residents, have little effect on others, and are probably harmful for still other individuals. The trick is to enlarge the first category and reduce or eliminate the other two, and most important, not to oversell the concept. Since panaceas are no more viable than the Loch Ness monster, advocates of TCs only diminish their credibility if they proclaim that the TC social structure meets all possible demands.

From the perspective of a corrections administrator, TCs increase the sale of Grecian Formula on a par with most other manipulations. This is not to say that TCs do not have a place within the correctional armamentarium—they assuredly do! The point is that they perform many functions, only one of which is helping some individuals exposed to the sometimes not-so-tender environment of a TC.

Prisoners (and some of their advocates) would have the so-called straight world believe that much of the effort of correctional administrators is directed by a "divide-and-conquer" philosophy. They contend that correctional managers have as an explicit, deliberate goal the setting up of one faction of inmates against another. This keeps the prisoners so busy that the staff can get the upper hand and maintain a semblance of control. While the statement contains more poetry than truth, it is at least partly true.

THE PARTS APPROACH

Typically, prisons are table-organized as a single whole. There may be teams, committees, departments, and so on, but generally all staff members deal with all inmates and vice versa, as in a prison-factory in which raw material comes in at one end and, through various processes, leaves at the other end as a finished product. Each of the sections within the factory has performed its function with every emerging product—and sometimes no one even has to send out an all-points recall bulletin. In this connection, the wonder of it, as Peter Drucker points out, is not that institutions work so badly, but that anything works at all.

A different institutional organization—having a "small is beautiful" orientation—would take a 600-bed prison and restructure it as six 100-bed "minifacilities," each of which operates in semiautonomous fashion. With this type of organization, the "factory" can continue production of Cadillacs even when the Chevy assembly line has run into some snags; GM, as a whole, is not shut down.

The establishment of mini-institutions—semiautonomous units— within a large prison has repeatedly demonstrated that this organizational structure results in a more smoothly functioning, safer, more humane, and (there is reason to believe) more rehabilitative institution. This approach capitalizes on much social psychology and group dynamic lore. It reduces the depersonalizing aspects of prison life. It establishes subgroups within both the inmate and the staff populations, which can productively interact with each other. Since every staff member does not have to know every inmate, some personnel and some prisoners can meaningfully get to know one another and begin to work together productively.

Within this unitized organizational structure, a variety of classification and treatment modality combinations can be tried out and among these the therapeutic community modality takes its place. The pitfall that must be avoided is thinking that TCs should be the only type of treatment used.

THE PROBLEM WITH TCs

Although viewed by their advocates as fine and many-splendored things TCs can be a source of worry to administrators who have responsibilities for running institutions as a whole. Questions arise such as "Is the staff still in charge, or are inmates running the show?" "How do we know they are not plotting a mass escape or take-over of the institution?" "Can we let them continue to dress down staff members verbally; doesn't that encourage disrespect and undermine staff authority?" "How come they don't have to follow the rules like everyone else?" Suspicions, tinged with paranoia, can be the source of a growing alienation between administration and the TC— leading to the administration's having to demonstrate its authority over the TC, and precipitating, eventually, the TC's demise.

Because of the suspicions they engender—particularly when functioning in an otherwise traditionally organized institution—TC's in prisons must be externally open. They need to invite in the rest of the prison world. This, of course can be very disruptive, particularly in the initial phases of getting a TC started. But some accommodation needs to be worked out, so that supposedly "dark deeds" by the TC can be viewed in a more realistic light.

Despite the unpopular and often unstated view, the fact is that inmates and staff are not coequals—particularly in a correctional setting. The staff has a responsibility that it cannot abdicate; staff members are in charge. How they conduct themselves in fulfilling this responsibility is an issue well deserving of exploration. True, to the degree that it can be achieved, one would encourage enlisting inmates' efforts in maintaining a safe, humane environment in which individuals are treated with respect for their human dignity. Correctional staff members may take off their ties and jackets, but that does not mean that they have become like any other member of the group. To pretend otherwise is to deny the reality TCs are designed to focus on.

This does not mean that TCs are unworkable in prison. One must, however, point out that the folklore is just that; prison TCs are not the true democracies some profess them to be.

One other aspect of TCs is also troublesome; do they disqualify their members for honest work? While this concern is expressed whimsically, it has been noted that many TC graduates want to become staff members or run their own community—some never want to graduate. In the setting up of an artificial community, are TC members denied the need to test their newly found strengths in that cruel world outside?

WHERE ARE WE?

Lest this essay create a "down with TCs" atomosphere, let me state explicitly that therapeutic communities have much to contribute in a prison setting. The intent here is not to denigrate them. Rather, the use of TCs is a mixed blessing, as is everything else. They can, and have, significantly helped both the inmates they contain and the staff responsible for running institutions containing them. They contribute to the decentralization of large institutions; this, too, is a benefit to both staff and inmates. They allow people to show that it's O.K. to care for one another—what could be better? They also create pain and *angst;* for both members and the administration.

While every institution should have a TC, I do not think that every institution should *be* one. If the decentralized organizational structure—functional unit management, as it is called in the federal prison system—is used, then other units can offer different types of programs. A TC experience may be "just the ticket" for some inmates; others would benefit more significantly from a different approach. The real task is to discover which of many approaches is best for whom. Let's hope that we have more than one note in our symphony!

PART II

THERAPEUTIC COMMUNITY PROGRAMS AND THEIR OPERATING ASSUMPTIONS

6

AN ENCLAVE OF FREEDOM: STARTING A COMMUNITY AT CHINO

Dennie Briggs

To grow or change, we need chances to try new things, to experience new ways of being. For prisoners, however, that is near to impossible: almost by definition, their existence is, as it were, held in abeyance—their past actions have seen to that. But there is another aspect of the prisoner's situation that renders any change a herculean task: this aspect comprises the prison's social environment—the other prisoners and the guards. The concentration of people and the accumulation of customs that are involved in running an institution such as a prison are not easy to overcome. Like extra shackles, the criminal code of ethics keeps the prisoner on guard (and in turn guards the prisoner) against officials and other prisoners. The code's most important rule is, "Never get too close to anyone!"

Of course, to survive, the prisoner must take risks—but these are usually calculated very carefully. Life behind walls is so precarious that it is almost impossible to be anything but devious. The rules seem to insure that the offenders continue to indulge in a life of petty crime, which in turn reduces their self-respect to bravado, to a macho image easily attainable by brute force or blackmail. All this occurs under constant scrutiny. That, in essence, is any prison.

STAFF INFLUENCE

Would a prisoner want to model himself after or look up to his captor? What inspiration does the prison guard offer his charge? The uniform and all its connotations, the gun, towers, the locks, the orders, and above all, the keys, constantly remind the prisoner of his state—of the contempt society has for him, of the unlikelihood of any decent future. On top of all this, inmates feel that prison administrators squander potential resources on almost nightmarish practices to control, correct, and discipline them.

The idea of a therapeutic community—as Maxwell Jones envisioned and practiced it—would in such a context seem Sisyphean in its absurdity, in terms not only of facilities but also of promise. True, there is no shortage of "subjects" for experiments in prison: prisoners are willing to risk their lives because there's nothing else for them to do. But a prison situation is unlike a hospital setting, where doctors always have an abundance of help. In correctional institutions, one must rely on prison officers, whom we have described as hardly acceptable role models to the prisoners. Of course, one can improve the odds somewhat: officers can be allowed to take off their uniforms, to develop some human relations skills, to gain some experience in trying out different approaches to the prisoners. However, this last gambit may be difficult in a large prison, unless the entire prison changes its focus.

Another option—to which we shall address ourselves primarily in this paper—is to use the resources of the prisoners themselves.

CHANGE THROUGH FEEDBACK

The importance of a therapeutic community lies in creating a setting in which people can see the effects of what they do and say on others. The goal is to give them a feeling of democracy, not by chance but by design, not by legislation but by an active part in execution. Individuals must see their reflections in a social mirror that does not condemn, interpret, or condone, but faithfully reflects. The assumption is that, when reflecting on the reflection, one might want to change the image—if it is seen as disagreeable. But change it to what? "I can be like you if I can do the things you do," is one way. But who is there around to be like? The other prisoners? But why be like other prisoners?

This last question has two answers. One is that fellow prisoners are more like fellow human beings. Another is that their reasons for survival are similar. There is, to some degree, a camaraderie. But the main reason is that changes in yourself are more attainable if the goal is to be like someone who is near you.

THE FIRST GENERATION

The therapeutic community at Chino Prison had a lifetime of almost five years.[1] During the first two of these years, we operated a transitional community, where we were concerned first with mere survival: ascertaining whether a prison could tolerate a very different approach to dealing with prisoners. This community, at any one time, consisted of 35 to 50 selected young men, many of who had violence in their histories. It had to operate within the confines of a rather traditional prison for 2,000 inmates.

The next stage of developing our community was one in which we were in, but not part of, the larger prison. It entailed having a separate building and staff, and evolving a tight, self-contained group of residents. Among these inmates, the first generation was a small group of "culture carriers." This role is familiar to students of Belmont, because Jones's unit had a core group of people who not only were highly trained in their former disciplines of psychiatry, social work, or nursing, but had learned the procedures of a therapeutic community along with Jones. They assured the stability of the unit, and were the carriers of the culture. Their role was to teach new staff members and patients. The teaching included supporting and developing the contributions each staff member brought into the on-going program. Part of the function of these "seniors" was to resist any new ideas they thought would change the program adversely—the term they used was "destructively." This sorting-out process is not an easy one (who is to say what is progress and what is resistance to change or different ideologies?).

The role, however, is important, and we developed variations of it for our staff members and inmates. In the next pages, I shall briefly describe our inmate culture carriers, and portray the first stages of their evolution.

TEN APPRENTICE PIONEERS

Ten of 50 prisoners decided that they wanted to be different from other prisoners and wanted the chance to help others change. Each one had his own mark, his own reaching for individuality, dimmed though it was by life in the institution.

There was Clay, short, with black, wavy, well-groomed hair and a muscular physique kept trim by pumping irons. He spoke up a lot in group meetings, usually commanding the others with veiled threats for noncompliance. He was self-employed after a fashion, in that he had a bakery route around the prison. His regular job was to pick up and deliver laundry from the housing units and staff areas. He used his laundry cart to cover up cakes and cookies that he bought from the personnel dining room and resold to prisoners. He made a neat profit and was considered an essential member of the community and the prison at large.

Wally was an associate of Clay's and helped him with his moonlighting. He was 19 years old, had dark curly hair, and was jovial, good-natured, and very popular with the other prisoners.

Jerry completed the trio. Young, thoughtful, handsome, he dressed neatly and read a lot. He was the business manager and collector when the customers' bills went unpaid too long.

The others were Bob, Cowboy Frank, who had managed to keep his boots and hat, Lee, Dane, Russ, Buddy, and Mike. They were a mixed bag, but they wanted to form a group, and felt that they could help the others, as well as be a bridge between inmates and staff.

As a group, they seemed to have more drive and open aggression than I had seen anywhere in prison. I was, naturally, uncomfortable, thinking that this group could be destructive, in the sense that they could become spokesmen for the community rather than the bridge they said they could become. And I wondered how they could project an acceptable image unless some of them changed their own behavior. But, I thought, why not give it a try?

THE CATALYTIC GROUP

The group wanted to know more about the social therapists at Belmont Hospital, which Max Jones had founded. I gave them some of Jones's writings and told them what I could, based on my visit to Belmont. They began by mimicking the therapeutic community process.

First, they set up a log in which they kept notes about behavior they wanted to bring into the community meeting, and meetings began each morning with one of the inmates reading the entries for the past 24 hours. At first the entries pertained to other men, not to the "therapists." The community might or might not take up the entries and discuss them and their implications. The "therapists" took an active part in the meeting, usually by prodding the others or making authoritative statements. They attended a community meeting after the staff meeting, and shared their observations on what had taken place. They attended small group meetings, and again were active in discussing the men's behavior. Some gave advice freely.

In the afternoon I met with them for a "tutorial," in which they wanted to learn more about what they should be doing to develop competence as therapists. The discussions began by talking about other men, but soon centered on their own behavior: the anxieties they were experiencing in their new relations with the others. They wanted to learn more about psychology and treatment methods, about human behavior, and about delinquency. They wanted to know more about me.

Who was I? How did I get where I was? And where was I going? What was I like as a person? As if the questions they put to me were also directed at themselves, they decided to keep journals, as they knew I did. Like the mirror in which they might search at leisure, these accounts they wrote reflected with increasing detail and perception their doubts, fears, and ultimate goals, both real and imaginary. Frank wrote:

Finally I had to sit down and look at myself and what I was really doing. When I did, I saw I was forcing myself to dodge my own ways and feelings. I saw I was too ambitious and aggressive a person to use just others' ideas. I asked myself "who am I?" and "what do I want?"—not he, or she—but me. Not for me to short change myself and not grow. That's when I really started to use what's inside myself as well as what was outside.

Of course, their development was not all smooth. There were ups and downs, and many crises. But there was a gradual progression, and soon the content of their discussions centered about their own delinquencies. Lee wrote in his journal:

We had such barriers. I feel strongly that delinquency and being a social therapist are not constructive mixtures. It's pretty shallow for Joe to steal and then confront Jack with Jack's stealing. To me the non-delinquency far outweighs what a social therapist says in the groups.

Clay identified closely with me, and became one of the strongest men in the community in terms of exposing delinquency. Where he had formerly been popular with the men, because his racket gave him power, influence, and hard cash, he was now enmeshed in constant conflict. As he said, he was a big man with the cons, but this cut no ice with me! He found he had to give up his moonlighting completely to become identified with me and with his new job. He discovered that the more he abandoned his delinquency activities, the more strongly he could expose the others. I asked him bluntly one day in the tutorial if it was true that one could be just a *little* pregnant? Giving up his business meant that Wally and Jerry were now without a source of funds, and they had to either follow suit or get another racket. Russ gave away a gallon tin of peanut butter stolen from the mess hall that he sold to the men evenings, for mid-night snacks.

These changes supported Max Jones's contention that there must be discipline in a therapeutic community to lend it protection from antisocial elements and to develop a climate in which more constructive liaisons can be worked out.

The men's reformation, of course, created serious dilemmas between them and other men, many of whom had not renounced their delinquencies. Of this, Clay wrote:

I have formed a warm personal relationship with Jim. This friendship has been a tremendous experience for me. I see Jim at a vital spot in treatment. He has experienced a great deal of responsibility, and has seen what it's like when others aren't as enthusiastic as yourself. He has tried to put this back on someone else, but still carried it inside. In this past week, he has been testing me as a social therapist and friend. He took bread from the mess hall and made sure I was aware of it. He made comments about getting away with something and making me aware of it, but I didn't put it in the log. When I fed this all back, his attitude changed. I had a feeling for a little while that I might have to make a choice as his friend—or his crime partner.

The social therapists were able to help our staff in finding their own way, for there were times when the staff members did not know if they were "fish or fowl or bright red herrings." They didn't know if they were to enforce discipline, ignore it and be friendly, or give advice when pressed. Frank summarized the issue:

> After going to staff meetings I have found that I'm also trying to help staff, and at this time they are still looking. I feel, in all this, I have gotten a better understanding of myself as well as staff and others. With this understanding, and seeing different things, it is for me to try and help staff get closer to the men, so they can help more and understand more. I may see something that the staff is too close to see. In letting them know what I see—this may help us all.

BECOMING A PEER CHANGE AGENT

One of of the difficulties the social therapists encountered was that they were identified with authority and their peers simultaneously. As we have seen, they had to set examples for the men to give some discipline to the project. Yet they had to be distinct from the staff. They had to be living, attainable examples of what the other men were striving for. Few were planning to pursue change agent roles in parole as a career, not out of apathy, but because at that time jobs like that simply did not exist. But they saw their new skills as effective in dealing with people—as more effective than their former ways, at any rate. Wally wrote:

> I see men in here every day who have abilities I don't have. I now know my own abilities and potentialties, like working as a social therapist. I don't want this kind of work the rest of my life, and yet I know I have the potentialities to be good at this work, as well as the field I'll be going into when I get home. I'll work as a social therapist until I go home and also in the groups I come in contact with outside, and apply what I've learned in life as I am back with my family and others I meet.

Jerry commented:

> Seeing and knowing these things has given me strength to do my work and feel good inside even when I know that the men are mad at me for bringing

out their behavior at the time and trying to get them to look at it. Out front, you see, you are not too popular with them. But then I go over and work with them five days a week and they keep coming back for more. This tells me they do want help. Also at night they want you to hear what they got to say, so you'll bring it up in the groups. And when you do, they act out front for a while that they are mad at you, to save face with the other men. And then, when the other men step in, they drop their anger some, and start trying hard to change their ways.

In time, the social therapists learned to take the brunt of hostility they continually bore, and, eventually, even to encourage it—to be like a sponge and absorb feelings, to take them all in. They grew more secure in their roles and were always wondering what new turn they would take. It was this constant spirit of adventure—"What new things should we try?"—that was one of the more refreshing attitudes they brought to the community. They continually wanted new ideas, and pressed visitors for theirs.

DEVELOPING CARING AND SHARING

The most difficult feelings for the men to handle—for both the social therapists and the community members—were warm, positive, and affectionate ones. I believe this difficulty was not manifestly part of their course of delinquency, but symptomatic of the larger, more human problem of a person's relation to other people, of prisoner to prisoner, of guard to prisoner.

Where emotions such as hate, anger, and suspicion abound, warmth is not easily dealt with or kindled. The difficulty the men had in accepting or giving any kind of affection was viewed askance. In prison, where the rule is "divide and conquer," any open display of affection is to be feared. It was understandable, then, that an outreach experiment early in the community's life by the peer therapists should prove a breakthrough.

While the rest of our residents were at work, we noticed that clean linen had been distributed on their beds, and someone suggested that we make their beds for them. We imagined them returning hot and tired to shower and rest before the evening meal. We set about making the beds—about 50—and even the correctional officers joined in. Everyone vied with each other in getting as many beds made up as possible. Bob, who had been a psychiatric technician in the navy, showed us how to make a bed properly: squaring the corners and so on. Soon we were done.

When the men returned from work, they were, naturally, surprised. But they were also suspicious. Some joked. Some were pleased. Others were embarrassed. But there were those who were angry, and three men ripped up their beds and remade them. True to youthful natures, a few beds had been "shortsheeted" in fun.

But the experience would not leave their minds. For several days it cropped up in conversations and meetings. One man, tearfully admitted that this was the first time in his four years in prison that someone had done something kind for him.

The act, spontaneous as it was kind, was difficult to accept. The display of affection, was, as someone said, part of the utter pain that kindness elicits when you are imprisoned.

A RETROSPECTIVE VIEW

What happened to the Chino "experiment?" First of all, it demonstrated that the therapeutic community method is more effective in changing the antisocial behavior of offenders than is the rest of their prison experience. The men who participated in the study were selected at random, and their behavior—as well as that of their "running mates"—was followed for one year after they left prison. They did better. But the most significant finding was that the men who participated in the program during the time the inmate social therapists were operating not only did better upon return to the outside community than their running mates did, they also did significantly better than the prisoners who had preceded them in the therapeutic community.

The prison in which the experiment was conducted also changed noticeably. Although the project ended abruptly five years after its inception, the superintendent saw merit in many of the ideas it developed, and tranferred them to the prison itself. The institution was decentralized into smaller, autonomous units. Counselors, who had previously been housed in the administration building and had not been easily accessible to prisoners, were assigned to the housing units. Correctional officers were given new roles that involved fusing behavior control with learning. The prison eventually became a community center, where men nearing the end of their prison sentences were sent to receive special training, going out during the day on work release to find a job, make family and personal contacts, and use the prison for sleeping and support until they were paroled.

The former administrator of the California Department of Corrections, Richard McGee, said that those who participated in the experiment went through a stimulating learning experience—that none of them will be the same again. McGee also added that it is out of such painful beginnings that significant movements toward constructive change take root.

NOTE

1. The therapeutic community in Chino has been described in several publications. The following summarize the experiment as a whole: Jones, M. *Social psychiatry in the community, in hospitals and in prisons.* Springfield, Ill.: Thomas, 1962; and Whiteley, S., Briggs, D., & Turner, M. *Dealing with deviants: the treatment of antisocial behavior.* New York: Schocken, 1974.

7

THE NETWORK PROGRAM: A CONCEPT

Stephen Chinlund

Many prison innovations of the past have appeared to fail because they have been inadequately sustained or insufficiently integrated with other work taking place at the same time. They have also suffered because usually they have failed to involve the correctional officer to the fullest extent of their potential. They have thus lost the value of the officer's years of experience and continuing face-to-face involvement with inmates.

There has been further appearance of failure because of the rehabilitation theory that once held that inmates were analogous to empty cups that needed to be filled with new education and understanding. In contrast, it is our working theory that inmates are responsible for their actions and that they have considerable skills and potential for leading responsible free lives. We also recognize that offenders have made choices that have led them to actions contrary to the law, and have brought down upon themselves the anger of the community, with resulting sanctions of punishment through the courts. This is the framework within which we must operate.

THE NETWORK OF NEEDS

As the nation has sought the cause of crime and tried to understand it better, there has been a tendency to isolate particular needs and to see each as the sole locus of inmate problems. For example, there was a time when it was believed that inmates needed only vocational training in order to straighten out and be responsible. As a result, vocational training programs were offered in various states and the impact was eagerly awaited. The vocational training should have been bolstered by a variety of other interventions. However, this was rarely done. In some cases, the research people said that it would be impossible to evaluate the vocational training impact if the same inmate also participated in other programs. In other places, it was felt that the offering of vocational training was sufficient for some; therefore, other programs were offered to other inmates in an attempt to be fair. The result was the same: one program (at the most) for one inmate.

Regardless of the reason, the good work performed in vocational training was undercut by the lack of counseling, education, and, most of all, improvement of attitudes, which was necessary if the vocational training was to achieve its intended results.

There is, therefore, in our projected program, a recognition that inmates have the same variety of needs as do those in the outside world. All of us have needs to express ourselves and understand ourselves in a variety of ways. Those ways include involvement with friends, with family, with our work, with a variety of mechanisms to help us solve the problems and crises of life as they appear. It also is important for most people to have some philosophy of life for participation in a spiritual community. Finally, there are many who draw sustenance for their lives from their involvement in a variety of cultural activities such as woodworking, pottery, weaving, dancing, making music, or in some other way enjoying the opportunities offered by leisure time.

The network idea is a dynamic one referring constantly to the developing sense on the part of individual inmates that they have needs of which they may have been only dimly aware prior to participation in a responsive program. A given inmate may enter the program making a contract with himself and the program toward the end of improving his vocational skills. As he proceeds, he may make new contracts having to do with the improvement of his reading, writing, and arithmetic, and still later he may make new contracts having to do with his relationships with his family. This is the pattern that we expect, and it should not be seen as a sign of vacillation or uncertainty. In short, the program must be designed to address all the needs of an individual inmate. No prison program can directly meet all those needs, nor will ours attempt to do so; rather, it will seek to direct each inmate to the most likely way of meeting needs for himself, whether that way is inside or outside the network program.

THE NETWORK OF RESOURCES

Just as there is a network of needs, so there must be a network of resources. Those resources are designed to meet the network of needs. To do so, the program of any facility must be fully explored and engaged by each network participant. They can be expected to be involved with the facility program during the program day and possibly also in the evening. Similarly, for those who are on parole there must be a maximum emphasis on involvement in the resources of the community. Every effort will be made to develop involvements that make the fullest possible use of time. There will be then three primary resources that will be engaged:

1. The institution's own program. This will include regular vocational training and academic programs, from literacy programs to college, as well as regular counseling programs.

2. There will be programs developed by the staff and the inmates themselves. Many will be able to tutor, lead seminars, discussions, physical exercise, meditation, or group sessions, and be otherwise engaged in network program activities.

3. There will be individuals brought in from outside, both as formal parts of the network program, as developed by the Commission of Correction, and as volunteers from the community who are regarded by the inmates and officers as valuable participants. They may run special group sessions, train family groups, teach ways of being with children, and share special life skills such as developing a sound budget, learning how to interpret a pay stub, understanding the social security system and the welfare system, and so on.

At every step of the way, there will be the maximum effort to integrate the network program with the facility, so that the two will not be seen as competing for the inmates' time. Rather, the network program will complement the variety of offerings made from time to time by the facility.

THE NETWORK OF FACILITIES

Over the past ten years, the New York State Department of Correctional Services has greatly expanded the number and variety of facilities in its system. It has done so under the pressure of extraordinary increases in the inmate population. It has therefore not been able to make the most creative possible use of the facilities in the statewide system. We propose to integrate and connect these facilities by developing network programs at all three security levels—maximum, medium, and minimum.

In the maximum-security levels, there will be primary emphasis on the life within the institution. There will be the greatest emphasis on increasing awareness of peer relationships and attitudes towards authority. There will be special opportunities to explore new and responsible behavior patterns.

In the medium-security facilities, there will be some of the same emphasis indicated above, but, as the time of release grows closer, there also will be special emphasis on family reintegration and adjustment to the problems of reuniting with spouses, children, and former friends and associates. These efforts will include couples' groups, and family groups for those inmates wishing to begin the process at that time.

In minimum-security facilities, there will continue to be considerable emphasis in the areas indicated above for maximum security, but there will be new emphasis on family and employment attitudes. Inmates will have the opportunity to explore their feelings about their families, about work, and about being supervised on the outside, with the intention of heading off the explosions and confusions, that have appeared in these areas in the lives of inmates who have been released over the years.

Finally, there will be integration of the parole involvement. Once an inmate leaves a minimum-security facility for parole, every effort will be made to involve him on a postrelease basis with other program graduates, who will meet with each other for the same positive purposes as have been intended throughout the institutional part of the program. Once again, it must be emphasized that many fine programs developed within institutions have failed in the past because there was inadequate follow-up. Inmates who themselves believed that they were ready for release and had developed a whole new set of strengths and honestly assessed themselves as ready for freedom were then surprised because the pressures of the community and their own homes proved to be more than they could effectively manage. It is crucial, therefore, that the parole portion of a reintegrative program be developed as early and as fully as possible.

For those inmates who are released directly to the community without any parole supervision, and for those inmates who finally are released from parole, the network program will make every effort to develop two types of continuing network involvement:

1. Community resources such as churches, settlement houses, and Ys will be sought for settings for a weekly or monthly set of meetings. These meetings will involve inmates as well as others (such as spouses and friends) they may draw into the program. It will resemble Alcoholics Anonymous, in that it will be run by and for the group that has been previously considered to be clients. In this context, however, clients will be providing their own resources as well as their own problems.

2. Program members may meet more informally, but, it is hoped, no less regularly, in each other's homes. They may meet in groups of any size that seems practical for the ongoing purposes of mutual support and airing of problems.

THE NETWORK OF PEOPLE

The primary definition of the network program is a network of people. It will succeed only if all those in the network recognize that they are responsible for themselves individually and for helping others who are in the program. Each participant will be expected to help in a way that continues to leave clear the fact that each person is ultimately responsible for his or her own life. To do that, however, the individual needs the support, encouragement, and criticism of a network of sisters and brothers in the community in which she or he lives. For inmates, that community is prison, but after release the community is as wide as the world.

It is hoped that husbands and wives of exinmates, as well as brothers, sisters, children, parents, and friends, will be involved in network meetings, especially those outside the institutional facilities.

NETWORK: SPECIAL POINTS OF EMPHASIS

A first point is that in our culture we are generally and properly taught that we should be modest in proclaiming our own self-worth. The network program seeks to make no change in that public posture; however, it is assumed that all of us, perhaps offenders most of all, tend to undervalue ourselves, our skills, and our potential. For that reason, it will be a continuing matter of emphasis in planned program in all its phases that all participants, including staff members, learn how to acknowledge to themselves and to each other particular qualities in themselves that they value. This may appear to be a strange point of emphasis. It does, however, grow out of years of experience with inmates and even with persons who might be expected to enjoy quite a high level of self-confidence but somehow undersell themselves.

Secondly, family reintegration work has been seriously neglected by the correctional system in particular and the social work and counseling community in general. One may speculate that this neglect reflects the uncertainties experienced by the professionals themselves in an area that has been fraught with changing emphases and new perspectives during the 1960s and 1970s. Regardless of the reason for the neglect, it is crucially important that it somehow be corrected. Inmates leaving prison have chronically recognized (in retrospect) that the disappointment for which they were least prepared came in the family area. In confinement they dreamed of the satisfactions of family life, often with an increasingly unrealistic point of view. When they were finally released and were once again reunited with their families, the lack of realism in their expectations may have come home to them with terrible power. They then in some cases reacted violently toward themselves or family members or toward the community at large. It is difficult to assess how many crimes are committed in the first year of release that stem ultimately from the frustration of not meeting needs in the family setting. However, the network program will have as a continuing emphasis a concern for realism and planning in the area of family reintegration.

The third point considered here is that correctional officers will be central to the program. There have been programs in the past where officers have played an important part, but none (with the possible exception of Briggs's work, described in Chapter 6) that have fully integrated the officers into their maximum potential roles. The network program will seek to do so by training officers who volunteer to participate in the program, by supporting them as they proceed through the changes and development of network environments in various institutions and, finally, by preparing some of them to train others in the work that they have themselves developed.

It is clear that many inmates have serious problems with authority. These problems lead them to mistrust anyone in authority, not least the correctional officer. It is the philosophy of our program that this problem is best solved by direct engagement. If inmates meet alone only, and do not confront the fact that, by prejudice, they mistrust an officer simply because she or he is an officer, then a great opportunity is lost.

Officers' primary responsibility within the network program will continue to be the security function. It will be their job to see that all, plans develop within the guidelines of the network community and, most of all, according to the rules of the facility. The officers have it within their authority to stop or modify the network program in any way and at any time, if that seems best to them. It is, obviously, the hope of those of us starting the program that abrupt changes will be avoided as much as possible, by ongoing careful supervision and by attention to the daily details of network life.

A fourth point emphasized by the network program would be that the inmates are responsible for their past, their present, and their future. It is recognized that the constraints of any correctional facility require that there be certain decisions that cannot be left to inmates. There is a danger in being unrealistic about the extent of inmate decision making. The network program is not an experiment in inmate democracy, since it is part of the philosophy of the program that such experiments ultimately are deceptive to inmates and lead to more problems than they solve.

However, within the necessary constraints of facility control, the program's philosophy does hold that inmates may learn much more than they normally do about themselves and about their capacity to make responsible decisions. There will, therefore, be a continuing effort to explore the appropriate boundaries between facility control and inmate responsibility, with a view toward enlarging the areas of responsibility as much as is realistically possible. As a start, all inmates participating in the network program will do so on a voluntary basis. There will be no coercion to enter. Moreover, simply participating in the network program will not be regarded as grounds for favorable parole consideration. Inmates who wish to participate must do so because they believe that there will be some intrinsic benefit to them. Care will be taken, for instance, not to link program participation with improved housing conditions or special honor-block privileges. Since network program participants will be expected to be involved in their own particular activities for virtually the full day, there will be no special gain from having increased television time or other such "privileges" that can cut into the concern of an inmate for making the most of the opportunities she or he has, even while confined.

HOPES AND EXPECTATIONS

It is not expected that a very large percentage of the total inmate population will volunteer to be network participants even in the distant future. Since network programs will continue to uphold the striving necessary for a full, free, responsible existence, that will in itself lead many inmates to choose not to participate. The same, in fact, is true in the outside community. For a variety of reasons, most of us choose not to participate in life to the fullest possible extent. We compromise for a variety of reasons and in a variety of ways, to make life seem easier to us at a given time.

Particular care will be taken to make it possible for inmates and staff members to come into the network program, leave it without blame, and then return at a later date if they choose to do so. This differs from the situation in therapeutic communities in the outside world. Such communities are able to enjoy the luxury of the anonymity of those who choose to leave the community. Unless clients are assigned to the particular community as a condition of parole, they have the option of simply leaving and going back to a regular private life. That is not the case in prison, and great care will be taken to make it possible to leave a network program and reenter it with maximum recognition of progress.

The network program is based on the hope that it offers a new opportunity to staff members and inmates. It will be possible for inmates who have some positive motivation, but who are unable to withstand the cynicism and hazing that dominates the yard and the mess hall, to proceed with their positive motivation, enjoying the shelter of the network environment.

Similarly, inmates who now are program participants to a considerable extent in the regular facility program will be able to have the benefit of criticism from their peers in areas that they previously neglected. For example, those who participate in the college program and still have serious attitudinal problems will have those problems challenged by other inmates. Many of those individuals remain unaware of attitudinal problems until they leave the prison and try to resume life on the outside. They are shocked to find that their progress up the academic ladder has not in fact solved all the problems that they previously experienced. If they participate in a network program, however, they benefit from their improved academic achievements and at the same time make necessary attitudinal changes.

The network program is not a panacea, and the prison system will continue largely as it is regardless of the success or failure of our program. However, for many hundreds (and perhaps, ultimately, thousands) of individuals it may make a difference. It is to that difference that many staff members have already dedicated themselves. It is both for the benefit of inmates and for the protection of their potential victims that the network program is offered. If it succeeds, for persons inside and outside the program, the network program can point to important new directions for the future.

8

THE PENETANGUISHENE PROGRAM: A PERSONAL REVIEW

Elliott T. Barker

The following is an attempt to explain very briefly the nature of coercive milieu therapy as practiced in the Social Therapy Unit at Penetang, Canada, and to translate that program into prison terminology. This brief description is followed by a tentative statement of ten basic principles that seem important to the success of this type of program.

A TOTAL MILIEU APPROACH

Underlying "the Penetanguishene program" is the unfashionable belief that the system is more important than the individual. We have tried in the Social Therapy Unit to alter the total milieu of the inmate, leaving nothing in his life that is counter-productive in terms of the reeducation process. Central to this process of reeducation is the fostering of a social system that embodies, to paraphrase Jack Seeley, "a number of complex simplicities: simplicities of relation, focus, value and product." According to Seeley, "a *relation* is one which joins the parties to it, in perhaps the greatest intimacy, combined with the greatest distance that is in the compass of human experience. One [inmate] must stand close enough to another to be his friend, [yet] far enough away to see what is happening. The *focus* is upon making what is unconscious, conscious. This is a two way street, a process of mutual education. What each [inmate] discovers of himself to his compan-

Dr. Barker's paper was presented in November 1978 as a Clarence M. Hincks Memorial Lecture at the University of Western Ontario. I am grateful to the chairman of the Clarence M. Hincks Memorial Lectures for his permission to reproduce a slightly modified version of Dr. Barker's lecture under its original title.

ion is part of his contribution, what he discovers of his companion to his companion is the other half. The paramount and only necessary joining *value* on both sides is the pursuit of truth, and the *process* is the continuous examination of the world as it is mirrored and distorted in the self, and the self as it is projected and distorted in the world." As Seeley concludes, "the product is, at the minimum, two people who know more about each other, each about the world, and each about himself. That is all. Perhaps that is enough."[1]

In this process we see the inmate as the principal agent of reeducation. Our experience suggests that the inmate is in many ways better equipped than the professional for a direct helpful encounter. For one thing, the inmate lives with the other inmates 24 hours a day: works, eats, and enjoys recreation with them. For another, an inmate is immediate to the others, has no formal power over them, and is much closer to their mode of experience than any professional. Finally, the inmate is committed to a parallel experience in a way that no professional can ever be. What perhaps may reassure those unaccustomed to thinking in these terms is that the shortcomings of individual inmates tend to cancel out in groups, where the correct administrative checks and balances have been established.

If one wants to try to change behavior, it is a gross waste of an inmates' time to provide them with a milieu that reinforces their criminal behavior 23 hours a day, and then to attempt in perhaps 1 hour of the day some sort of experience aimed at reversing the process. Ideally, the inmates should be allowed no experience that does not in some way contribute to their reeducation, and every minute of their stay ought to be designed to bring about a change in their ability to cope when released.

To make the statement that inmates should not be allowed any unhelpful experience is, of course, to stumble into the thorny question of coercion. To what extent is force legitimate in reeducating inmates who are incarcerated because of attitudes and behavior they do not recognize as self-defeating and may not wish to change? We think that all inmates should be offered the opportunity of a reeducation program aimed at reducing recidivism, and those who accept the offer ought to be committed to the program for a fixed period of time set in advance, probably a minimum of six months, with no possibility of opting out during that time. To go further, we believe that throughout the entire prison system sufficient coercion to keep the system open (so that the weakest inmate can without fear report abuses from other inmates) is justified. The so-called humane warehousing or "hands-off" approach, with an absence of mandatory open discussion by inmates about significant interpersonal events within the inmate mileu, is not a humane way to run a prison. It is our opinion that the covert coercive practices of the more powerful penitentiary inmates (and guards) are far more dangerous than the open and obvious coercive practices we use in Oak

Ridge to guarantee everyone's protection and freedom of speech, though we recognize the obvious paradox that to preserve freedom of speech, some things cannot be said.

SOME PROGRAM FEATURES

The most basic program in the Social Therapy Unit at Penetanguishene is the Training Unit, through which all new inmates are admitted. This unit is run like a school, with a principal and teachers, who are inmates. While the explicit function of the Training Unit is to teach material related to the reeducation process, the implicit purpose is to demonstrate to the trainees that the full weight of administrative authority will descend on him if he retreats from our principles of openness and communication to the traditional inmate subcultural norms, which postulate that the most important thing in the world is to "do your own time": you mind your business and I'll mind mine, except when I want to take your tobacco or money, in which case it's every man for himself, with the provision that *nobody rats*. A rat is a person who tells things to the staff.

After four to eight weeks in the Training Unit, inmates graduate, and become members of one or another of seven or eight member committees that run our program. The Inmate-Staff Liaison Committee is responsible for program planning and organization, the Small Groups Committee is responsible for selection of ad hoc groups built around individuals experiencing current problems, the Clarification Committee is responsible for clarifying and reporting to the ward meeting the precise details of instances of interpersonal difficulties on the ward, the Sanctions Committee is responsible for deciding the action to be taken for particular deviant behaviour, the Security Committee is responsible for immediate physical control of any threatened or actual incidents of physical violence, and the Ward Committee is responsible for housekeeping functions on the ward—laundry, cleaning, and so on.

Twice a day, seven days a week, the entire community assembles for community meetings of one and one-quarter hours each. The first of these serves as a feedback center for committees: the preceding 24 hours are reviewed, committee decisions relayed and discussed. The second is concerned with the discussion of small-group activities, focusing upon the problems of individual inmates. For an hour and a quarter each day, on six days a week, the entire ward subdivides into small groups that are assembled on the basis of individual inmate needs. When a ward member is "shook-up," as the inmates say (that is, depressed or hostile, threatening to act out, and so on), the Small Groups Committee forms a group of from four to eight inmates who are considered the most suitable group for him to talk to under the particular circumstances of the crisis, selecting from among people who were involved, people who had experienced similar situations, and the inmate's current friends or enemies. Small groups are assembled to make periodic reviews of an inmate's progress, to examine his motivation for a particular act, or to make specific recommendations that a committee did not have the time to consider at sufficient length.

For an hour each day, seven days a week, the ward subdivides into fixed dyads and, for a further hour, fixed triads. That is, each inmate is locked in a room with one (in a dyad) or two (in a triad) other inmates. No inmate is allowed to write, read, or sleep. He is expected to talk or to listen. These dyads and triads remain constant: that is, the same groups of two and three people meet for an hour in a locked room each day for as long as they are in the unit. This sort of grouping is based on the assumption that in any close relationship a person will encounter obstacles to communication from which the person may unhelpfully choose to withdraw. If, however, the individual is forced to stay with other persons involved in the situation for an hour a day indefinitely, the individual is forced to solve the problem, usually by identifying those aspects of self and others that created the difficulty.

The status of dyads and triads is dicussed in dyad and triad groups of six inmates, which subsequently feed back into dyad and triad ward meetings. Much of the most meaningful interaction takes place in these groupings of two and three people, where the evolution of a relationship is made much more apparent to the partners by its forced continuity.

Perhaps the most important structural characteristics of the inmate committee system is the way it operates, with little dependence on guards to initiate and sustain proceedings. Recommendations are made to them directly, and the ward supervisor maintains close contact with all developments, but in practice seldom has to exercise the supervisor's unquestioned power to veto any committee decision.[2]

The inmates often remark that the unit is in the business of upsetting people, and that is true as far as it goes. The processes of anxiety arousal, recognition, and change are central ones, and are aided by a number of other procedures and programs.

We have a closed-circuit television video tape recording system that provides a powerful resource for the objective observation of group dynamics. Small groups, dyads, triads, and ward meetings can be observed live without intrusion, and can be recorded and played back for analysis. The use of a zoom lens enables a sophisticated inmate cameraman to concentrate on many events that might be lost to the most alert participants. Others of our program features that observers find of interest are:

1. Demystifying drugs:[3] We have found Sodium Amytal-Ritalin, Tofranil-

Dexamyl, Scopolamine, LSD, and alcohol useful either in exposing to people the nature and quality of their antisocial behavior and attitudes and making such behavior more clear to their fellow inmates, or in general, heightening the morale in the unit and focusing attention on caring behavior.

2. Physical restraints:[4] Inmates who are assessed by their fellow inmates and by the staff as potential homicide or suicide risks are observed closely and conscientiously by their fellow inmates, and if necessary are secured during the day by a locked canvas wrist strap attached to the wrist of another inmate, who observes him for a four-hour shift and is then replaced by a third inmate.

3. Total-encounter capsule:[5] The capsule is a specially constructed, soundproof, windowless, continuously lighted and ventilated room, eight feet by ten feet, which provides the bare essentials—liquid food dispensers, washing and toilet facilities—and in which it is possible for a small group of volunteer patients to interact for many days at a time totally removed from contact with the outside.

GUIDING PRINCIPLES

I shall now list the guiding principles I have distilled out of our 13 years' experience with the coercive milieu programs at Penetanguishene. All of these principles seem important to me, and they are not listed in rank order. I feel that although some inmates and guards, and occasionally professional staff members, may not believe in or follow these principles, the program innovator—that is, the person in charge of the program—must both believe in these principles, and practice them; otherwise, major difficulties will result.

Genuine, Not Merely Token, Support Up the Line

It must be assumed that introducing milieu programs into a custodial institution will cause friction and tension at all levels of the system, and that this will cause repercussions up the line to those in authority. No matter how skillful the innovator, troubles in the system are inevitable and, if the type of support from above is such that the innovator is simply given enough rope to hang himself, he should not begin. The other side of the issue of receiving support up the line is to give support up the line. It is essential that the authority to whom the program innovator reports be kept totally informed of all matters that may potentially create difficulties. It is clear that the program innovator must earn the confidence of those by whom he is employed. This requires a working partnership in which the principal innovator is competent and conscientious with regard to the difficulties one can get an employer into, and the employer, on the other hand, is sufficiently mature to take reasonable risks, confident that the long-term benefits outweigh the inevitable short-term problems.

Aiming to Strengthen, Not Lessen, Static Security

All too often, "progressive" innovations in custodial institutions are measured in terms of increased physical freedom for the inmates. This seems a very short-sighted view, in our experience, for two reasons. (1) Psychological freedom is a more important ingredient in a total institution than is physical freedom; and (2) increased physical freedom, when it goes wrong, is the quickest route to retaliative repressive measures stemming from public reaction, political reaction, and reaction by those in authority farther up the line.

Since guards in custodial institutions see themselves primarily as security staff, it is a direct assault on their identity to do anything that, in their eyes, weakens security. Our strategy has been to accompany any new program variation with heightened security, that is, security slightly in excess of what the guards would deem reasonable, until the decision comes from the guards themselves on what is an adequate level of security. In our experience, guards (who know more about security than other prison employees) *do* have good judgment in these matters when it is not clouded by real or imagined threats from therapeutic staff innovations..

Losing the Battles but Winning the War

Other staff members must operate as mediators to prevent polarization between inmates and guards. This mediating function is clearly not possible if the staff members are themselves polarized either against inmates or (more likely) against guards. In our experience, no individual battle over a particular inmate or a particular incident is worth winning (even if winning is possible with structural authority) if it jeopardizes the acceptance in the guards' eyes of the staff member as a reasonably trustworthy ally. If one can comfortably lose ten battles a week (before they are even seen as battles), it seems much more possible to be able to achieve a long-term (five years') objective of shifts toward more enlightened life within the institution.

Emphasis on What Is Best for the Group

At all times, what is best for the group or system as a whole must take precedence over what is best for the individual inmate. Clinical training is so heavily weighted toward individual care that this type of system programming comes hard. It seems morally wrong and is certainly emotionally very trying to see a particular inmate suffer because of the injustices of the wider system. No inmate will receive any assistance independent of the wider system, however, and it seems a matter of logic (rather than emotion) that steps taken to improve the system as a whole take precedence.

Support of the Guards

In conflicts with individual inmates, the guard is always right, especially when he is wrong. A guard in a reeducation program is likely to experience more stress than either inmates or professional staff members must endure. The guards do not have a role that permits symptoms (as the inmate role does) or a role that compensates for high stress by high salaries, high prestige, and relative ease of mobility (as does the role of the professional staff). In our experience, all guards must know that in any battle vis-à-vis an inmate, they will always be the winner and always be supported by line authority. Obvious exceptions, of course, are contraventions by a guard of the rules of conduct for guards. Only when the guard knows he will be supported, no matter what he does, can he have the internal strength to learn by his own mistakes.

Limiting Program Participation by Guards

Guards must be instructed not to participate directly in programs. Since inmates become more skillful at covering up their emotionally vulnerable areas and more adept with words than the guards, it is unfair to allow guards to participate in the verbal exchanges in reeducation groups. Inmates must frequently be reminded that at all times they are to respond to the guards as though they were always right and always knew what was best in any situation. In our experience, this dictum has been accepted well by the inmates when it has been put forward as being as immutable as the architecture. The guards feel supported by such a policy and are able to admit mistakes and function more helpfully under such an edict.

Responsibility for Security and Reeducation

Both professional staff members and the guards must feel responsibility for security and reeducation. Any splitting of the security and reeducation functions seems clearly destructive. If professional staff members scapegoat the guards as the bad guys who impose silly rules, and hold themselves out as the good guys, they maliciously and directly undermine security. From a strictly theoretical point of view, such an artificial division is unrealistic and a bad model for inmates. In practical terms, when guards see the professional staff genuinely concerned about security, their sense of confidence in the staff is increased. The other side of the coin is that when guards see the professional staff genuinely impressed with a guard's real ability to help inmates, the working relationships between the two groups are improved.

No Changes without Consensus of Key Guards and Key Inmates

One of the easiest traps is to get lured into a coalition with those guards and inmates who are most sympathetic with the program innovator's views. This is clearly a suicidal course of action if those inmates or guards do not have at least formal (and, more importantly, informal) power in the system. The power axis must always be between the program innovator, the most powerful guards, and the most powerful inmates. The programs must develop at the pace set by these persons if it is to survive.

Maintaining a Balance of Power between Introverted and Extroverted Inmates

In inmate-run coercive milieu programs, one of the most powerful checks and balances is the mixture of introverted and extroverted inmates. The relative inability of introverts to describe the way they feel and the relative inability of extroverts to draw on analogous emotional experience have created a situation in many ways poignant for both personality types. We have found this polarity of personality types to be a major impetus toward change. Intelligent extroverts display great ability in observing details of behavior, correctly describing it, proposing practical alternatives, and organizing activities. The introverts offer much in terms of emotional support and empathy. For individuals, introvert or extrovert, this combination provides a multidimensional picture of their situation, and a wide range of resources within which to fulfill their needs. The program seems to be stabilized by this combination, which provides checks and balances, softening the raw practicality of the extrovert with the dreaminess of the introvert, introverted idealism with extroverted politics.

Modest Numbers of Professional Staff Members

Too many professional staff members make programs inoperable. The professional staff is trained to help people. It is hard to be a "good" professional staff member unless one sees oneself as helping people. If the inmates are to be the principal agents in the reeducation program, the guard staff a back-up resource, and the professional staff a third line only, there is room for only a few professional staff members to work closely as a team, primarily with key guards and key inmates, to make alterations in the system as a whole. Since large numbers of professional staff members are not required for this job, any in excess of the absolute minimum will fall back on their training and hunt out individual inmates to help. No more effective undermining of the system of inmate helping inmate can occur, since inmates often have the belief (probably delusional) that professional staff persons are better at helping people by virtue of their training.

NOTES

1. Seeley, J. R. Guidance—a plea for abandonment. *Personnel and Guidance Journal* May 1956.

2. Barker, E. T., & Mason, M. H. Buber behind bars. *Can. Psychiatr. Assoc. J* 13, (1968): 61–72; Barker, E. T., & Mason, M. H. The insane criminal as therapist. *The Canadian Journal of Corrections* 10, 4 (October 1968); Hollobon, J. My therapist, the psychopath. *The Globe and Mail Magazine* (Toronto), March 18, 1967; Mason, M. H. *Contact, this magazine is about schools* 1, 4 (Fall 1967): 89–98.

3. Barker, E. T., Mason, H. H., & Wilson, J. Defence-disrupting therapy. *Can. Psychiatr. Assoc. J.* 14 (1969): 355–59; Barker, E. T., & Buck, M. F. LSD in a coercive milieu therapy program. *Can. Psychiatr. Assoc. J.* 22, (1977): 311–14.

4. Barker, E. T., Mason, M. H., & Walls, J. Protective pairings in treatment milieux: handcuffs for mental patients. Unpublished Monograph, Ontario Hospital, Penetanguishene, 1968.

5. Barker, E. T., & McLaughlin, A. J. The Total encounter capsule. *Can. Psychiatr. Assoc. J.* 22, (1978): 355–60; Valpy, M. Naked in the box. *The Globe and Mail Magazine* (Toronto), December 1968.

9

A SELF-CONTAINED COMMUNITY

Robert H. Scott

This account describes the origin and early history of Camp Brighton, a conservation camp operated by the Michigan Department of Corrections for convicted young offenders. Included are the principles upon which this experiment was based, as well as the story of how those principles were implemented and with what apparent results.

The setting for our program was the Michigan Department of Corrections, which has responsibility for all state penal institutions, parole, much probation, and jail inspection. In the early 1950s, the director of the Corrections Department's Bureau of Probation and Parole[1] asked me to help design the program for a new parole camp to be established across the road from Michigan's main prison. The camp was to be an open institution similar to army barracks or a mess hall or day room. Bright colors and curtains were to replace steel bars and gray walls.

We brought together a planning committee, which designed program features, including a schedule of outside speakers on employment, police, parole rules, community assistance, Alcoholics Anonymous, and the like. The atmosphere was to be relaxed and family visiting (especially picnics in clement weather) was to be encouraged.

GENERAL PRINCIPLES

The three principles described below guided the program plan.

Involvement

Basic to the process of change and growth is the voluntary involvement of the "changee." This principle came to me first from Alcoholics Anonymous and the religious group from which that remarkable organization sprang.

For example, in my contacts with the campers (as an "outside speaker") I opted to employ a group discussion technique developed by Professor Donald Phillips, president of Hillsdale College. It involved forming groups of six persons with six minutes to present six answers to a question posed to all groups. Predictably, it became known as the "Phillips 66" method. I had used this technique with a wide variety of groups—including students, church groups, conferences, and PTAs.

My conviction was that the real experts—the ones who best knew the needs of inmates—were the prospective parolees themselves. So I asked (1) that the corrections officer leave the room; (2) that the group divide into groups of six; (3) that each group elect its own chairperson and secretary; (4) that each group answer the question, "What do you think is most needed in the parole camp program?"; (5) that the secretary record and report *anonymously* each suggestion to the entire assemblage. Then I invoked the second guiding principle.

Confidentiality and Anonymity

Two factors meet here. First, inmates tend to support each other and to resist in subtle ways administrative purposes and pressures. Second, inmates do not want to be identified. So I carefully cautioned all secretaries against identifying the author of an idea when reporting it. Such a caution must be made early and often.

Improvise: Be Spontaneous and Flexible

On that first experiment, I was moving from group to group to observe process, taking care not to eavesdrop. One group was bogged down. "What's the problem?" I asked. "I can't write," said the group-elected secretary. (That says something about institutional behavior.) Turning to the group chairman, I asked "Can you write?" "Yup," he replied. "O.K.," I suggested, "why not swap jobs?" They did and the group moved ahead.

The process went smoothly and well. The total group behaved very much like any other with which I had worked. They divided quickly into groups of six, circled their chairs, elected chairpersons and secretaries, and talked as easily as any group outside the walls. Among the happenings were these: Group secretaries scrupulously preserved anonymity. A rich harvest of suggestons resulted. Many were excellent. None was frivolous or insulting. Suggestions included "getting the kids out of this joint," job furloughs just prior to parole, and so on. This and subsequent sessions showed that the offenders were indeed a valuable source of ideas, that they appeared genuinely involved, and that, assured of anonymity, they expressed ideas freely. Incidentally, many of those ideas were implemented, and we gave visibility and credit to the parolees (albeit anonymously).

FILLING IN A BLANK CHECK

I next received an invitation to head a new youth division, a recommendation growing out of the Jackson prison riot of 1952. I cautiously obtained an 18-month leave (which was to become 19 years) from my academic position. I was given a blank check but with *no* amount and no *signature*. I lacked definition, goals, authority, personnel, and budget. My sole directive came from the Michigan Corrections Act: "There shall be a youth division with an assistant director of corrections in charge." The corrections commission defined the age group as 15 years (the age at which juveniles could be waived by juvenile court) to 25 years. Obviously, this was an administrative category, not a statutory or diagnostic classification. I was given "program responsibility"—a vague term—for that group. For my staff, I was to have two assistants (a sociologist and a psychologist). They came later.

A survey of the inmate body of about 8,500 inmates showed a young offender population of about 2,400—half of whom were under 21. The latter I termed youthful offenders—the others, young offenders. Again, these age categories were for administrative purposes.

Institutional spaces for those age groups then consisted of only Ionia Reformatory (a virtually maximum-security institution), with a capacity of about 1,200, and its satellite, Cassidy Lake Technical School (75 miles distant). The "Lake" was a former National Youth Administration institution with an unfenced lakeside campus with small eight-man cabins and rustic facilities. It then accomodated approximately 180 youths.

Theoretically, there were youths in various conservation/correction camps (the department ran a total of ten). But investigation revealed that all inmates were codified by *age on admission.* No one ever aged a day, according to the records. So only slightly more than half the young age group were housed in facilities specially designed for them. Moreover, all males went through the reception center at "Jackson" (officially the State Prison of Southern Michigan, which then had 4,500 cells, the remainder of the inmates being housed in farm barracks). To me, it was a highly undesirable situation. It was, I believe, the factor referred to by the parolees' suggestion "Get the kids out of Jackson."

THE EXPERIMENTAL CAMP: INGREDIENTS AND PRINCIPLES

It seemed that a beginning solution to our problems of space and program would be separate youth camps. I asked for and was given "program responsibility" for Camp Brighton, as the most accessible place to begin. Camp Program (the official designation for the management of all corrections-conservation camps) continued to administer and supply Brighton (more will be said of that later). Camp Pontiac was added subsequently.

I did not encounter Maxwell Jones' writings about the therapeutic community until several months after the youth division began its Brighton program. The program innovations there were the result of religious involvements and exposure to programs such as Alcoholics Anonymous. The discovery of Maxwell Jones's book encouraged us immensely and contributed important insights. The book became our basic training manual and greatly enlarged our horizons. We added new principles to the three discussed above.

Autonomy

Earlier, I had been invited by the warden of Ionia Reformatory to begin our program at that institution. The invitation was politely but decisively declined, for two reasons. First, the reformatory was essentially a maximum-security institution of the "Bastille" type. It was the second reformatory built in the United States, and was modeled after Elmira. Second, institutional operations were a major industry in the small rural town of Ionia. Several generations staffed custodial and administrative posts at both the mental hospital and the reformatory. The cultural conflict between the staff and the population seemed an insurmountable obstacle to community. Moreover, the ingrained attitudes and inherited culture would, I felt, be so subtle and pervasive as to make our task difficult, if not impossible.

Autonomy at Brighton was far from complete. Camp Control (the headquarters for all camps) was still in overall charge of the operation. Differences in philosophy, objectives, and style sometimes hampered programs.

Most of the department's 100-man camps were then staffed by a sergeant and three or four officers—a skeleton crew. But during the day, most inmates were out on crews assigned to forest tree nurseries, fish hatcheries, park clean-up, rough construction, and the like. Crews were bossed by foremen on the staff of the State Department of Natural Resources. The corrections department had no direct voice in the selection, training, and supervision of these foremen. The arrangement worked well, for the most part. However, it would have been preferable to screen crew foremen, train and supervise them, and involve them in case conferences. Moreover, an additional counselor/officer seemed a necessary addition to the staff. He could spot-check and observe the crews, change crew composition, and "trouble shoot." (One crew foreman had a distinctly negative attitude toward inmates and was quite outspoken and heavy-handed about it. On one occasion he was heard to send an inmate to a tool shed to get a length of rope. "Be sure to get enough to hang yourself," he is alleged to have said. His humor—if such was intended—was not appreciated. Not long afterward he forgot his lunch. Without a by-your-leave he proceeded to help himself to some of the crew's lunch. A few days later, several of the trucks had sugar in the gas—a rare incident.)

We obtained the following changes: (1) A camp supervisor was selected by the youth division. This position encompassed programs as well as administration and custody. The selection of a person qualified by philosophy, temperament, style, and experience was essential. We were fortunate in finding just the right man—Edward Green, now head of a coed training school in a western state. An addition to the staff was the camp counselor—also a professional position. The counselor was to perform custodial duties (take count, enforce rules, and so on) in the evening, as well as oversee the program and counsel individuals. This combination of roles was viewed with cautious skepticism by Camp Control, but worked well. Again, we were fortunate in recruiting an ideal corrections counselor Charles (Chuck) Bowditch, a warm, cheerful bear of a man, now working in the California system.

Shifts were arranged so that the supervisor was on duty from 8:00 A.M. to 4:00 P.M. and alternate weekends. The counselor was on duty from 2:00 to 10:00 P.M. and alternate weekends. The three corrections officers were scheduled in various ways to maximize staff coverage during the times of crew arrivals and departure and the hours after dark.

Treatment is Everything That Happens to People

Maxwell Jones gave us important insights into theory and practice. The reader is cautioned not to confuse experience with expertise. My efforts were distinctly amateurish. We learned by doing, always careful not to push custodial limits unreasonably far. I held this principle (that treatment is everything that happens to people) and those that follow as essential to the way offenders should be dealt with. Each of these principles made sense as we accumulated experiences of success and failure.

The first subprinciple we deduced had to do with dignity of the individual. We concluded that respect for the person is not inconsistent with security, and should be clearly and consistently practiced. In other words, discipline can be maintained without the demeaning putdown. One can be careful without being cynical. Both staff and residents must be aware of the realities of the situation—taking count, "shakedown" inspections, and the like. But in taking count, I asked for and received the cooperation of camp staff in using *names, not numbers.* Moreover, in small camps, the staff can take count inconspicuously most of the time. Of course, there are lapses: once an officer taking count was confronted by two identical surnames. Instead of calling Smith, Adam, and Smith, Fred, he called Smith, 1234, and Smith, 5678 (names and numbers fictitious).

Another illustration: One member of the camp was a holdover from the former older population. He asked to stay on since his family was closer to Brighton than to most other camps. Yet this individual's record and age made him an inappropriate member of the new group. I felt obliged to explain to him the unsuitability of his remaining. I felt he merited a candid statement and told him that in a hitherto untried experiment we could not afford a man of his reputation. He appeared to accept the explanation philosophically and without rancor.

When guests came, we introduced them to the camp. We wanted to avoid the spectator/curiosity seeker complex. Campers were used as guides and escorts for visitors. From another state came a visitor looking at special programs for offenders. The camp clerk acted as his guide and mentor. "I would like to talk to an inmate," requested the visitor. Replied the clerk, "Sir, I am an inmate." The confusion was flattering to us.

Another corollary of our total treatment philosophy was the resolve to keep people fully informed. I made a practice of informing the entire population of our philosophy, purposes, and plans at our Monday night camp meetings. Not only is secrecy unnecessary—it is usually impossible. The most rapid means of communication is the institutional grapevine, and what is not known will be imagined, distorted, and circulated. Privacy concerning an individual inmate's personal matters is carefully protected, but staff concerns must be shared.

Our Monday night sessions were a time to introduce guests, to inform the campers of plans, progress, and problems—to answer questions, respond to gripes, and get input from campers.

It became clear that it was important to see that campers got "a fair shake" from us. Treating people fairly seems axiomatic—unfortunately it is an axiom that is not always strictly observed. This means that "being fair" sometimes entails going to bat for people treated unfairly by others.

For example, "Junior" N. was unceremoniously removed by Camp Control. The reason was that Junior was considered a sex offender, and convicted sex offenders were prohibited by law from placement in an open correctional setting. But Junior had been charged, not convicted. An inoffensive, undersized farm boy, he was alleged to have had intercourse with a girl under the age of consent. There was no indication of assaultiveness. The case appeared to have been weak and the charges were dropped. So the camp staff pressed for and obtained a reversal of Camp Control's action. Word got around that we had gone out of our way for Junior, and this increased our credibility.

REQUIRING GROUP COUNSELING

I gave high priority to group counseling as the focal point for small-group interaction, focusing upon questions, concerns, and insights. At first we emphasized content, having been influenced by New York State's "social education" program. Slowly, we began to see that content tended to inhibit, so we shifted our emphasis to an unstructured yet purposeful process. Our goal was a significant encounter. We envisaged two stages—the first a required 12-week elementary series, and the second a voluntary 12-week "advanced course."

Required Participation

Required participation lessens the reluctance of inmates to participate in programs put forward by the administration. This point is conjectural but, to us, persuasive. We suspected that inmates tend to resist covertly administrative goals. If so, required participation would reduce the stigma of "playing ball with the man"—of being a "front-office" man. We found that participation in the voluntary advanced sessions was regular and frequent.

At first, there were only two of us—a counselor from the main prison at Jackson drove over on Monday nights. Working in the prison in the daytime, he became our first "volunteer" at night. I was the other "volunteer."

THE COMMUNITY AS A MANPOWER POOL

Our neighborhood university (Eastern Michigan) was helpful in many ways, but especially in providing students as group leaders. Several attractive young women volunteered. They conducted themselves with friendly dignity and were a bright and healthy highlight in an all-male environment. There were no untoward incidents—a tribute to both the women and the campers.

We soon discovered that college students were usually restricted to one-term participation. The turnover interrupted group continuity and kept us burdened with selection and training. So we veered toward recruiting volunteers from nearby communities. Some remained with us for years and became valuable unpaid colleagues.

Too often, volunteers are used as "hewers of wood and drawers of water." As a frequent volunteer, I often felt imposed upon—made to feel guilty if I said no. We strove valiantly to avoid both these pitfalls.

Three important aspects of working with volunteers were their selection, training, and supervision. We sought leaders with natural skills rather than formal training. Easiness with self and others; conversation without condescension; and courtesy that forebore the asking of such questions as "What trouble brought you here?" We wanted listeners, not teachers or preachers. Easiness with self included ability to recognize and accept, without becoming disconcerted, testing by the group. While groups built their own agenda, we wanted leaders who could sense underlying interests, questions, and problems. Our goal we termed a "significant encounter." Recruitment was largely accomplished by the volunteers themselves.

On-the-job training was our principal training method. Prospective volunteers were invited to visit, to be shown the camp by a camper, to participate in our Monday evening general camp sessions, sit in with a group as an observer, and to join the "aftersession" (more on the last point, in a moment).

A volunteer who wished to give it a try would assist the group leader until she or he felt comfortable, and then undertake leadership with another group for one series of sessions (usually 12). At the end of the series, either party was free to terminate the arrangement. We wanted the volunteer not to feel trapped without "terminal facilities," and we also wanted to feel free to terminate without embarrassment to the volunteer. I cannot recall any occasion on which we exercised the latter option, but I remember several volunteers who excused themselves when things obviously were not working out. Thus, training became self-selection as well.

A camp staffer or I would explain the camp's philosophy (such as preserving anonymity and confidentiality—except where camp security was involved) and program. We would caution against taking out letters (those were the days of mail censorship) and contraband (money, drugs, "booze"). We would explain testing by the group, "bitch-and-gripe" sessions (which were not censored but were discouraged after a reasonable time). We encouraged the reporting of gripes after permission had been obtained from the group and anonymity had been assured.

There were three methods of supervision of volunteers. In the first, a staff member visited a group. The second was the aftersession—attended by every group leader. At first we also asked each group to send a representative—this to ensure the camp that anonymity and confidentiality was respected. It was soon discovered that attendance by a group member was no longer necessary.

Basic to this work was the conviction that volunteers are not just "cheap help," but were valuable, although unpaid, staff members, and that consequently the corrections department was obligated to supply the leadership, selection, and training, and supervision without which volunteer programs might flounder and fail.

ENSURING HONESTY AND PROVIDING ANONYMITY

Volunteers are frequently imposed upon and made to feel guilty. We made it clear from the onset that we asked a volunteer for commitment only to one series (12 weeks) of sessions. After that, they were free to leave with our gratitude and without obligation. Neither side had any further commitment. In fact, many community members stayed on for years and were valuable colleagues, their only recognition being a certificate of service and our genuine appreciation.

Job finding—essential to parole—was hampered by a perceived prejudice against "ex-cons" (a word the staff did not use). The felt injustice rankled. In one of the first sessions, a camper asked me if I would knowingly employ an ex-offender. I replied in the affirmative. (As a matter of fact I had previously attempted to, but he had opted for a better offer.) Then the camper asked the clincher: "If money were missing, would you suspect the ex-offender quicker than others with equal opportunity?" He had me. If I said no, I'd be lying (and I'm a poor liar—as the group would quickly detect). If I said yes, the group would see me as a phony—pretending a trust I did not feel. Either way I'd lose the group and maybe the program. In any case, I'd lose my self-respect if I didn't speak my thoughts.

All of these thoughts occured in a fraction of a second. Finally I said, "Well, I know this sounds inconsistent, but I would suspect the ex-offender first." Contrary to my expectations, rapport increased. The group may have thought me stupid but they knew I was trying to be straightforward.

We continued to stress anonymity with great care. We assured group leaders we did not want group confidences revealed. One exception—we told the leaders, and the *entire* camp, that actions threatening camp security were not protected.

Here is another example: Rarely did a two-time prison offender come to camp. One did arrive—rather hard-bitten and self-contained. It seemed a good idea to tape-record a session for training purposes, but first I asked the group's permission. For my part, I would play back the recording, and if any member objected to any portion I would erase the offending sections. If that did not satisfy the objection, I would erase the entire session.

Only one member objected—our "two-time loser." "No way," he said, "I got trapped by one of them things once." "That's O.K.," I said, "Let's forget the recorder." "Wait a minute" was his response. "Did you say we could listen and then erase?" When I assured him that was indeed the case, he gave the go-ahead. "Don't use last names," I cautioned the group.

After some early self-consciousness because of the recording, the group settled down, and we recorded a typical session. As we listened to it play back, other groups were breaking. Our objecting group member called to passing friends, "Hey, you guys, listen to this."

At a camp Christmas party, our then nine-year-old son, restive, asked if he could get some fresh air. As I weighed the advisability of the request, this same two-time offender said to me, "Don't worry, I'll keep my eye on him." So out they went—I confident that our son was in good hands.

INVOLVING THE GREATER COMMUNITY

One of our initial mistakes was a failure to involve the neighboring community. Later, a walkaway occurred when two young campers high-jacked a neighbor's car, forcing the neighbor to drive them to Detroit. The seriousness of the incident was somewhat ameliorated when the campers, learning that the driver lacked gas money to get home, gave him a couple of dollars.

The community, alarmed, circulated a petition to remove the camp. A meeting was held by the county board of commissioners. My superior, the director of the department, attended. Wisely, he suggested the appointment of a committee, urging that it include our critics as well as our supporters. The idea was acclaimed.

The committee assembled in the camp mess hall for its first Monday evening meeting. While waiting for all members to arrive, committee members proffered suggestions such as "In the event of a walkaway, notify the neighbors so they can put on the yard light and let the dog out." Perhaps my faulty memory suggests that loading the shotgun was hinted at.

The first item before the formal meeting was a tour of the camp—each committee member was escorted by a camper host. The tour was followed by a supper consisting of the regular camp menu.

At the usual Monday night camp meeting the committee was introduced and its purpose explained. The usual meeting announcements, explanations, questions, and answers followed.

Then the guests divided themselves among the various groups, later attending the customary aftersession. The climax was a meeting of the committee, at which there were expressions of confidence and support. Most encouraging were comments to the effect that "Now that we understand the camp and its people and program, we support it." We were heartened as well when several committee members volunteered as group leaders.

The lasting effect of our belated community involvement was demonstrated when a petition was circulated objecting to the building of a juvenile training school in the general area. Neighbors hastened to assure us that the objections did not apply to Camp Brighton.

Another program was family-group counseling by husband-and-wife teams. We queried prospective parolees on the interest of the camper *and* his wife in meeting with a volunteer couple. After talking with their wives, three campers responded. The sessions were productive; our wives were a distinct asset. After a certain amount of sparring, the couples got down to what was on their minds. Wives no longer claimed all was serene but expressed their anxieties and frustrations. Husbands voiced their resentment against suspicion. Unfortunately we tried only that one series—I wish there had been more.

The program at Camp Brighton was experimental, but not a before-and-after, test and control group experiment. We were testing the feasibility of such a camp for young offenders—the workability of tentative principles, and their apparent effect when applied. These principles and effects converge with "reintegration models," which are described by Clarence Schrag as follows:

> Presumably, then, leadership in a close-custody prison is often exerted by its most negativistic and least improvable members. The asocial offender types tend to give a strong minority of its votes to inmates from its own ranks. This suggests that leadership patterns can probably be modified by changing the composition of the prison population. If the less criminalistic offenders can be housed in separate institutions, they may be protected in this way from criminal socialization. Some support for this view comes from studies showing that in minimum-security institutions the prosocial offenders tend to play a relatively dominant role.[2]

THE PROBATION RECOVERY CAMP, AND TWO MORE LESSONS

The Probation Recovery Camp was instituted for young offenders for whom community placement was deemed inappropriate. The Youth and Probation Division shared program responsibility and the department's camp program staffed and operated the camp. The program included passes (six hours' absence within a 25-mile radius in the company of an approved adult) and furloughs (three-day leaves to the home community to maintain family ties and arrange future employment). The success of the furlough program prompted its extension to Camp Brighton. Problems in its administration at one of the camps caused the suspension of the furlough program (with some exceptions) at Camps Brighton and Pontiac.

Another spinoff from Camp Pugsley was the Resident Home Program, designed for community placement. Subsidized by a grant from the McGregor Fund, the program underwrote boarding homes as an alternative to halfway houses.

The Brighton lesson of involving the community before starting a new program was not lost on us. Careful arrangements were made well in advance to bring together community leaders and the press. The McGregor Fund also underwrote a program that provided a second-hand bus and arranged a cooperative program with the Traverse City Public Schools. Under this program, teacher salaries and classroom costs permitted a modest offering of courses during evening hours.

The probation camp program included the features developed at Camp Brighton. The former had a somewhat larger staff than the latter, since more processing and paperwork was required. The staff included a female secretary and a husband-and-wife cooking team. The camp supervisor was transferred to Camp Pugsley; a probation officer was added to the staff; the custodial staff was headed by a lieutenant specially skilled in counseling young offenders. As in Camp Brighton, work crews in the forest tree nursery, fish hatchery, and state parks were supervised by foremen employed by the Department of Natural Resources. Case conferences at regular intervals measured progress by and with the probationer.

The special nature of the camp required reporting and release procedures different from those in other corrections camps—all residents of which had been processed through a reception guidance center at the State Prison of Southern Michigan. Maximum stay at the camp was one year. Depending upon progress, the camp recommended to the sentencing court return to the community in from six to nine months. Walkaways and maladjustment cases were referred back to the court.

Two final principles can be stated. One is that involvement of the community prior to inception is essential and the second that program and administration/operation are intimately interconnected. Divided responsibility requires compatible philosophies and procedures. Our goals and those of probation were indeed compatible, but differences with Camp Program frequently arose. Patience on both sides was necessary.

We concluded that—especially if the above principles are satisfied—the concept of the probation camp has considerable merit. It provides a placement resource for acceptable young offenders who might otherwise be sentenced to prison.

Today, many of the graduates of the first class at Camp Pugsley are successful men. One has graduated from college with an engineering degree; another is a highly paid designer with a large automobile manufacturer; yet another is involved in nuclear physics. Some have returned to the wrong road, but the program has paid for itself many times over, not only in money but in terms of lives that might otherwise have been wasted.

NOTES

1. The bureau's director was Gus Harrison, who later headed the corrections department and encouraged the work described in this chapter.

2. Schrag, C. *Crime and justice: American style.* Publication no. HSM-72-9052. National Institute of Mental Health, Center for Studies of Crime and Delinquency, 1971. The study included Camp Brighton.

10

DEMOCRACY AND JUSTICE IN A PRISON THERAPEUTIC COMMUNITY

Peter Scharf

Some have suggested that perhaps the fundamental task facing corrections is *not* to reform or reeducate, but rather to control the psychological and moral damage imprisonment inflicts upon prisoners, and to provide for a reasonably benign quality of life for its charges.[1] In this context, the justification for the therapeutic community is not to rehabilitate, but to create a social community in which human beings can reasonably endure for long periods of time. Its rationale lies in the "warehouse" prison's failure to provide the prisoner opportunity for a secure, democratic, just, and orderly existence.

DEMOCRATIC PARTICIPATION IN PRISON THERAPEUTIC COMMUNITIES

Many prison therapeutic communities strive toward a degree of inmate self-governance and democratic participation. In some communities, this goal is seen as a means toward some other end. For example, in prison communities that use "reality therapy," democratic participation can be seen as a means toward greater reality testing. In other therapeutic communities, democratic participation is seen as a central element in an altered prison environment. To explore the possible tension involving democratic participation in prison therapeutic communities, I will describe a few of the ways in which prison reformers have sought to implement democratic participation as a component of a reeducative prison. In the experiments initiated by such men as Alexander Maconochie, Thomas Osborne, and others, the prison is to be viewed as a living school whose main lesson is to be civic democracy. Osborne declared:

Outside the Walls, a man must choose between work or idleness. . . (Why not let himself teach these lessons before he goes out). Such things are best taught by experience. So inside your walls you must have courts and laws to protect those who are working from the idle thief. And we must rest assured that the laws would be made and the laws enforced. The prison must be an institution where every inmate must have the largest possible freedom, because it "is liberty that fits men for liberty."[2]

Whether it is seen as a central or as a subordinate goal, democratic self-governance is often essential to the success of the therapeutic community. For a therapeutic community to thrive, there must be a sense of "oneness" and "we-feeling": a sense that the community is a viable social unit and that the inmates and staff control its destiny. This "oneness" and "we-feeling" are best fostered in a community where individuals feel they have a sense of ownership and control, a community that at least in spirit reflects the democratic will of its members.

Of course, prison democracy must always be defined as "limited" democracy. Inmates cannot legitimately vote to free themselves, nor can they vote to neutralize their captors. Images of a New England town meeting are somewhat misleading. Democratic prison reform is always limited by the judicial, economic, and psychological, as well as physical, walls of the prison.

In spite of such limitations, there have been numerous efforts to share power systematically within a prison community, in an at least quasi-democratic manner. One of the first prison reformers who systematically created a democratic prison environment, as well as recognized the importance of community in the reformative process, was Alexander Maconochie. In 1840, Maconochie was permitted to implement an experimental model of prison reform called the "mark" system, in the Norfolk Island prison of the Australian transportation colony. Maconochie proposed to have a group of six men work together in a partially democratic and interdependent work and living community, with the men receiving jointly the profits and rewards of the work that was achieved by the group. Inmates had a hand in imposing discipline within the work group, as well as in actively spurring it toward greater effort and mutual support. In this experiment, which lasted nearly four years, Maconochie was able to create an island prison community that established a "community feeling" and a level of political involvement unknown in any other prison of his day.[3]

Roughly 70 years later, Thomas Mott Osborne established a prison-wide democratic community known as the Mutual Welfare League.[4] At Auburn Prison in New York, Osborne proposed that all internal disciplinary offenses be turned over to a committee of 49 inmate representatives, one from each of the prison workshops. These men would form an inmate court as well as a rotating grievance committee. Predictably, at first inmates balked at punishing "their own." They, however, soon were able to exercise freely in the yard, an "experiment" that had never until that time been attempted. Fights became rare. Hospitalization for injury decreased. Escapes were few. Assaults on guards were nearly nonexistent. Work production continually increased.

In 1914, the experiment was moved to Sing Sing Prison, a larger and more difficult prison. Here the results were even more spectacular, altering almost every aspect of prison life. The Sing Sing "screws" shifted their role from that of hostile warders to something akin to the modern, counselor-correctional officer. Osborne also organized an inmate fire department, which on numerous occasions was credited with the saving of prisoners' lives. A bank with assets of over $30,000 was chartered "by inmates, for inmate benefit." Following a constitutional convention, the inmates elected two men from each workshop to act as their representatives. This "congress" of delegates became Sing Sing's working governmental body. When the men in the foundry shop needed special shoes or when a guard needed money to visit a sick relative, the request would be addressed by the executive committee. Conflicts between inmates and staff were adjudicated. When the workers in the shoe shop appeared to be malingering, an order to return to work was delivered to them by their executive committee.

THE JUST COMMUNITY APPROACH

Several years ago, Dr. Joseph Hickey and I sought to create a participatory prison environment in a Connecticut female prison, the Niantic State Prison for Women.[5] Our goal was to create a reeducative community in a single prison cottage that would be perceived as legitimate by inmates and staff, and that would function in a democratic manner. As an initial step, we proposed a "constitutional" meeting where inmates and staff could air differences and, most importantly, where they could begin to explore bases for mutual collaboration and cooperation. The goal was to create a community meeting format that would provide inmates with an opportunity to share in political decisions relevant to the program. In community meeting sessions, which would last over six hours, inmates would create and enforce cottage rules. The entire cottage staff and inmate group would jointly decide any disciplinary action to be taken against particular members (either inmates or staff). The meeting would also determine important policy issues for the cottage. Inmates routinely designed educational and recreational programs. Other common topics included interpersonal conflicts and tensions between inmates. Inmates might "call up" other inmates for anything from being "snobbish," to stealing from other inmates, to attempting to escape. Every six weeks, inmates participated in a "marathon meeting" in which rules for the next six weeks would be proposed and negotiated with the prison administration. Finally, inmates would discuss parole plans with other inmates and staff members in the program.

CONSTRAINTS AGAINST DEMOCRATIC COMMUNITIES IN PRISON

Despite its centrality for the prison therapeutic community ideal, democracy in the context of the prison faces difficult constraints. Some of these constraints are unique to prisons; others apply to almost any "political" island that attempts to assert itself within a larger bureaucratic labyrinth. In even quasi-democratic prison communities, staff members face difficult tensions regarding loyalty and identification. For example, experience with the Just Community program indicated that the "giving away" of democratic control to the inmates depended greatly upon the type of offense involved. It was often difficult for the prison administration to allow inmates any degree of democratic control on matters that involved either potential legal felonies or major threats to prison authority. Offenses for which inmate rule offenders might face serious consequences made inmate responsible participation improbable. Issues such as prisoner use of heroin, for example, were rarely successful topics for democratic discussion, because the inmates in the program often suspected that no matter what the "democratic community" would decide, the inmates involved in the offense, if convicted, would be sent back to the maximum-security prison. Offenses such as inmate fights or theft from inmates made better topics for democratic dialogue, because enforcing these rules was perceived to be in the inmates' self-interest. This was rarely the case for matters involving contraband, drugs, or alcohol, which were presumed to offend primarily the staff or administration. There was also the assumption that fights among inmates were "self-destructive," and the inmates believed it was reasonable to use the democratic process of the prison community program to arbitrate such inmate conflicts.

Many prison democratic communities become dominated by inmate elites who govern largely for their own economic and political interests. The notion that inmates can act responsibly toward the prison staff and other inmates is difficult for the public to accept. The disrepute of the prison, combined with public hostility toward prisoners, makes domocratic prison reform a difficult political cause. The prison's administrative organization also forms a massive constraint against democratic reform. Democratic rule making conflicts with the hierarchical order characteristic of most bureaucratic prisons. The powers granted to inmates also tend to conflict with bureaucratic jurisdictions or administrative territories. Finally, the powerlessness of inmates provides an overwhelming impediment to democratic participation. As the inmates possess no goods, perform no valuable service, and have no outside lobby, they can only *request privileges*; they cannot demand the *right* to democratic participation. As long as the inmates accede to the administration's wishes, everything runs smoothly. When there is a difference of opinion between the therapeutic community and the prison's administrative powers, the prison administration usually wins.

In the Niantic Just Community experiment, the reality of a few inmate elites' "controlling" the democratic process of the program was often a serious problem. In one episode, a powerful female inmate leader was caught by another inmate shooting heroin in her room in the presence of three other inmates. When the incident was reported at the nightly community meeting, all three of the witnesses indignantly swore that the inmate was wrongly accused. Much to my surprise, the rest of the inmates in the group voted not to punish the inmate, while privately admitting that she was obviously guilty. It should be noted that in almost all democratic prison communities, inmates can (through sheer numbers) outvote the staff members on any given issue. The program's staff in this case was so enraged by the abuse of democratic discipline that they collectively threatened to resign.

On various occasions, agreements made between the Just Community program and the prison administration were reversed when key administrators objected to the inmates' decision in the matter at hand. In one incident, the inmates had been allowed to formulate a parole policy for their unit. When they developed a policy that *might* have included a particularly "objectionable" former inmate (then a parolee), the administrators reneged on their agreement to give permission to allow the inmates to formulate the parole policy. The inmates were generally aware of the limits of their "democratic" powers. Unable to enforce their democratic rights, they were at the mercy of a prison administration that could unilaterally withdraw the privilege of self-governance. In this context, democratic self-governance was often extremely difficult to "sell" to inmates. At several points during the program's history, inmates indicated they preferred a return to unilateral staff control. These tensions in the program say something about the structural position of the prison therapeutic community vis-à-vis the larger prison and correctional system. The democracy of the prison therapeutic community is always a democracy within a larger correctional bureaucracy, ultimately subject to its laws, rules, jurisdictions, and norms. In this context, the democracy of a prison therapeutic community is in a tenuous position, subject to powerful forces beyond its control. Such forces must be faced, because democratic participation represents a central element in the prison therapeutic community, both as an ideal in itself and as a means toward social cohesion and group solidarity.

SOCIAL JUSTICE IN PRISON THERAPEUTIC COMMUNITIES

The idea of social justice is a concept distinct from that of democracy. Where democracy deals with a form of decision making, social justice deals with both a moral process and its outcome. *Formal justice* refers to the means of attaining justice; *substantive justice* is the outcome of a distributive or retributive decision. The dilemma of both these aspects of social justice represents an important issue for prison therapeutic communities.

While most prison therapeutic communities articulate the hope that in their bosoms social justice will be achieved, the achievement of social justice often proves elusive. In practice, many prison therapeutic communities deny inmates and staff members what appear to be the rudiments of procedural or actual fairness. This tendency toward moral abuse in the therapeutic community seems important to exemplify and understand.

One type of abuse in prison therapeutic communities is the problem of seemingly capricious decisions. In one episode, two inmates in the Just Community program decided to go for an illegal nocturnal walk to the prison storehouse. One was a popular inmate who also happened to be a mastermind safecracker and "lockwoman." The second (despised by the other inmates) was feared for her often heavy-handed and "indiscrete" behavior. After the two inmates were discovered in the act of "escaping" from the prison unit by another inmate, a hearing was held to determine the punishment appropriate for each of them. Not surprisingly, the inmates voted to give the popular "lockwoman" a mild punishment. (The inmates said "she needed help.") They voted to expel the more obnoxious inmate to a rather undesirable maximum-security prison. The staff members' appeals that the decision was "unfair" fell upon deaf ears. It seemed impossible to convince the community as a body that equity required a like punishment for a similar offense.

Another issue of social justice relevant to therapeutic communities involves the abuse of psychological criteria. In 1972, I visited an intensive prison therapeutic community (now defunct) that used transactional analysis as its theoretical guide. In community meetings and small-group counseling sessions inmates would point out each others' "games" (such as "Tom's angry child hooks Harvey's domineering parent . . ."). One session involved a discussion of a fight between an inmate named Bill and an inmate named Sam. It was a fair fight, and neither inmate was hurt. In the community meeting, one of the unit's counselors advocated locking Bill in the "wetbox" (the segregation cell) and placing Sam in a lifescript analysis session. The counselor reasoned that since Bill's problem was his "hostile child" he *needed* punishment. Sam's problem was perceived quite differently. Diagnosed as a rather supressed young man with an "overweaning parent," he required, according to the counselor, "a more supportive treatment." Interesting to me was the absence of verbalized criteria of justice other than those derived from the therapeutic axioms of transactional analysis. No one seemed concerned about the seeming injustice in treating Sam and Bill differently, as dictated by the "psychological" ideology of the prison community.

A related abuse rests in the difficulty of ensuring impartial review of decisions made by a therapeutic community. In small intensive communities in general, and in prison therapeutic communities specifically, there exists no independent body to review decisions made by the group as a whole. This at times results in decisions that are unappealable except to the community that originally made the decision. An example is the case of Hilda, an inmate in a therapeutic prison "alcoholic" unit. The prisoners in the program had decided that Hilda's daughter was "bad for her" because she had given Hilda a drink on her last furlough, and they refused to allow Hilda to see her, even during visiting hours. Hilda begged the community to reconsider the decision it had made, but they refused. Finally, it was discovered that Hilda's daughter was ill with a serious disease. Hilda beseeched the community at its meeting to allow even one "short controlled visit." Finally, in desperation, she turned to the psychiatrist running the ward and asked him to "make the inmates change their minds." The psychiatrist (who was sympathetic to Hilda's problem) said he had "but one vote on matters which were not medical in nature, and that the group had made a final decision."

Another abuse of social justice relates to the problem of individual autonomy in a cohesive group. In one "Concept House" drug program I visited, the leaders justified the intense pressure upon members to dress the same way and to adopt the "concept" philosophy, in terms of a need to build group morale and the necessity of breaking down the fronts of addicts in the group. Toward this end, mail was censored, as were books from the prison library. One young man was "brought up in group" for having hidden a copy of Camus' *Myth of Sysyphus*, which the leader called a "negative book." The book was promptly confiscated, and I observed that no one in the group protested the action. Inquiry among the members indicated little sense that the young addict had any moral right to read a book that was judged to inspire "negative" ideas. This lack of respect for individual freedom exists in many therapeutic community programs, and is justified by some therapeutic argument or other.

A final moral ambiguity deals with the problem of equality of rules and law in a given institution or correctional system. In many therapeutic prison communities, a prisoner who is caught smoking marijuana, sniffing glue, smuggling mail, or fighting will not be judged by formal institutional or legal procedure, but rather by the "town meeting" of the therapeutic community itself. This practice raises two difficult moral issues. First, it is clear that different therapeutic communities might have radically different rules, and inmates in therapeutic community *A* might receive penalties for the same offense substantially different from those in therapeutic community *B*. Both therapeutic communities might also differ substantially from the penalties to be expected from a formal prison discipline board.

A more serious problem deals with the "usurping" of legal powers from the judicial system. During the seven-year history of the Just Community program, the inmate "town meetings" dealt with issues ranging from assault with a weapon to homosexual harassment and escape. This practice, while it has its own justification, creates the problem of a "shadow" community justice system, which may operate with substantially different logic and outcomes from the constitutionally legitimate judicial system.

The bureaucratization of justice in prisons clearly serves some positive functions in the prison: social justice is "removed" from the hands of particular individuals. Bureaucratic rules, in theory, bind both inmates and staff. The guard who violates these rules is liable to sanction or punishment by the prison. Inmates can come to anticipate treatment and consequences for particular actions. Typically, there evolves a regularization of rules across institutional subunits and across particular staff members. In bureaucratic prison systems, the discretion of the individual guard is greatly limited. Arbitrary forms of action by guards are restrained by centralized structuring of inmate-staff interaction. Guards' actions are scrutinized by higher officials through a review of reports and complaints and through close hierarchical supervision. On the other hand, the bureaucratic organization has been rightly associated with a form of moral blindness. "Moral" decisions are broken down into small "technical" decisions. Rules are, for example, often enforced whether or not they make sense.

In the context of the prison, a wise leader of a therapeutic community, given a committed group of inmates with a high level of mutual trust and a willing correctional system, *might* arrive at decisions that are in some sense substantively (if not formally) just, in that they reflect moral respect and seek to maximize human liberty and equality. However, Max Weber saw the justice of the autonomous community as potentially degenerating into what he articulately called "Kadi justice"—the justice of the mythic Moslem wiseman who dispenses justice from an inner, almost mystic vision: "Every prophetic verdict is in the end Kadi justice unfettered by tradition. It is written, *but* I say unto you . . ." Weber points out that such justice cannot ensure equality under the law, provide for judicial appeal, or result in anything approaching a rational or empirical mode of justice.[6]

Weber, were he to observe the modern prison therapeutic community, might well ask if the autonomy enjoyed by such communities permits anything we might call rational or empirical justice. He might also suggest that *some* of the conflicts experienced between prison systems and prison therapeutic communities might in fact be tensions between two oppositional modes of justice: the justice of the bureaucratic prison and that of an administratively autonomous prison therapeutic community.

I should add that the structural autonomy of most prison therapeutic communities *need not necessarily* lead to the kinds of abuse I have described. With leaders (both inmates and staff members) concerned with justice, equity, and a sense of due process, such communities can, with the cooperation of a just and democratic correctional system, approach the ideals of a true and just community. I believe it is possible to balance intensive community with social justice—even in the context of a prison. I also believe that such a task represents an extremely formidable and difficult accomplishment.

NOTES

1. Fogel, D. *We are the living proof.* Cincinnati, Ohio: W. H. Anderson, 1973.

2. Osborne, T. M. *Society and prisons.* New Haven: Yale University Press, 1916, P. 26.

3. Maconochie, A. *Norfolk Island.* London: J. Hatchard, 1847; Maconochie, A. *Australiana.* London: John Parker, 1839.

4. Osborne, T. M. op. cit.; Osborne, T. M. *Within prison walls,* New York: Appleton-Century-Crofts, 1914; Osborne, T. M. *Prisons and common sense.* Philadelphia: Lippencott, 1924.

5. Scharf, P., & Hickey, J. *Democracy and prisons,* San Francisco: Jossey-Bass, 1979.

6. Weber, M. *From Max Weber,* Edited by C. W. Mills and H. H. Gerth, New York: Oxford Press, 1948.

PART III

DIALOGUE ABOUT THERAPEUTIC COMMUNITIES IN PRISON (CONFERENCE EXCERPTS)

11

THE THERAPEUTIC COMMUNITY AS A SOCIAL LEARNING ENVIRONMENT

Jones   I've learned over thirty-plus years in this field that there is no such thing as *a* therapeutic community. There is no such thing as specific criteria one has to follow, in the shape of a detailed prescription. Each therapeutic community is unique, has its own unique challenges, and has its own unique clients and staff. To me it's become inevitable that if we seek common denomination of therapeutic communities we have to begin to follow simple principles, like there must be interaction at every point between whoever is in the particular setting. There must be a capacity to listen, which is very frequently lost in any kind of group process. And there must be willingness to confront, with the purpose of helping the learning process.

Confrontation, seen as a positive part of learning, is painful. It takes perhaps six months for a group to get to the level where they can honestly hear a hallelujah chorus when someone says "that's bullshit." I try to train myself to hear celestial music when I'm exposed to profanity because if someone is saying "that's bullshit," they're really challenging where I'm at, and I can find out where they disagree with me, and that's part of learning, whether we're talking about clients or staff.

The two segments of the community (clients and staff) are inseparable. I'm tired of talking about "treatment" and "training." To me they are the same process. I think that often you are treating the staff and being trained by the clients. The two terms can be lumped together into learning as a social process.

In any therapeutic community there must be regularly scheduled meetings. By "regularly scheduled meetings" I mean daily, so that you can begin to get process. What happened today must flow into tomorrow. What happens tomorrow must be part of a continuum, so that if, for instance, we're discussing the presence of visitors in a correctional community, we don't finalize the decision on Monday, but it follows through to Tuesday. And if process means anything, it means that we slowly move in an evolutionary direction, so that things become clearer and we're striving towards an ideal of consensus. All too often the process is not followed, and unfinished business is forgotten the next day. I think a group gets credibility by its capacity to resolve problems and to follow through on unfinished business.

A third general principle is that if you are dealing with some problem area, such as the selection of clients, everyone must have their chance for input. Information sharing is an absolute necessity. And what information sharing means is that everyone has a right to input, and that listening to input is part of the dynamics of change. When Doug Grant starts to talk, I will hear him, and I'll hear other people questioning some things that are not clear, and the position that I started with is inevitably modified. I cannot stand still if I'm really listening, and hearing 12 to 15 inputs. Something is going to be modified in my perception of a particular idea that I came into the room with. In other words, that is process also. And that is what I like to call social learning.

Now, "social learning" is a term used in different ways by different people. To me it means that if the inputs from everyone in a room are matched against my own position, I can't stand still, and I must begin to modify my attitudes, values, and beliefs so that I change, in some tiny, almost imperceptible way. That's something happening to me which is affecting my personality, if you like, in a tiny way.

This idea of social learning, of course, has to be linked with sharing of information not only at the cognitive level, but also at the *feeling* level. Information sharing, and the sharing of content and feeling, is one of the later developments of communities because it takes considerable time, whether it's in a fourth-grade classroom or in a new group in a prison. It takes time before it is safe to share feelings: You've got to be certain that there are going to be no reprisals. You've got to be certain that everything said in that group is confidential, and remains within that group. So you've got to build a system for change where it is safe to criticize, where you are going to be listened to, and where you are a participant in the process of change.

The question of leadership enters here. Someone's got to start as a role model. Someone has to have an idea of the goals and of the objectives: ideas are not born in a group womb; someone puts them into the pot. And leadership must be a changing pattern, where any person in the group is a potential leader, and has his own area of competence. I think that a well-balanced social structure assumes that everyone has his area of competence, and recognizes it. In Chino Prison, for example, leadership emerged from the most unlikely places, and was changing hands daily. There was no assumed authority structure. That happens to be one of the most difficult concepts to get across in our society, because we all grow up with the idea of an authoritarian hierarchical structure, and if we really believe that leadership can change hands within any group session this is contrary to basic ingrained assumptions held in the universities, and elsewhere.

Another issue is that it is a dirty word in some fields to be called a professional, but you can't help it if you've had training. It may be pretty chancy and inadequate training, but the fact remains that you've still got it. And the fact also remains that we need inputs from every facet of education. Here the important thing is that the professional must be competent in his small area. At Henderson in the early days, professional criminals had to be our interpreters: I didn't know the East End of London; I didn't know what it was like to get status through stealing, and about being a car thief and sharing the loot. The offenders had to tell me, because I didn't understand their culture. Now, given the willingness to listen, interact, and learn, professionals can have input in their own area of competence.

But how do you avoid the prejudice against you as a professional? Obviously, by the role that you play and demonstrate. And to follow this prescription is, as we know, incredibly difficult. I am not surprised when I visit hospitals, industry, schools and meet the same resistance everywhere. I don't know a clear, easy entree to a social system. So I'll end by saying that one principle I've learned is to get away from the concept of a consultant, and introduce the concept of a facilitator. A facilitator must be someone who helps people to help themselves, and does not pontificate.

THE PRINCIPLE OF ABSOLUTE CONFIDENTIALITY

Levinson   Are there any limitations on the extent of confidentiality? If they, for example, tell you about a plot to kill the warden, how confidential is it?

Jones   I once had a murderer surface in a group in a mental health setting, and I kept confidentiality. I was terribly torn, but I had no doubt that I had to keep that under my hat.

Levinson   But let's bring it back into a correctional setting, because I think that helps.

Jones   Yeah, well I would do the same thing. I would think the group would probably take this upon themselves, and if the group said, "Look, we can't hold this. If there's going to be a riot, we're bloody well going to snitch," I think that I would trust the group to have enough investment in the survival of that system to decide it for themselves.

Levinson   In the groups somebody says, "I know that somebody's going to kill the warden," or "Someone will start a riot"—not necessarily a group member, mind you. What do you do with information that has come out in the group, where somebody else's life is going to be put in danger?

Jones   My point is that if you put it to the group, saying, "Look, what are we going to do about this," meaning "what are *we* going to do about this," I trust the group is willing to accept an exception to the confidentiality, and then it's not destroying the group structure. That's the way I'd look at it.

Levinson   Even if they decide to keep quiet, you'll accept that too?

Jones   I have to accept that, that's all I can say.

SOCIAL LEARNING STARTS WITH RISK-TAKERS

Jones   The first principle that I've learned from my experience over a lifetime is that people are sick to death of conformity, of restrictions, of hierarchies. And everywhere I've gone, I have found that first-rate staff accumulates.

Toch   Latent risk takers?

Jones   Latent risk takers, disenchanted youth, people who have dropped out of college because they're fed up with being treated like children. Social workers, psychiatrists, people who want to get out of the hierarchical structure.

Wright   They sometimes get too far out of it, don't they?

Jones   Well, there's always a danger, of course. The point is that risk takers are around, and they really do like this kind of a challenge, so recruitment is relatively easy. In Scotland at one point we had four American psychiatrists working for nothing. It attracted them, that kind of a free system, because the big pay-off even in corrections is, that if it's truly a good social organization, the test of its effectiveness is the extent to which people feel fulfilled. The concept is that in a truly democratic, open system everyone's latent potential has a chance to surface, whether it's in the direction of skills or leadership, or some special work assignment. I think that's the pay-off.

Toch   Earlier, you indicated that the creation of a therapeutic community culture was a long and laborious enterprise. Wouldn't that suggest that these idealistic individuals might burn out when they see there's a long, grinding process ahead, with few immediate payoffs within a short time?

Jones   That obviously is a fair point, and I think it's a test of motivation. I don't see any short cuts. I think these are long struggles.

Rosenthal   One of the shortcuts is if you bring in a significant infusion of people to begin with. By that I mean if you go into an institution you bring along other people who by their presence and by their own actions are participating in the kind of behavior that you want the others to participate in.

Toch   Does your model presuppose the existence of a prior therapeutic community from which you draw this invading army, or can you create that from scratch?

Rosenthal   No, it does demand that you have a talent bank to draw on.

Devlin   Cross-fertilization leads to germination.

Elwin   I've had some strange luck where in the early stages a unit is under siege, and we got to get together because we've got a common outside enemy, which threatens both staff and the residents. Now I don't know if you could create that.

Wright   I think far too many crisis intervention teams are created. What are needed are some crisis creation teams.

CRISES AS SOCIAL LEARNING EXPERIENCES

Rosenthal   We had a very interesting experiment two and a half years ago, when a crisis was imminent through a cut in state funding to drug abuse programs. We ended up with a mass of 200 some people who camped out 60 days on the banks of the Hudson outside the state capital, and during that time functioned together as a working therapeutic community. No one would have ever thought that that was possible, given the history of competition and backbiting with the programs that were involved.

Jones When the patients at Henderson wrecked the local pub, which was a terrible thing to occur, that crisis was turned into a very valuable learning situation. The patient peer groups said, "Get stuffed, guys, go and give yourselves up to the police. We're not going to be suffering because of your silly behavior." The incident did in fact lead to a learning situation which helped to establish limits which people were not going to go beyond.

Toch Mitch raised the question about that first lonely full-time staff member, and how insecure he must feel. That brings to mind that poor lonely therapeutic community in its first week or two of life. It doesn't get any sense of being accepted in the system, it doesn't know what its goals are, it doesn't have that sense of mission. Wouldn't that be a very vulnerable stage, and wouldn't one have to build in some sort of support system?

Levinson The warden or whoever runs the institution should be meeting with the head of this therapeutic community once a week, and the news would get around the institution.

Toch At least at first, I suppose, which is the critical phase?

Jones Because if the authority is invisible, then all the pretensions, all the fantasies, congregate around that invisible figure.

Barker My experience is in some contrast with what was said. In retrospect, I think there was some strength in being alone, though the blessing of the top man would seem to be indispensable. If there had been three or four of us who had a clear plan and had come from somewhere and were going to deliver a system unto this new place, I don't think it would have succeeded. Being alone and rather frightened, I had to turn to the patients and the guards for survival, and I think that's a very important dynamic. If I had three or four people I could go and get sustenance from, I wouldn't have been turning as honestly to those whose help I needed. And I wouldn't have felt I was their guest, even though I had formal authority.

CONFRONTATION: AN ALTERNATIVE MODEL OR A SUPPLEMENTARY ONE?

Jones I'd love to find out at some point, how we can begin to look at Synanon-type games, which are a violation of most people's psychother-apeutic ideas and ideas of process and learning. It's a kind of persuasive technique, where a condition that's beyond my belief, nevertheless has got good results. And I would like to look at that.

Chinlund   I think the question has to do with the appropriateness of confrontation techniques.

Jones   Absolutely. Because to me it's one of the discrepant practices that are going on under the heading of therapeutic community. On the one hand, the Synanon games with their violent confrontation seem to be effective with some people, and on the other, so is the more familiar pattern we have been talking about involving peer group-based processes. But the two mean a very different thing.

Levinson   Having to do with the nature of the patient?

Jones   Well, that's what I want to know, because it's obvious that at Marion, Illinois, they were in the worst of the federal prisons, and the inmates were a highly volatile and explosive group. And one thing I want to know [is] if that kind of technique is relevant only to that population.

Rosenthal   I think we use a range of techniques going up to the strongest kind of confrontation groups, that you would characterize as violent, as verbally violent. And at the other end of the spectrum is a much more supportive, analytic, nurturing, slow-moving type of process.

Wright   Is it self-selecting?

Rosenthal   No, it isn't self-selecting, except in that some patients may feel more comfortable in working in some areas or in some settings than in other areas. But all of the patients are likely to be exposed to all the different kinds of therapy groups that go on. It is also self-selecting in that people can leave who are uncomfortable in that kind of setting. Now I have really been in both camps, and I've been involved with a wide range of patients, from those who are closer to a psychiatric population, borderline schizoid, to patients who have much more typical characterologic distur-bances with a strong history of antisocial behavior. I think that strong confrontation groups are tremendously effective, and we have ample evi-dence of this right now. I also think that these kinds of groups have a potential for very serious abuse. As long as the group is focused responsibly, and their mandate is the long-term well-being of the individual members, it's okay. Even if somebody may go in there and the style may get them upset, I think that the group can still be responsible. However, when the group starts to use its techniques for sustaining the institution or toward the adoration of a charismatic leader, we move from therapy to cult or thought reform. Then there's a significant danger beyond the danger to a particular participant, which is that the technique might become too harsh and too brutal. But it is the perversion of confrontation techniques towards a religious movement and an ideology of totalism that is the serious issue.

Jones   I cannot understand the process in the Synanon-type game. To me it's persuasion or "join us or else" or something very powerful which holds people together in that setting. But I can't yet see it as a growth experience where something is learned.

Devlin   I don't know that it's as much a growth experience as it is a measure to prevent physical hostility. I also don't know any therapeutic community that uses only that technique in this day. You're talking about Synanon of the '50s.

Chinlund   How harmed do you feel the work of Cortage, Daytop, or Phoenix would be if that piece were eliminated, and you were to say "from now on we will not use the sharpest of the violent confrontations?" Do you think it would lead to physical violence, because they no longer have that opportunity?

Rosenthal   Worse than that. I think that you would render the community very ineffective. It would be like taking a scalpel away from your surgeon.

Devlin   Aside from the possibilities of physical violence increasing, I see it as a release valve in that pressure cooker environment.

Wright   But why don't you just go out and get a punch bag?

Devlin   Some places use that technique also.

Rosenthal   I'll tell you why you just don't use a punching bag. The amount of denial and rationalization that most of our patients use in being comfortable with their self-destructive habits is not very easily stripped away, unless you use techniques that are as forceful, as searing, as these techniques that have evolved.

Wright   But you have a different way of doing the same thing, don't you, Elliott?

Barker Well, as you described these groups, our patients have developed the terminology much as you laid it out—supportive, analytic, and confronting groups. When they form a small group, the small groups committee will designate which of the groups they want, and they'll form a composition for it. And I'm not familiar with Synanon and Daytop and so on, but I've always been uncomfortable about confrontation groups. They exceed my personal taste buds with regard to aggressiveness. However, the patients seem to like them and the staff certainly like them. I always think there's more heat than light generated from the point of view of a learning experience. But both groups like them and feel it is the only way you can get at character disorders. To undermine denial, and the capacity to rationalize and keep people at a distance, they would want that technique. Where it can get off the rails in our system is if it's used as a way of attacking some individual on the basis of some personal agenda and not for his welfare or the welfare of the community.

Rosenthal It tunes in very well to one significant aspect of the unconscious, which is rage and anger. It is just as Freud said, "Dreams are the royal road to the unconscious." That kind of verbal violence and profanity, that kind of catharsis, opens up aspects of people's feelings. And it teaches them that they can handle that sort of drive without violence, and without threats of physical violence. Now, if there are counterbalancing forces that are loving and nurturing, this sets up on the other side groups that put people in touch with their need for love, their need for closeness, their need for trust, and it does it in very emotional language, rather than in the more intellectualized language that we are more comfortable with. We now have regular confrontation groups, two, three times a week, sometimes a fourth. But then, almost on a monthly basis everybody is in a long group called a "marathon group," and those groups have very little to do with expressions of verbal violence. They are attempts to get people back to their most fundamental feelings about themselves. It's when you don't have that counterbalance that you're in trouble.

The point is that if you were just running long groups and just opening up people in terms of their softer types of needs, you'd be missing a whole dimension of aggressive violence that is also a part of their psychic experience. In order to get a full picture of somebody, you have to see all of them.

Barker The part of the confrontation groups that I feel is most sinister is that they can be prescribed, so to speak, by professionals or quasi professionals for other people. I think there's great safety in having a group being the master of its own destiny. And if a group of inmates who have been living together for a period of time decide amongst themselves that they want to utilize this technique, and it's discussed amongst themselves, I see that as safer, providing there's checks and balances within that system, than if a group of professionals who believe they know what is best for those people, lay it on the inmates. But if you have an ongoing group, and they read or hear about that as a particular technique and want to try it, I'd keep an eye on it but I wouldn't feel like stopping it.

Rosenthal   We're not talking about outside staff coming in as some hired guns and doing it. We're talking about 12 people who sit down, who live under the same roof, work under the same roof, and share all experiences together. They're now sitting down with a contract that they're going to help each other. And so there are built-in checks and balances.

Jones   I think this discussion has helped me because Mitch was very reassuring when he added the component of tender loving care. I think it's very necessary to propound it the way you've done, linking it with conflicts of a highly submerged kind.

Rosenthal   I think very few people would sit around and have somebody come in and call them names if there wasn't another level of concern and ability for tenderness and a whole other range of interpretation.

Jones   I would call it a technique of containment, that you contain people's violence and make it safe to bring it out. But how much learning occurs for the future? It is hard to look at the process and say "there is something that they take out of it." It may be that they can help handle potentially violent situations outside better than they did before. I think we need more information about what is learned.

Rosenthal   There is a fairly fixed relationship between time in program and outcome, looking at people two years, five years, and seven years later. And when you talk about containment and strong groups, these are all important dimensions. Another very significant part is a structured, stabilized environment over a long period of time. Most of our people have been in the most chaotic, wild environments. And stabilization itself is a very important factor, the chance to deal with problems below the belt—with sexual problems. The fact that we have been locking up many people for many hundreds of years who have significant sexual disorders, and we have basically been treating those people above the belt, is something that we must look at.

Jones   I think it needs to be expounded far more in terms of learning theory or any other process we can think up. Because the dynamics need to be understood.

SOCIAL LEARNING, SELF-STUDY, AND NEW CAREERS

Grant   A key problem I see is the linkage of what one does in institutions, with the postconfinement world. In our early studies with offenders in the navy, we were very fortunate to have a built-in postinstitutional job and postinstitutional climate. You may not call it the ideal climate, but everyone of my population, after they got through with whatever we were doing with them at Camp Eliot, went back into the military service. And they had a job, and they had a role.

In a recent workshop in England, they had representatives from Poland, who discussed this same built-in feature. In Poland, everybody had a job, whether they were serving a sentence or not. It's quite a different ball game when you have that as a given. In our prison work, we trained offenders as program developers. We had built in that we would work with them while they were confined, to enable them to play roles in the correctional system, in the Youth Authority and the Department of Corrections. They were not to go back as assistant custodial officers or as assistant counselors, but as assistant training officers and as assistant administrative analysts. They were to go in with the idea of playing a role in trying to promote continual change within the organization. That's one of the goals, incidentally, that led to my rather early and abrupt departure from the correctional scene.

In the navy, we had moved from trying to work with the offenders themselves to a total study of the confinement experience. I had a naval captain who bought into this enough to let us do it. We had everybody attend a plenary session, where we called them all to attention and the captain entered. We broke up into study groups afterwards, the staff and inmates together. Very early in my thinking there evolved this concern with expanding the effort at studying what's going on in your program as a way to improve both the organization and the mental health of members in it. That, by the way, is extremely well documented, that you can use this process to improve mental health, and have fewer undesirable incidents, fewer problems, fewer suicides, and higher morale.

I see this merging now with the concern for what's being called the quality of work. There's a task force report out of HEW that ends up with the ringing recommendation that we work towards becoming an experimenting society, where everyone spends some of their time studying and working on how to modify and improve what they're doing. And this means not just that you have an elitist planning office that develops how we're going to change, but that you get total employee participation in program development. Let me just say for the benefit of planners, that there's a tremendous role for some competence in total planning that fits into that system. But I think it's more than conceptually that you can talk about total participation. For example, many of you know that in Sweden and in other European countries, there's a great deal of work getting employees to become competent in planning what they're doing. And in America, the Department of Commerce has two demonstration projects within the department, where they are studying their own operation in accounting and audits, and in their publications department. They have had a similar study going on in the World Bank, where the staff systematically spends part of their job in adjusting the problems. And there's a fair amount of thought within the Department of Labor on the implications of employee participation on problem of health and safety of the workers. It strikes me that you could very plausibly defend custodial officers studying prison survival problems.

Hans Toch and I worked for five years with police officers, to get them to become students of their system. And I think there is a good deal of know-how here, relating to how individuals can simultaneously improve their own competencies and the competencies of their organization.

One thing we stole in the way of a conceptual idea from Maxwell Jones was the issue of new careers. Jones brought Scandinavian women as social therapists into an all-male institution. This experiment, and its positive impact, started Dennie Briggs and me thinking about other new roles that can be played. We know that there's a leadership role, a priming role of stimulating things. There's the administrative role of keeping the roof on the place. There is also leadership as social learning.

As I understand it, Max Jones doesn't just say that you get together where everybody feels comfortable and can swear at each other. He says that you take a natural crisis, a natural incident, and you study that, and you learn from that incident as opposed to panicking and making a lot of new rules, which you tend to do in that situation. And that social learning fits very much with the critical-incident technology that Flanagan pioneered a good many years ago. He was concerned with arranging that as you approach a problem you center on actual incidents and systematically study these, as well as focus your discussions on them. We have applied the logic of this procedure in our prison work, where we had a research unit of about 35 inmates, not all of whom were nonprofessionals by any means. We always had a few MDs or a few certified public accountants, a few almost-doctorates of sociology and so on. But we had many men who had not had much formal training at all. And we wanted to augment this deficit by having what you might call a research utilization component. We had people out in the organization that helped develop the questions and helped to expand the study. We brought these people in to help us develop confined men as what we originally called social change agents. They quickly changed their name to program development assistants and then program developers. And they did a lot of studying of incidents and events in the prison world. One of the things we did with them while they were still in training was to have them help Toch and me study institutional violence, as an example of the use of a product of a problem (some of them had been pretty violent themselves) in coping with the problem.

What I think should not be forgotten in our looking at implications is that those men not only contributed appreciably to our knowledge of the system, but that they also developed change in it. We moved the program into the larger community and the men went on working as program developers. Fourteen of them are now in responsible positions around the country.

What I'm saying we should not lose track of is that you have resources in both staff and inmates, particularly once you get some kind of living-learning thrust, to start doing quite formal studying of the nature of the institution itself, and particularly the linkage of the institution with the community. In this way, you could start to think of linking your corrections involvement with other agency involvement, including the private industry concern with employee participation. This could lead to the building of new roles for staff and inmates that move into a postinstitutional structure or career.

THE THERAPEUTIC COMMUNITY AS A SOCIAL MOVEMENT

Elwin   My experience with therapeutic communities is that whether it's by design or by the very process, they tend to turn out individuals who see themselves as change agents. Very unfortunately, out here in the so-called real world, there are very few jobs for change agents, particularly if you're not credentialed. So the graduates of therapeutic communities come out to change the world, and after a short time, in practical terms, they get a file clerk's job, and then the whole thing goes.

Wright   The problem that Ed's talking about is that you get the accusation made that when somebody arrives outside of a therapeutic community, they don't go *into* a therapeutic community. Therefore, what are they going to do? The point of that being that too many therapeutic communities are not therapeutic communities but just a different or better way of running an institution. We go through this therapeutic community motion as a way of keeping the peace or as a way of being innovative, or any of a whole lot of other things. That isn't what the point is. A therapeutic community should be like thorazine, in the sense that it alters a person's way of functioning rather than being an instrument to keep an institution happy. Now, often, when therapeutic community graduates go out, all they try to do is to create bigger and better therapeutic communities, one vast therapeutic community in New York, or the world, or the universe.

Jones   Well, this points up the whole illusion that you create a therapeutic community quickly out of whatever you have at the time. When I was superintendent of a hospital in Scotland it took me seven years to develop a decent open system. I don't want to sound too pessimistic, but I think that's one of the factors that we overlook. I'd much rather train people for small-group work or even psychoanalytic work than for a therapeutic community, because it's an extremely demanding and extremely disciplined approach. And I think open communication, let alone information sharing and decision making and so on, are enormously exacting exercises that we're not used to.

Grant   I'm not as upset as it sounds from the comments around here that the whole world ought to be getting more like a therapeutic community. I'm very much interested in strategies for the human race to have some role in determining its future as opposed to just being the recipients of it. And that's what's so exciting about this employee participation. I by no means want to belittle the issue that's raised, because I think it's extremely crucial to have roles for people to go to. But it seems to me there's a real model, where you get the skills and the knowledge and the orientation out of a program into a larger world. Some of our inmates have voluntarily gone back to truck driving or something like this. And I think it's another move if they decide that themselves.

Those first 18 offenders all had had case records several inches thick. And within the relatively simple interventions we were able to supply—very much including the opportunity structure—they moved from being extreme liabilities to society to being extreme assets. You can measure it several ways, one of which is their tax returns. But as they developed by becoming involved in social change, they also established new relationships, including heterosexual relationships, and were able to get a new identity with new groups of people. We need to think much more about that.

You could be a secretary, you could be even working in the Volvo assembly line, and you can still put in a fair amount of respected time for your own development and to try and develop the organization for which you're working. And I think that merges the development of the human race with the development of people.

Rosenthal   I think a lot of us have been responsible for idealizing, romanticizing, and marketing that concept, which isn't to say that it isn't true, but it is to say that any change agent has to be part of a larger system, and has to be part of a context and organization of change. And when a person is taken out and his magical expectations start to be reciprocated with someone else's magical expectations, then you really are set up to have everybody disillusioned.

Devlin   I don't think that the traditional evangelism, even the term change agent, exist today like they did some years ago. I think young people coming out of the TCs today really do want a job. You know, years ago in the life of every young Catholic boy there was a period where you wanted to become a priest. And in the life of every TC resident, there's an aspiration to be that change agent, super star, or staff in the therapeutic community. But life today in the therapeutic community is not as romantic as it was years ago. It's almost become a civil service job, and not everyone wants to work in a TC. But it's jobs that are the problem, because it's not that easy to be the secretary or the truck driver. Because there are ten guys in front of you who did not use drugs and were not offenders, who are applying for that same job.

12

CREATING A SOCIAL LEARNING
ENVIRONMENT IN THE PRISON

Briggs   Maxwell Jones' remarks are a good introduction to my own, because Max helped us plan our project and served as ongoing facilitator through the four years it was in existence. The other guiding spirit in our project was J. Douglas Grant.

When Doug Grant became the first chief of research of California corrections, he inherited some small ongoing projects, which were all projects having a look at the effectiveness of individual interventions, and mainly at psychiatric casework, with control groups and follow-ups on parole. And we were concerned, in talking with counselors, parole agents, and other people, about the contaminating or masking effects of the institution itself. One of our concerns was seeing to what degree you could minimize these contextual effects and (if you could) how you could do so. Another concern was to have a look at interventions other than individual approaches. Here we were immediately drawn to looking at the total environment, to see what we could do with it. A third concern was the length of exposure, because many inmates we were interested in were serving long sentences, and there was a question about how much time was needed for effective or long-term change.

So we set up three controlled experiments to test out these ideas. The first related to the issue of the effect of the institution itself. To try to examine this effect, we took a small new unit of 100 that was being built in a mountain setting as a forestry camp, where we had a chance almost from the point of architecture to design a small environment that might be self-contained, where we could have control over relationships, such as at work and in housing arrangements. By way of contrast, we set up another unit within a large institution, a 2,000-bed minimum-security institution. And we used the same selection criteria for the two units.

We were involved at this time with the young, aggressive offender, from age 18 to late twenties. And these men were especially of concern because they made up about 40 percent of admissions to prisons and cause most of the disruptive behavior. They had to be housed in higher-security settings, and we wanted to see if this was really necessary, if we couldn't handle such men in a program from a management standpoint as well as with long-term effect. In the two units we were also interested in looking at the maturity-level concept, and we selected inmates with higher maturity levels. In a third unit we were interested in older, more recidivistic inmates in their thirties who had long histories, and who were of lower maturity levels. All three groups were selected at random, each with a control group. We tried to set up as likely a working model as we could, between what we thought a therapeutic community should ideally be like and what was possible within the institution. One interesting thing that happened was that as we began the first unit we inherited a half-dozen trained psychiatric social workers from projects where they had emphasized individual casework approaches. Maxwell Jones was very helpful in training the psychiatric social workers, who were quite a mixed group, with some interested in the therapeutic community concept, and some interested in pursuing individual treatment.

We looked into many things, including the use of work and the use of education and recreation. And we considered these things, thinking that we ought to study them rather than having preconceptions about their impact. We started with work because we wanted to build as much of a community as we could within the prison, with a common work project. Most of the newer people hadn't held down any kind of steady job in their lives. So the prison gave us a common work project. We ran a laundry for the institution. The superintendent thought he could see the effects of higher production and maybe through that the inmates would learn something. He was wrong—they learned very little.

The other thing that the administration thought was that you have to have separate discipline and rehabilitation. And the kinds of inmates we chose were constantly in trouble, one way or another. We thought that in order to give the program more freedom, the inmates should be dealt with by the outside custodial force when they got into trouble. We were also wrong on this issue.

The project was divided into two phases, by evolution and not by planning. At the end of about two years, we had a crisis among the staff. The counselors weren't working out, and they didn't like it very much. Within a period of two or three months we lost all counselors but one, through promotions or transfers. And when we put out applications for replacement, we received no applications. Our image within the social work field was tarnished enough so that social workers didn't want to work in our setting. We had a crisis around the question of what to do. And it was at this time that a very exciting thing happened, in that the custodial officers filled in the vacuum. They decided there wasn't anything the social workers were doing that they couldn't do with some training. And Max Jones and other people helped us to supply such training. As the correctional officers became less concerned with discipline and custodial matters, a strange development occurred: the inmates became concerned about custodial issues and escapes. In fact, they took on the role of guards. From this point on, really awesome things happened, because now roles were always in flux, and Max Jones' ideas of leadership could come forth. As the correctional officers became interested and developed skills in counseling, the inmates were taking my job away from me. We actually set up a system where the administrator of the project rotated from day to day, so that all of the correction officers had administrative responsibility, and the inmates moved into counseling positions.

. We followed up our groups of inmates on parole, for one year. None of the three projects did better or worse than the others, when inmates were compared to their control groups. Isolating one unit in a beautiful country setting did no better or no worse than having the unit in the middle of a large traditional institution. And there was a significant difference when you put all of the treated group together as against the control groups. But the most exciting results appeared when you compared all of the inmates from the first phase, which was largely run by the staff, with the second phase, which was largely inmate-run. There was a significant difference between those two groups favoring the second phase.

Incidentally, the optimal time of treatment turned out to be about eight months. There proved to be no benefit in staying longer than that.

Jones   Can you expand on the point of the inmates' assuming responsibility for discipline overnight?

Briggs   In California, which may be unique, some inmates were worried about what would happen to them custodially because of earthquakes, which I didn't know. They were terrified about what would happen to a high-security prison in an earthquake, because all the locking devices might be neutralized, and they'd have no protection. Our inmates were also concerned about suicides and escapes. In the first two years of the project we had three successful escapes, and the men were concerned because if a man escapes, he can never come back to a unit like this. And they felt that they had some responsibility to the men, especially because while one is undergoing this kind of a project, the escape potential rises. So the men set up a regular custodial system of four-hour watches where they were responsible around the clock for running the unit's security. And that was seen as an indication of inmates' progressing in the program: they were expected to take on responsibility. There were no escapes in the last two years.

STAFFING A THERAPEUTIC COMMUNITY IN A PRISON

Jones   You want to have some people who really have the skills, I think. And I think that the authority structure has to trust the people who are going to be given this delegated responsibility and authority. Within the social organization there must be consensus through the various levels that these are the appropriate people to be given this opportunity.

Levinson   It's hard to talk about staff selection if you don't know what kind of inmates you're going to be working with.

Briggs   With our young inmates, we tried older, experienced correction officers, and we tried psychiatric social workers. It ended up that the best people within the unit were young correctional officers just coming into the system, with one senior officer who was very experienced and almost forced himself into the unit. We didn't especially want him, but he was an absolute gem, as it turned out.

Jones   Someone knows quite a lot about the officers, presumably. Someone knows about their kinds of group skills. And that's where I would have thought you could get some pretty good leads about the kinds of people who can interact sensitively and do planning and other things that really fit the job.

Chinlund   Dennie had just said that he did best with his brand-new staff, which doesn't frankly come as a surprise. I mean, if you've got people who are not yet set in certain ways that are counterproductive, and that's true of group skills too, they can't say "this isn't the way we did it back wherever."

ORGANIZATIONAL EFFECTIVENESS, AS OPPOSED TO THERAPEUTIC SKILL

Barker   I lost the kind of notion that anything I was ever involved with ever got anybody any better. It seemed to me that "better" or "effectiveness" has to do with the morale of the inmate while he's doing time, and the morale of the institution, which reflects itself in a lower suicide or mutilation rate within the institution, and increased security, and less deterioration of people within the institution. And I think those three things are really very basic, and much preferable to whatever this "cure" business is, which seems to me unmeasurable anyway.

With regard to selection of staff, the criterion is not who can help us to cure a particular bunch within the prison, but who can contribute to infecting the whole prison system with a disease that's healthier than the one you've got. And as part of that strategy, I would say it's critical to pick correctional officers who have some clout within the institution. I assume we pick a warden who in fact runs his institution, but has for his own reason, some interest in playing along. And we don't pick correctional officers who are most interested in "therapy" but ones who have credibility within the system and are also game, for whatever reason, to go along. And we work with the first such officer and let him pick congenial work-mates or friends. Some inmates may volunteer because of those correctional officers, but some wouldn't because those officers are going to become involved. And I would accommodate this fact. I would also let the guards have some say in who (among inmates) comes in, if not total say in the first inmate group.

What I've described is the only way that I have ever done it—which is just once—and that seemed to make sense as far as the longer-term objectives of infecting the whole institution were concerned. If we had taken the officers who agreed with us to start with, it would have fed nothing back to the harder core.

THE CONGRUENCE OF STAFFING NEEDS WITH STAFF MOTIVES

Toch   In an abortive effort to get some estimate of the prevalence of mental health problems among inmates, we interviewed a largish sample of correctional officers in New York State. I say "abortive," since the officers didn't prove to be a good source of information about the prevalence of inmate difficulties, because of the tremendous variance in their estimates. Now as is usual in science, we extracted out of adversity a piece of scientific information which to us seemed quite valuable. This had to do with differential sensitivities and interests among officers in the mental health area. It was particularly dramatic when you had two officers dealing with the same inmates, giving us different estimates of problem prevalence, ranging from no problem to 20 percent of inmates.

It became obvious that some officers define their role very narrowly. They see themselves, in terms of their mandate, as having no business becoming interested in inmates who ought to be referred or counseled, who might have problems one ought to inquire into. But there were other officers, and they were a significant minority, who had an amazing amount of interest in the area. I say "amazing," because there wasn't any reward system for this. Their peers, as far as they knew, didn't hold their concerns in very high esteem. The department certainly didn't reward them, and didn't mandate them to do this. They were swimming against the tide; they were trying to mobilize the system on behalf of inmates, in a sense feeling that they were using up credits in doing so. Is it conceivable that an option might be to select officers who have àn initial concern and a broader definition of their job? Officers who might not volunteer because they might not realize that their concern coincides with the opportunity structure you provide?

Elwin   I think one of the problems is that we really have no hook on what talent we have in the system. In terms of the number of people who have some kind of prior experience that may not be completely what you want but may be close enough to say, "Hey, that's a good one that I could build on," we might be pleasantly surprised in terms of what we pick up.

Toch   And such officers would be able to contribute to their training by drawing on their prior experience, which would make the training experience less passive and academic.

Jones   Though this sounds plausible, I'm always uncomfortable when wise people sit around determining other people's fates. Before you do that, I would very much like to think that you would give the prison officers a chance to discuss this whole matter and advise you.

Briggs   Before I turn to the subject, may I say a word about my upbringing? Spending a month with Maxwell Jones at Henderson was a real turning point in my life, because I knew that there was nothing I could ever do that would replicate Henderson, but at least now I had a model in mind—something to work toward. I knew it wouldn't be the same, but I knew what could happen. And I also learned a great many things in that unit that, to this day, I use continuously. Jones is the best example of his own point that leadership is very important.

THE ROLE OF CORRECTIONAL OFFICERS

Briggs   The correctional officers who had volunteered to work in our project came with expectations of doing something different than custodial work, and were immediately involved in all activities with the prisoners. They not only had little expertise to draw upon, but little custodial training and experience as well. They were nice young people, some just out of the armed forces, experiencing and exploring their own lives and unsure of their future careers. One older and more experienced officer chose to remain when the new ones came into the project. We all looked to him for help with custodial matters, and the training was done on the job.

Each officer met with a small group where he saw the need to develop additional group skills. These groups were concerned with interpersonal and social relationships of the men who were in them, and often went more into depth on matters raised in the community meetings. We met weekly for a seminar on groups, where one officer would present material from his group as the core for the training. Where the morning and the afternoon shifts overlapped, we held daily meetings lasting half an hour, to share communication about what was happening that day.

Once each week, I met alone with all the officers. Here we discussed what was happening to them in the project: their worries about their capabilities, their anxieties about inmate situations in which they became involved, their relations with other officers in the prison, their families, their personal lives, and their expectations for the future. They compared how they did their job in the past—even though they had not had much experience—with what they should do now. They had many uneasy exchanges with other officers in the prison, and they felt they had mistreated prisoners, and knew of other officers who had also.

It took about six weeks before they could talk about sensitive matters in the group. They went through a period where they thought they were discriminated against by fellow officers. Then they went through a phase of feeling guilty for mistreating prisoners, and they had to unburden themselves. I was a little startled myself to hear them "confess" to mistreatments. The prisoners had talked many times of such injustices, and I had heard their stories so often, I was prone to thinking they exaggerated.

One day the officers brought a young lieutenant to their meetings from the main prison. He had been transferred from a high-security prison where he had a notorious reputation for being the unappointed leader of a "goon squad." The administration realized that he had leadership potential and also that he was ultimately dangerous to public relations; hence they had transferred him to us for "softening." The officers—realizing he was a key to the acceptance of the project in the prison—had been able to convince him to come to their meeting. He attended regularly over a period of time and eventually began to tell of some brutalities he had committed at the former prison. His acceptance of the program and personal change was a key event, because after the officers "converted" him there wasn't as much trouble as before with the custodial staff—he simply began to "put the word out" to the others. One sergeant who was especially troublesome to the project began to come around, and he, too, made a radical turnabout. He was later appointed a member of the Adult Authority and was very helpful.

The superintendent brought in a newly appointed captain who backed the program openly from his arrival. He eventually spread aspects of it into the rest of the prison and sent other correctional officers around to learn from it.

We didn't do all of the training alone. We had a number of regular consultants, among them Doug Grant and members of his staff, and

Maxwell Jones. And we had occasional consultants who helped us with specifics in the development of the program. These were people like Albert Elias from the Highfields, New Jersey, Group Interaction Center; LaMar Empey from the Provo, Utah, Pinehills Group Project; Bruno Klopfer, who had just returned from Europe with an existential frame of reference; the late Eric Berne, and others.

And the training of the inmates, you see, followed simultaneously. As they began to get new roles, Max Jones came and talked to them about social therapists, and they read up on social therapists. One social therapist just happened to be living in Los Angeles and we had him come out to a seminar on what the role of a social therapist was. We developed a role of social therapist which included training. And we set up university extension courses for the inmates that eventually merged with the officers' course, so that they were learners together. We brought in students from the university, made a connection with the outside, and helped to change the image of an officer and an inmate into a learner.

Barker I'm afraid I never had a meeting with any of our guards to discuss anything we were doing. I didn't want them to become more sophisticated psychologically. I saw that as a step backwards, in the sense that we as middle-class, psychologically oriented people are not of the population we're dealing with, but that the guards basically have a healthy lower-class orientation where a punch in the mouth speaks more than some sophisticated psychological argument. We weren't allowing punches in the mouth, but verbal punches of the same order, whether they were psychologically cute or not, seemed relevant. The danger that the therapeutic community is a cocoon and a protected sort of place is my argument for not trying to make staff more "therapeutic," meaning more sophisticated, like social workers or psychologists. I liked the fact that in the midst of the patient's talking about matters psychodynamic, the guards could always come up with the comment "you're still a goddam rapist to me." Which is very therapeutic, and reflects the outside culture that the inmates would be going to, so that they never left that base too far.

In the selection of staff, I've mentioned that we started with a key supervisor who had clout, physical clout in the local cultural center. He could beat up most people. I mean, he had moxie and standing. And when he got interested in the process that was going on in the ward, the institution really followed. I wonder in retrospect whether it would have been a mistake to offer higher pay if it were possible within civil service, to seduce that kind of person into the original model. Under civil service, staff are used to being moved where they're told to move, and I don't know what the chemistry is of getting someone involved originally.

As to never having staff meetings, one of my rationalizations was that we never had enough staff to man the place. And there was a problem of staffing to meet with staff. It wasn't my cup of tea to meet with the guards anyway, and I never had any illusions but what I was running was a dictatorship. We argued for maximum freedom for the patients to talk between themselves without limitation, both negative and positive, about what they were doing. But when it came to security, clearly the staff were in charge and always had a veto.

THE INMATE CADRE FOR THE THERAPEUTIC COMMUNITY

Levinson   I think there's danger on both ends, of getting all the bad guys, or getting all the good guys.

Briggs   We only picked the cream of the crop. We had about an 80 percent prediction that they'd be back. We did a base expectancy study to compare them, and they were comparable to any group that was in the prison at that time.

Chinlund   But it was staff selection?

Briggs   The first two years it was all clinical decisions by six psychiatric social workers, a consulting psychiatrist, a Ph. D. psychologist, you name it! They read folders, they interviewed volunteers, they held weighty clinical staff meetings, they went on and on and on. And one day they went off to a professional meeting and I was left alone. The superintendent called and said he's got a bed shortage, you've got to take an intake tonight, pick the five people. The inmates overheard me on the phone, and said, "We guess you need a hand." And they went along and took the intake candidates over to the unit, put them through a sort of behavioral test, and did all sorts of worrying. Then they gave me the names of the people we should put in.

Levinson   But they picked from a pool of people who had volunteered?

Briggs   Right. But when we ran the expectancy tables, they were comparable to the average inmate.

Levinson   Yes, but there's a difference between those who volunteer and those who don't, isn't there?

Rosenthal   I think selection should be self-selection. When the navy was trying to determine who would do best in the Antartic, they did extensive psychometric testing, interviews with anthropologists, long, complicated procedures. In the end the best predictor of who did well in the Antartic was the people who wanted to be there.

Toch   Are we saying there are no sensible criteria other than willingness or eagerness to participate?

Rosenthal   If you have the willingness or eagerness to participate, and then allow the group, as in Dennie's case, to apply its own standards and criteria, I think that's the best way to do it. It doesn't accommodate the concern from the point of view of science and controlled experimentation, and it doesn't answer the concern for are there other things that you're trying to accomplish. You're talking about who is most likely to benefit from being in that system—it *does* answer that.

THE PENETANGUISHENE MODEL OF THE PATIENT-RUN COMMUNITY

Barker   With regard to the inmates for the original unit, I was trying to load the dice in favor of survival. I'm glad there weren't any researchers around trying to randomize the place, or it never would have gotten off the ground. It seemed to me that we needed all the help we could get to keep from blowing apart. So we picked the patients in the institution who were willing to come to the unit, and gradually transferred them in while transferring out people who seemed disenchanted or ill-equipped for what was going on.

Once the original colony or beachhead was established and had some reasonable status within the institution, there was less of a problem getting staff and patients, and moving out to the other wards.

Toch   It's been said about you that your principal skill consists of putting people together so that significant things can happen without anybody getting hurt. And that you have improved on the model by devising new ways of putting people together, such as in those very intensive experiences. I suppose at least one item is the Penetang feature of having techniques of change originate with inmates, where part of the social learning process is to evolve a change technology. I think it might be useful to get your experience in this matter, since it's unique.

Barker   On the first ward, we had a mixture of psychopaths, schizophrenics, and retarded people with either of those illnesses. As I said earlier [Chapter 8] in the social structure that evolved there were half a dozen committees that ran the business of the ward. There was an attempt to balance the schizophrenics and the psychopaths on each committee. The prevailing ideal was to have the balance of potency in favor of the schizophrenics. Potency always seemed tough to define, and the patients talked a great deal about it. If you asked them to rank order, in terms of potency, the people on the ward, they could do it with tremendous consistency. And it usually meant the capacity to sway others verbally. And if in any committee the balance of potency lay with the schizoprenics, it seemed to be a safer kind of operation.

One of the things that we had as a preoccupation was to have the patients run their own show independent of professional "expertise." In the early days we had none, and later we thought we were doing better without it. So the programs that evolved were strategies that would work without the safeguards of a trained person within the group. And that's one reason I speak of this balance. We thought there was less scapegoating and a safer, healthier climate if we had that balance, because we didn't have trained persons sitting in each of the groups to monitor what was going on.

Within the committee system, some patients were clearly better at certain jobs than others—as chairman of the treatment committee, for example, or on the staff-patient liaison committee. And you could get a selection of patients who could run the ward exceptionally well. Since there's always the tendency to want to keep the ward running well, it took administrative fiat and pressure to make sure the committees changed each month, always in the direction of inefficiency but increased usefulness from our point of view. We also had the problem of how persistently potent people would get "treatment" within the system. Even if you buried them on the housekeeping committee they would have influence. Various attempts were tried by the patients to cope with that.

Many of the patients had killed people and been found not guilty by reason of insanity. And they really didn't know why they'd killed people, and they didn't think they were going to get out. They were on an indefinite sentence, until they had shown some change. And if they looked the same as the day they killed the person and the week before, which many of them did, they were interested in demonstrating some kind of change in the hopes that they might get out. So they were interested in procedures that would somehow get below what they were thinking about or feeling about, or tap into some internal reservoir of whatever it was that caused them to kill. And they had an interest in certain drugs. They seemed safe chemicals to use, in the sense that they didn't seem to make anyone worse. The patients also had interest in exciting events around which to interact and care for each other on the ward. As those procedures developed and the risks of homicide and suicide seemed to increase, there was a preoccupation with protection against suicide and homicide. And they developed a system of staying up all night with a rotation of observers if someone was very disturbed. But during the day, with the possibility of a fellow punching out a window, the patients decided that they should use handcuffs to cuff a sane partner to an insane one—one who was most upset to one who was least upset. And the caretakers would be rotated in shifts through various committees. That procedure is still used—it was developed some 10 or 11 years ago. The original idea came from a schizophrenic patient in a ward meeting and everyone laughed, because it sounded like a crazy idea.

The group system that I described, the committee system, is a fairly rigid structure. The patients wanted to learn new roles within the system, but basically nothing was happening. And they wanted to experiment with getting out of the role given them, the job they had to do. They wanted to move to a roleless state, and some 31 of the original 38 volunteered to go into a room, and just go in with nothing, no furniture, and minimal clothing. And they stayed for about 100 days. It was called the 100-day hate-in. It was a failure, but it was an attempt by the patients to try an experience which broke out of the tight role definitions that had been in the original program. Following that, the patients devised a thing called the capsule which is just a small room, eight by ten, where groups of four or five or six volunteers could go by themselves. Again, this occurs without professional staff monitoring being involved. It could go for up to two weeks at a time, and there was no contact with the outside, and they wore no clothes in that group. It was another attempt to plumb the depths, and many of the patients asked for and got some kind of sleep deprivation procedure.

By this time, the committee structure system was being maintained on one ward, but there were other attempts on other wards to modify the modalities for different people at different stages. And a tribal system evolved as a group where all the decision making was to be done by consensus and by almost continuous ward meetings, with some subdivisions into dyads and triads, and a rotating chairmanship or moderator of each. The patients themselves saw the tyranny of the rolelessness, and the tyranny of the articulate, the potent, which was a worse tyranny because there wasn't the structure to limit the power. But the tribal system has continued with modifications as another aspect of the program, and patients will go from the highly structured system to the tribal system and on to some other program.

The patients can come up with different modalities. I saw my job as being a kind of mediator between what the patients thought might be helpful and what the attendants, the guards, could tolerate. I'll give you a concrete example that I still find embarrassing. The patients, in the early attempts to live together in a roleless way, wanted to move to this room, naked. And they did that one weekend when I wasn't there, so when I came in on

Monday morning, some of the senior attendants were wondering what was going on with all this nakedness and its overtones of homosexuality. I reacted by firing the nominal leader of the inmate group and set him to polishing brass as a demonstrable demotion for having done this crazy thing. What was at stake was that the security staff had an enormous concern that there would be fellatio or worse taking place if the patients moved into this room naked. But the patients designed a monkey suit, of the kind that garage mechanics use. It was made in our industrial therapy shops, and the buttons didn't go up the front, but went up the back and were padlocked. They really were chastity suits, and they were incredibly strange. But it's what got that program delivered, until the guards, after about a month and a half of conscientiously locking everyone into these things before they would go into this group program at night, thought it was all kind of foolish and wasn't really needed, and abandoned it.

I think throughout the history of the hospital, I saw my role as a facilitator mediating between what the patients thought made sense, and the resulting guard anxieties. And I tried to mediate in what were often very strange ways, so that the two groups could live together in a way that made sense to both of them.

Chinlund   Maybe I'm alone in this, but what you've said sounds extremely far-out and very hard to connect to what we've been talking about. You describe it all in such a wonderfully sane and matter-of-fact way, but I just wonder where the connecting link is.

Barker   I think the principles are perhaps relevant, but not the activities. I mean ours were patients who were trying to get cured of something that was keeping them incarcerated. So the ground rules don't apply elsewhere. But the principle of listening hard to the guards who can shut the place down when they feel like it, and listening to the inmates, and mediating, I think is relevant to other programs. And when it's working right, the morale goes up and the security problems go down. What is the selling point to the guards? After five or ten years, I think it's clear to my guards that there's less worry about security because the patients are busy doing things that they're interested in doing. The guards don't have to worry about plans hatching and so on, and their morale is higher. One of the things I wonder about is whether you can sell this kind of program without devotion—I speak of it cynically now. At the beginning I was a true believer, I was the truest of the true. We were all going to get cured the next day, the next month, or the next year. And perhaps the people involved have to believe that if you're on the cure model.

Wright   On the one hand you claim an absolute dictatorship, and yet most people visiting you for an afternoon would feel that it's the most liberal prison society that they have ever seen, where the patients in fact make every decision pertaining to their daily lives, as long as they don't go through that door to the outside. The patients have power within certain generously circumscribed areas, you've got a wide periphery. Did this discretionary realm start off in a natural way and gradually get bigger and bigger as you found that the patients could define it better than you could, or better than the guards could, or better than God could?

Barker The periphery of psychological freedom within the institution varies, I think, to the extent that you meet the needs of the guards. If you begin crowding the guards with program innovations that they have doubts about, that periphery shrinks. And their weapon is to say that the area is not secure and lobby to shut down the program. And freedom expands as you meet the guards' personal and psychological needs, so they feel confident and comfortable and in charge of what's going on. Then they just seem to melt back and allow anything. That, I think, is the key dynamic, and the fellow that followed me didn't believe that dynamic, he felt I mollycoddled the guards.

Levinson The point that Elliott was making was that he decided that the participants in the program should have the say as to what the content of the program should be. And that he was dealing with some crazy people, and maybe they came up with some crazy ideas. We're dealing with inmates, who may come up with some con game ideas. But somehow this becomes part of the therapeutic community too, when inmates can decide what's going to go on.

Saunders But there was something to add onto that—as long as it didn't disturb the guards, or the climate of the guards.

Levinson Yes, the same thing would happen in a prison, no question of that. And I think one of the points is that the people outside, the third parties, and the people watching what's going on in this therapeutic community, would want to feel that the staff ultimately is in control of what's going on there. Or else, I think, we'd have some real problems.

Rosenthal The point I'd like to dovetail on is that it is more difficult to run a therapeutic community when you have to deal with the vested positions and roles of traditional people than it is if you just have to deal with the clients, or enable them in fact to deal with themselves.

Wright I think that except for differences in the use of officers in the two corners of the table, both of you were saying that the more the inmates were involved, the better. Isn't everybody saying that?

Briggs   On certain things.

Wright   Oh sure. I mean not on opening the doors and things like that.

DIFFERENTIAL PROGRAMMING AND SUPPLEMENTARY PROGRAMMING FOR CLIENTS WITH DIFFERENT PROBLEMS OR NEEDS

Redl   One problem that concerns me is the problem of either-or-itis, which means that a program has to be either this or that. No' given population falls into one and the same category. Many of the categories which we originally had to deal with when I was trained in analysis, for instance, don't exist any more. And if we would make such people, they couldn't survive. We have produced different pathologies and different mixtures, just like in our drinks we combine all sorts of ingredients which would have been regarded as indigestible years ago. Traditionally, in our programs we never mixed extremes which we felt to belong to different specialties. But we do it now in setting up programs and selecting clients for them.

For instance, in one of the hospitals in this state, you have a closed unit for youngsters who have to have at least rape or murder on their record to qualify for admission. And they have to be between about 14 and 17 or 18 years of age. But behavior alone doesn't mean very much in describing a problem. There is one youngster, for instance, who is in the unit because he killed an old woman. And he knocked her down, tried to take her purse, and killed her, though he says he didn't mean to kill her. After he killed the woman, he tried to rape her, and couldn't manage. And then he got mad and defecated in the most bizarre fashion. Now that isn't the same killing as that of another inmate in the unit who wanted to steal somebody's purse and got extremely violent, because he doesn't quite know how to do it. The first youngster does not fit in the same program as other kids. And some of the things he needs are markedly different from the treatment requirements of an aspiring gangster who tries to get a reputation through violence so the Mafia will protect him or hire him or trust him with a job. And yet the unit does not ask, "How do we group?" and, "which youngsters should be in the same project?"

Another good illustration of the difference between offense-related selection and grouping according to dynamics is the wide range one can describe of fire setters. Some fire setters I know are quiet kids, and any group home that happens to get them would be delighted because they are nice to have around. They are dreamy and not difficult, neither rough nor tough. In fact, they are too dreamy, they forget when to get up and you have to remind them. These are kids who typically grow up in neighborhoods that look like Nuremberg after the bombing. So the kid spends time standing around in a place where half the buildings are bombed out, and there's nothing to do. So he smokes a cigarette, which need not contain tobacco. And after a while he gets bored, and has fantasies: daydreaming is his major problem. In the daydream he has a cigarette, so he throws his cigarette into a container which has some rubbish in it. After a while the rubbish starts burning, and after it burns a little bit, he concludes, "I think I can put it out." So he tries, but the fire gets higher and the young man gets scared and figures, "Well, I don't know what to do so I better get out of here." This is the only good idea he has, but it is good reality perception. But by the time he gets out of his daydream and runs, other people get killed, which he didn't want at all. He feels very guilty about that, he didn't want to destroy anybody. In fact, there was nothing to destroy, it was already all destroyed.

But then of course the fire department arrives and then come the hero daydreams, the gamblers' fantasies. The gambler fantasy is "Let's see whether something happens or not." And "Here are all these fancy guys with their machines and I am the only one who knows what's happening. I'm standing right here, these police are all around, and they don't ask me for nothing. And here I might even help them." And these are rather unusual, powerful, omniscient daydreams.

And of course the youngster gets caught and gets placed somewhere. And since he's a nice kid you don't put him in an institution, because nice children shouldn't be in an institution. So the kid fits in some group home which has no concept of what kids who are that crazy really need. So the kid sits around the group home, and after a while he hangs around closer to the door, and sooner or later the staff let him go out, because after all he is bored and you can be sure he won't steal anything. So you let him walk and he ends up in the wrong place with the wrong kind of fantasy, and with the temptation input from the situation, and you have another big fire.

Disturbances such as the one I have described are not visible clinically, unless a young man is quite psychotic, which is obvious to everybody. But in the beginning they are not. And if this young man is incorporated in a program of group therapy it may not be obvious that for this youngster you need more than that. You need something else besides, because he has an *extra* problem over and beyond that of other kids who benefit from living with each other and being able to learn from each other—he can do that too, but it doesn't stick, because he has another problem at the same time.

What concerns me is the question of how the rest of a program reacts to this kind of an enriched syndrome. How do we know who needs what else besides? What special staffing do we need, and what special kind of a program? And how can you create a group which has enough deviation tolerance for different kinds of clients?

Another problem which comes up is the issue of differential improvement. What do we do if (God forbid) one or two of the sons of guns improve? The moment some inmates improve in terms of character of learning, your program can't fit everybody the same way. Assume that an inmate in a prison community improves in terms of the way we live together, the way we talk together, the way we act together. But we can't let anybody out because obviously the others are not ready for it. If one inmate is ready too early for a wider range of programming leeway or trustworthiness, you've got a problem. Because from then on what happens within that institution is wrong because a client has outgrown part of it. While if you do what's right for one man, you do things for the rest which are not all right.

One problem I experienced was when some youngsters in one of my programs improved so much they made a very positive relationship to some of the adult staff. They wanted to be proud that they could be trusted. But the unit was on the fourth floor of a 500-bed psychiatric hospital with all sorts of activities going on, and we couldn't let our people off the closed ward without somebody else with them. It so happened that one of the child-care workers was skillful, and had an especially good relationship with one of his clients. That kid suddenly had changed and felt bad because he could never really do anything for his special child-care worker. Not doing something wrong was not enough, because if you do something wrong somebody grabs you anyway or is around to stop you. The only thing you could do was beg staff to give you the keys, let you go downstairs, pick up a Coke, and come up, without running away. And of course it's against the rules. On the other hand, you cannot provide certain positive experiences unless you have a wider range of possibilities. And that kid was ready under certain conditions for a wider range of spontaneous experiences. That's what he needed to become healthy, or to become normal. Because if you really improve you need to feel that improvement, and that improvement has to be fed. So here again, if individuals have different levels of improvement in certain areas, the program must be designed so that you can regroup people, or throw in special experiences which can be provided without making the program of the rest become wrong or too embarrassing or so struck that they cannot change or cannot improve.

Clients don't promise you which way they will improve, and particularly which way they will improve in areas which are relevant for your operation. Some improvements are no problem. The fact that someone is more friendly or more grateful or more reasonable is fine unless he changes into a goody-goody, and loses his friends. Even such improvement is dangerous for him and for nobody else. Certain improvements, however, if they happen too fast, become a problem. To accommodate such contingencies, what needs to be built into the design is flexibility which permits the modification of programs or of grouping, under conditions where some community members do not need program elements any more or have enough of what was previously available.

ESTABLISHING THE BEACHHEAD

Rosenthal   Fritz made a point about what happens when you have some kids getting well and having residual needs, and suddenly you can't handle them because you have the balance of your population that are somewhere else. I think most therapeutic communities have to come to a critical mass where they can handle individual differences without a significant number of their participants' suffering because the community can't accommodate them. So you must have a community that is large enough—I think that is minimally somewhere around 60 to 75. When the mass gets below that, it gets too small, too precious, and you don't have enough leeway to take care of the individual differences. You also have a critical mass when you start to talk about single-handedly developing change in a specific institution. There is a real danger, as I see it, that the single person on line is being called on to do too Herculean a job—you're looking for a kind of psychological Renaissance man who can incorporate all the conceptual brilliance and experience that is embodied in this room and bring it to an institution, and then with great patience, great wisdom, tremendous amount of concern and love, begin to weave his magic.

Chinlund   We can use that as a job description.

Rosenthal   I could identify with doing that job myself—and I have started from point zero, I know how hard that is. And boy, you need some other folks there with you. You need some critical mass so that there is some start of brotherhood that is going to establish a beachhead and begin to do the work; otherwise I think that one can get wiped out very quickly.

In 1967–68, Phoenix House was running a program for 600 inmate adults and for 100 adolescents on Riker's Island. And for a short period of time we had terrific cooperation from the Department of Corrections, until other parts of the system became so crowded that the department had to say, "Guys, we appreciate what you're doing, but we can't make the accommodations in our system any more for your system." And then things began to break down very badly.

Chinlund   How do you help the one Renaissance man who's subjected to this?

Rosenthal   Well, for openers, it makes sense to focus on a single institution and use all one's strength in a single institution. As quickly as possible, take all of your change agents and all of your staff in, and get as many recruits—staff, inmate, whoever's going to join you in this venture—working with you, and develop a critical mass that can go on with the dynamics. Then maybe, maybe, your one Renaissance man will have a small chance of success.

Toch   Was the issue how to establish a beachhead in such a way that the first guy on the shore doesn't feel vulnerable and lonely? The question of what sort of support system can one generate to make sure that it isn't too cold out there?

Rosenthal   I'm not even too worried about his feelings, being lonely and cold. I'm worried about his being able to become effective.

Wright   What makes him effective?

Levinson   If you're going to have a job description, the first qualification should be, can he walk on water? And you know, in prisons, it may not be a matter of creating the ideal therapeutic community. It's been said that a lot of things get put under the rubric of a therapeutic community. We have certain things going on which we think are approximations of therapeutic communities.

Rosenthal   Are you talking about Marion, Illinois?

Levinson   That's one.

Rosenthal   But you had a lot of juice there. You had a lot of well-trained people who started it.

Levinson   We had one. He happened to be a guy who almost walks on water. But that's only one example. There are other things going on in other institutions which may or may not fit your definition of therapeutic community, but they are impressive. The point is, what can you do to help the innovator? One of the most critical things in an institution is where the top man is. If you have a warden who's going to be supportive, while you might have a lot of discontent among the line staff, you've got much more going for you than if you have a warden who is not supportive. If you have an outside agency that's supportive, it's not as good as having the warden, but it'll help. If your man is just in there on his own, you do need the Renaissance man you're talking about. I think they're in short supply these days.

Rosenthal   But let's look at Marion, because that was a terrific experiment [Chapter 3].

Levinson   In the early stages, when Groder asked for space, they wouldn't give him any. He was asking for resources, and the only resources he had were those that he could steal from the hospital budget. He actually set up the beginning of the community in the hospital, because they wouldn't give him a ward. I mean, he did not have support, though things have changed a lot since. Which means that if you get one program started, it's much easier to get the second going. And if you have an institution set up with units, it's a lot easier to specialize one unit. But maybe the first man in the first unit does have to be an unusual person.

Wright   In what way unusual? For instance, what should a psychiatrist be like in this kind of thing? Is the fact that he's a psychiatrist a useful thing? Does he need an obsessive personality, or does he need to be paternalistic—are there any common qualities?

Rosenthal   There's one that we might pass over too quickly, that doesn't have to do with personality characteristics. Groder had rank and a vested position in the administration; he had some command. When I started a project at Oak Knoll, I was a lieutenant commander in the navy. I was in charge of a unit, and I was vested. When I started the second Phoenix House at Beth Israel Hospital, I took an appointment as a staff psychiatrist at Beth Israel in order to be in charge of the unit so that I fit into that chain of command. It's important.

Eisenberg   Everybody knows that in every institution there's a lot of gatekeeping going on, no matter what the high man wants. There's always sabotage through low levels. And the question is, how can you walk into an institution and get the majority of correction officers working with you as opposed to against you? What strategies seem to be the ones that pay the most dividends?

Devlin   Asking for help.

Saunders   When we went into Arthurkill, the seven people who went in presented themselves to the staff, communicating that they wanted their help and their involvement. They admitted they didn't have the answers but were going to try and do something. And that unit became the most popular unit in the facility. Everybody wanted to work on that unit, without any help from the warden.

Toch   In other words, you suggest that potential sources of resistance be approached as problem-solving, intelligent people?

Saunders   Yes, as helpers.

Rosenthal   But at some point somebody's got to give an order. At Arthurkill the boss gave an order that "there shall be space." And "These 25 beds in one unit shall be for this project." Without that, it wouldn't have happened.

Elwin   As you tend to pick wardens or superintendents, there's a tendency to pick those that are "with it." That is not necessarily good, because those that are "with it" don't necessarily control the institution. The very fact that administration perceives them as "with it" may mean for the rank and file, that they don't run it.

Toch   That's saying, apply the same logic to the administrator as you apply to the guard? Pick yourself the powerful and credible one?

Elwin   My best operation came with the worst of the hard-noses, who clearly ran and controlled his facility. I think it took me a year to con him into going where I wanted to go. But I could walk away, because if the man made you a promise, he'd give you 110 percent, to show that he could do better than he promised.

If you get the kind of superintendent who runs a facility, which tends not to be the kind of superintendent that we look for, you get a good thing going. When you choose a very liberal superintendent, most likely he's got problems with his own staff, in terms of trying to get them to go along with him. And when he brings you in with his imprimatur, you also get all of the negative connotations that the staff perceives in him.

Levinson   I hope we don't equate incompetence with liberalism!

13

UNIT MANAGEMENT AND THERAPEUTIC COMMUNITIES IN PRISON

Levinson   The federal government became involved in the therapeutic community "business" when a law was passed called the Narcotics Addict Rehabilitation Act. There was considerable interest around the country in trying to do something about addicts. Congress passed this statute which defined a group of addicts meeting certain criteria, and sentenced them for treatment—that's the way their commitment read, "sentenced for treatment."

When this law was passed, many people in the Bureau of Prisons thought that a catastrophe had been unleashed, because we knew nothing about treating addicts. There were some of us, however, who entertained the idea that this might be an opportunity. Because people were being sent to us for treatment, resources were to be made available explicitly to develop programs for these individuals.

We began with three units, one at Danbury, Connecticut, one at a women's institution in Alderson, West Virginia, and the third in a federal correctional institution, Terminal Island, which had both a male division and a female division. With a rich staffing pattern we developed, these programs were set on their own. Their mandate was "Go do your thing." The law said that the addicts would come in for a period of study. The study was to determine: (a) were they addicts? and (b) were they treatable? If the answer to both questions was yes, a recommendation would go back to the court, which would then commit the inmate under the Narcotics Addict Rehabilitation Act.

The first therapeutic community developed at Danbury with a big assist from Daytop Lodge. As a matter of fact, one of the program's criticism was that Daytop was running it and our people were not. As the number of addicts coming in under this law increased, we developed additional programs (using a variety of models) in other institutions. And we began to wonder whether, if they worked (as they did) for drug-addicted people, what about programs for alcoholics? To test this question, we developed a few programs—using the same kind of model—for inmates with alcohol problems.

Parallel developments were taking place elsewhere. In a juvenile institution, we tried to develop a program where all the inmates assigned to one unit, stayed in that unit and had a staff who worked in that unit. We developed a concept called a correctional counselor, which entailed taking some correctional officers, training them to no longer function as correctional officers *per se* (there were others who handled that function) but to be available full-time to work with the inmates.

When the National Training School in Washington, D.C., was closed, we opened an institution at Morgantown, West Virginia. There inmates were assigned to different units with specific kinds of programs for each type of offender. Our classification was based on a system (developed by Herbert C. Quay) which differentiates among inmates those who are primarily neurotic, psychopathic, immature, and subcultural delinquents.

That was the beginning of what we called *unit management*. In this model, we take an institution and subdivide it into smaller components, usually around 100 inmates. We identify a staff for each unit to work with the inmates. We build their offices where the inmates live. And, we try to eliminate the six grills that people usually have to get through before they see their caseworker. The staff is available.

We dropped the idea of having to develop every program for the whole institution. Under this new structure, Unit A could run one kind of program and Unit B, Unit C, and D could select another. And if whatever Unit A was doing didn't seem to be working, they could change only that program, while the other three programs could continue functioning. In other words, you run four little "institutions" in a big facility.

We tried to sell this concept throughout the bureau. Initially the whole idea was pooh-poohed by the people in the big joints—the "big tops," the Atlantas and Leavenworths. It was all right for the "kiddie joints," but would never work in a *real* institution.

The next thing that happened was NIMH decided to get out of the drug treatment business, and said, "Well, we've got this place down in Fort Worth. . . ." We successfully unitized Fort Worth, and then tackled the NIMH plant in Lexington when it was made available. Lexington was a much bigger institution, and what developed there is now pretty much what happens generally—namely, that we have both specialized units and general units. A general-purpose unit would be for random assignment of whatever kind of inmate comes into an institution. There are also what we call special units. At Lexington they have three special units: a drug unit, an alcoholic unit, and a geriatrics unit. In this last type unit we have older inmates, many of who have physical problems (but some don't). It's tough to get these individuals out on a handball court or to a VT program; you have to develop other kinds of programs for them.

The next development was that Wisconsin wanted to divest itself of an institution while we were interested in buying one; so we acquired Oxford from the Wisconsin Department of Corrections. At this time we were beginning to get an influx of young offenders with long sentences—too long for our traditional institutions for young offenders, where programs run for about 15 or 18 months. Therefore, we created an institution where the entrance requirements were that you have a sentence of more than 7 years and that you be under 26 years old. Naturally, we felt that we were going to have some real problems, because that's a deadly combination. Also, when we went through our data we found that the blindfold of justice may slip just a tad, because these criteria were going to give us an institution with an awful lot of black inmates. It was therefore decided to use a system similar to what had developed at Morgantown; namely, that we would differentially assign inmates to the units at Oxford, depending upon what kind of people they were. Basically we used Quay's approach—only with these older inmates the four groups became a three-fold breakdown: the weak inmates, the strong inmates, and a middle group. One of the major objectives—and accomplishments—was to keep the "wolves" from the "sheep," geographically isolating them by living quarters assignment. They would all participate in the regular part of the program, in all activities, but efforts would be made to schedule them at different times.

PROGRAM-RELEVANT CLASSIFICATION

Toch When you say "strong," "weak," do you mean exploitive and exploitation-prone?

Levinson Yes, wolves and victims. And we had a way of identifying them soon after they came in. This developed out of a lot of work that Quay and his colleagues had done—factor analyzing profile scores. He started working primarily with delinquents. We tried to stretch this to an older group (as at Morgantown). Eventually he felt it couldn't, with integrity, stretch anymore, so he began all over again.

Essentially it is a matter of using three different sources of information about an individual. You get a large item pool, and you have people check off, from the individual's social history, what kind of background behavior he has shown. Then you use a factor analytic technique to find out what dimensions this preliminary questionnaire is picking up. You try to identify items that are most appropriate for picking up that particular dimension. Then you go to a source on the individual's background. Does the presentence investigation indicate that he has engaged in aggressive activities in the past? Yes or no. The approach is very behaviorally oriented—you don't have to figure out what was he thinking or how did people feel about him. Did he, or did he not?

The second kind of information is supplied by somebody who observes the individual in the admission setting, usually for about two weeks. And the staff member responds on a different check list in terms of "Does the individual engage in this kind of behavior? Yes or no?" Sometimes you end up with very few checks, and you wonder, "How could such perfect specimens of humanity get in here?" This may mean your observers need some additional training.

Question   Was that because they're very purist about identifying behavior under direct observation?

Levinson   That's because the inmates might not display much symptomatic behavior during the first two weeks.

Question   At least, in front of the staff.

Levinson   Or in front of the staff. Anyway, the second kind of information is, What can you observe? And the third kind of information is true or false information that the inmate himself has filled out on a questionnaire. Do you do these kinds of things? Do you think these kinds of thoughts? Yes or no? This is an MMPI type of approach.

Each of the three instruments were factor analyzed and the same dimensions showed up on all of them. What we were getting was a convergence of information from different perspectives, and we had a way of putting it together. Quay's position, which we bastardized, is that all of the dimensions are present in everyone—me and thee, as well as all inmates. The question is, How much is present and how well is it controlled? You can be high on the psychopathy scale and be a used-car salesman or a president, rather than a prisoner.

Since on the original scale you have four times three times two permutations of the different types—too many to work with easily—we just took the high score, and said this person is primarily neurotic, primarily a psychopath, primarily immature, or primarily a subcultural delinquent. We made our classification only on the high score. What it did is give us in a short time a way to identify potential problem cases and potential victims.

And here we were—to get back to Oxford—with what we expected to be a very difficult population coming in, and much concern about how we were going to handle these men when we put them together into one institution. A new warden was assigned who initially was opposed to the whole approach. On the other hand, he was also concerned about what kinds of people would be put into this institution, and was willing to go along with anything that could turn out to be a good management tool.

A variation on the theme that Oxford introduced was the idea that while we would initially assign people to units based on how they profiled on our scale, we would also provide an "out." The inmates could opt to participate in two programs. One was an Aesklepieion type of program, and the other was a Carkhuffian (Robert Carkhuff) type of approach, based on facilitative counseling. The inmates would be assigned to one of three units. They could opt to go into the Aesklepieion program or the facilitative counseling program. If they didn't work out for some reason, they went back to the unit from which they came.

Toch   So two units could be characterized as specialized treatment or training programs, whereas the rest were ways of subcategorizing the population to minimize destructive interaction?

Levinson   Right. And it worked.

Toch   What about the wolf-wolf environment? You created one subsetting in which you put all your "toughies," or the ones you thought were going to be tough. That worked harmoniously?

Levinson   What tends to happen is you have stand-offs. "I don't have to prove anything to you, you don't have to prove anything to me."

Toch   Is it like Elliot Barker's psychopaths' neutralizing each other, as opposed to creating a new set of sheep among the wolves?

Levinson   Our problem was to try to protect the real weak ones. And of course among the weak ones, the stronger-of-weak dominated— none of this is perfect. But it did reduce the number of serious management problems we had anticipated would develop at this institution.

Question   Bob, will you be saying something about how they selected themselves?

Levinson   The inmate would talk to a staff member of the team or the case management person, and arrange for an internal transfer—within the institution. There is a trial period in the opted-to program which included resolving the issue of whether the program was going to accept the individual or not. This would be worked out between the two unit managers—between the manager of the unit where the man was living, and the unit manager who was running, say, the Aesklepieion program.

Question   So the shopping problem would be cleared up by the unit managers, if the inmate was bouncing around?

Levinson   Right. And always with the understanding that if the man didn't work out, he would come back. It really wasn't a way to permanently get rid of somebody, because if you were referring somebody who obviously was going to bomb out, in a couple of weeks he'd be back again.

Question   Did the inmate himself participate in this?

Levinson   Yes, each unit has team meetings in which the inmate sits and is a part of this decision-making process about himself.

The next development was that we began to have a lot of problems at Lewisburg. This is a major penitentiary in Pennsylvania. Inmates started killing one another in such numbers that we were in the newspapers very frequently and prominently. Somebody had to do something about Lewisburg; it was decided to introduce the management classification system and the unit approach. This was the first time we had attempted to subdivide a major penitentiary and bring in a classification system that would assign inmates. One grand and glorious weekend they began to move 1,500 inmates from where they had been living, some for many years, into where they would live based on the classification system. And as a result, Lewisburg went 13 months without somebody killing someone. Now, there were other changes as well, but unit management made a significant contribution, so much so that when we began to get similar problems developing at the Atlanta, Georgia, penitentiary, the executive staff of the Bureau of Prisons said, "We will unitize Atlanta, and introduce a management classification system."

SUBDIVIDING THE MEGAPRISON

Question   What made it possible to get from the rather neat, small, and easily managed units in Oxford to this mammoth total institution?

Levinson   Architecture of course plays a role here. Some people will say that architecture is the be-all and end-all; I don't think that is the case. Architecture will help or hinder you, but it won't make or break you.

Lewisburg was certainly not designed or built so that it could be easily subdivided. And as a result, we have some big units at Lewisburg—200 people to a unit. I mean, we have stretched the concept to some extent.

Lewisburg, in turn, was a little bit easier than Atlanta. Atlanta is an institution with a big cell house and 600 inmates living on five tiers; the architecture *is* presenting a number of problems. Nevertheless, they will find a way of subdividing the institution. It is easier if you have independent units or "naturally" formed "pieces" in the facility's structure.

For example, one of the things they did at Lewisburg was to create an industrial unit. Working in industry is one way to get out of the initial classification system. If the inmate gets himself a job in industry and maintains it, he no longer has to live where he was originally assigned; he can live in different sections of the institution. His unit staff is located where he works. Now they're in the process of building offices for staff people that are near the units. This, I think, is an important feature, but it involves some construction money. Other places, they've emptied a cell and turned it into an office. Getting the staff working with the inmate, close to him, so there's a lot of interaction; that is the critical thing.

So what we have, I think, is two different streams converging. We have the idea of trying to develop therapeutic communities for specific kinds of inmates, primarily beginning with drug addicts but going on to the alcoholic and then to other kinds of problem areas or types of inmates. The other theme is the management style of subdividing institutions. Instead of having staff deal with 600 inmates and inmates deal with all the staff, have six 100-man "institutions" operating on the same reservation, sharing many of the resources. As a result you don't build six vocational training areas, but the units can develop their own individual programs in other areas—like counseling.

Toch   The one thing they have in common is they are communities, aren't they? The staff is attached to them, and know the inmates, the inmates know each other.

Levinson   Now the potential is there, and some go further down the therapeutic community road than others. A lot depends upon the staff. This gets to the point that when this management style or organization of the institution is set up, what begins to happen depends upon the inclinations of the unit managers. You get some people who are interested in developing intensive programs. They either have monies available to get consultants, or they use the psychologist, a teacher, or some caseworker who has taken a course some place and got tuned into something.

STAFF LEADERSHIP

Question   How far do inmates have an input into this evolution? Is it all determined by experts or do the inmates have a real say in the process?

Levinson   We control it.

Jones   But isn't it to some extent based upon the inclinations of the manager? If he wants to he can have a democratic unit, whereas another one might be authoritarian?

Levinson   What I can now talk about is the difference between trying to set up a therapeutic community, as opposed to having a therapeutic community develop. What happened in a lot of places is that we would have a unit operating in a very traditional institution. That unit was there because central office said it would be there, and the prison received additional resources that we put there—staff resources as well as money resources. For the people in the unit, this was great, but it generated enemies within the rest of the institution. But the fact that the central office said, "There will be a drug program at Danbury," meant that there was a drug program at the Danbury, Connecticut, institution.

Now, in that circumstance I think we did need a super-human kind of person to take all the gaff, to be the one who's operating differently than anybody else in that setting, and to absorb overt as well as covert hostility. It takes a pretty strong person. We were able to find such people and they were able to develop and survive, in a rather, at times, unfriendly atmosphere. The situation we have now is easier. Everybody is in units: to run your own program is accepted and has recognition across the board.

Now, if there's a psychologist or a caseworker on the team who pushes a program, that unit can go ahead and do its own thing—as long as it doesn't get too wild and stays within accepted policies. If they want to develop a more democratic, therapeutic situation such as would more closely approach a therapeutic community, they can. And so you begin to have these communities popping up here and there, depending upon local initiative, with the blessing of some central-office people, and the shaking of heads by some others.

Then we called them up on the telephone and asked, "Do you have any therapeutic communities, and if you have any, how many have you?" And they tell us that in the system we have 15 of them, in different institutions.

CONSISTENCY AND AUTONOMY

Wright   Might you have three TCs in one institution?

Levinson   About two is probably closer. Then we get into a definitional problem. Some are just somewhere further along than running the traditional kind of program you find in an institution, and many are pretty respectable kinds of therapeutic communities.

Question   Do you have a problem in the system when you have a unit functioning and the unit management chooses to leave or goes someplace else?

Levinson   Yes, that presents a problem. People get promoted: you do a good job so management won't let you do that anymore. Somebody else comes in. We would hope that in the selection process, it's somebody who would be friendly to this particular approach. Unfortunately that does not always happen, and we can lose a lot of ground.

What I just talked about is not new as far as mental health settings are concerned. It's not even new when you talk about juvenile institutions, because some juvenile institutions have been doing this kind of work for a long time. But to do it in penitentiaries may be an interesting development.

Wright   The difficulties you're talking about are precisely the same as the difficulties we found when we were trying to unitize hospitals. But hospitals were always functionally divided, they had a geriatric unit and a chronic unit. And we made them all heterogeneous, based on geography.

Levinson   I think if you're going to differentially assign inmates, it ought to be on some basis which gives you a way to "hook" the inmate. The fact that they all come from New York City doesn't tell you a great deal, whereas if they all have a similar problem it gives you an "in" around which to design a program.

IS A HUMANIZED ENVIRONMENT A THERAPEUTIC COMMUNITY?

DeLeon   I think Max's irritability around "Do we have a therapeutic community?" in some of the efforts you're describing should be highlighted. It goes something like this: if you're talking about setting up some kind of counterforce in the institution, maybe we should drop the term therapeutic community. It's true that the problem is a very special technological one, in psychiatric hospitals and in the prison system. Can we set up some kind of counterforce? And we ought to talk about that. But if we talk about using a therapeutic community as a counterforce, we're wasting time if we don't clarify the essence of therapeutic community, and spell out some of its guiding principles. If we have something else in mind, it should not be called a therapeutic community. One set of TC principles was introduced by Max Jones, when he defined the therapeutic community of democracy, which has its own community healing principles. And then there are the beneficent hierarchical therapeutic communities that we've seen in drug abuse treatment, which have their own community healing principles.

Chinlund   In that sense I don't care whether our program is a TC or whether it's something else. I'm interested in what can be done now, practically speaking, within the system, to improve the system enough that inmates have a different kind of opportunity to direct their own destinies than they now have. And that's one reason why the opportunity to wrangle about whether a classical TC includes four irreducible qualities, or five or six, or whether we fall 80 percent or 83 percent into a classical mode, can distract from an already complex task. I would rather keep my eyes fixed on the goal of change, however small, of the total system, than bring in an external model and stick it somehow into a system which could resist it to the point where it would be bad both for the system and for the model.

DeLeon   I wouldn't want to go into an empty lecture on therapeutic communities, but I think that without a model you run into serious trouble ultimately, even though you're beneficently attempting to impact the system. I'm waiting to hear the federal data to tell me that even impacting that system had a positive measurable effect, although there might have been some changes in morale.

Levinson   There are such data.

DeLeon   I think that's important also, the fact that "impacting-the-system" data are measurable and useful to get. And my second concern is that if we have models that are pretending to be therapeutic communities in the federal system, and they aren't working, I don't want that to redound to the hard work of therapeutic communities over the last 20 years. I don't mind that we have to impact first within the limits of the system. But I don't want that misnamed as an authentic therapeutic community effort, because in high probability there's a 70–80 percent failure rate in these programs. You're entitled to that experiment, but I don't want that shadow to fall on some of the hard work that has gone on in therapeutic communities.

Toch   Does this mean that something has to be sanctified by a therapeutic community ingroup to call itself a TC?

Comment   Outside of the prison setting, there are outfits calling themselves therapeutic communities that are not even reasonable facsimiles of what you and I know as a classical therapeutic community.

DeLeon   Yes, and we pay a price for that.

Question   But who are "we"? We use that language when it's expedient.

Chinlund   Basically, I see the argument as one between going in, in effect, with our package and a whole list of procedures, and "This is the way the program is going to work, so inmates, line up, because this is the way it's going to be." The other approach being one in which we go in from the earliest possible date to move with them according to *their* agenda. And we keep that agenda moving along as the inmates change and upgrade their agenda. Maybe those alternatives are not as contradictory as I have presented them, but I have the feeling that that may be the way the dialogue would evolve.

Levinson   What I've described primarily is a situation in which people, because they are committed under a certain law, will be in a drug treatment program. And that drug treatment program can take a variety of forms. One such form is what we think is close to a therapeutic community. If you don't buy that, fine; but there it is. But these people have no choice, because the law says, "You will be committed for treatment."

Now, we have had some problems, in that we have had inmates who have come back for a "graduate course." And some offenders who face 20 years suddenly get very interested in having their drug problem treated, until they get the final sentence, and then they're no longer interested. But that is one way that people get into the program. The second way is that it's voluntary, and people are assigned to units but can then opt into these programs. We have a third approach, which is what we call "optional programming." And there we have a situation in which the staff and the inmate sit down, and talk about a program. It could be that the staff thinks it would be important for a man to get some treatment for his drug addiction, and they will put him in a program. At the end of an explicit period of time—30 days, 60 days—he can opt out with no negative consequences. It's nice if people volunteer and you get the right people to volunteer. But there are other kinds of ways of approaching how they get there.

MANAGEMENT IMPACT

DeLeon   I was interested in the data you mentioned about program impact.

Levinson   Everything I've read indicates that if you have some system in which you differentially assign inmates to units, that institution, no matter what else happens to those inmates, has fewer management problems. We felt that by having a systematic way of subdividing inmates, and assigning staff to work with those inmates, you should get fewer management problems. And that means inmates are generally living in a more humane environment—and some may even get some help. There are pre and post data to show this. The data show, for example, how we used to have the annual spring "riot" at an institution of a thousand young offenders. And after we went into unit management, no annual spring riot. A lot of other things also happened, but this showed what management can do to make living in these environments safer and more humane. Plus inmates benefit if you do more than just subdivide them, but begin to add programs.

Barker   Did you say subdivide on any basis?

Levinson   On a reasonable basis. I mean, you could take the fat inmates and put them in one place, or the blue-eyed ones, or sort for tall ones and short ones. I'm assuming you divide them with respect to problems or personality types. One thing this does is that the staff begins to feel that they've a handle on a task. They may or may not really have one, but if they feel they have one, they *do* have one. And it is very important to get staff to feel on top of the situation, to feel they know what's going on, and have a way to control a little piece of their world.

PRISON COMMUNITIES AND GROUP PSYCHOLOGY

Redl   I want to make a comment about the question of group psychology you are hinting at. What you are talking about is groups that are really groups. So if they feel like a group they are in fact groups to deal with. And once you have that group to deal with, it's different than many people assembling somewhere and being a large mass, in which everybody goes haywire, which is totally unmanageable. What you are forming are groups, and the next question is, are they meaningful on the basis of wanting to get to know each other, or because of the kind of project they are interested in, or on some other basis?

In many of our schools we have used this image of lots of people. There is nothing done to make a classroom feel like a group because it's too large a mass, and nobody knows each other any more, and therefore things go out of hand. We have a case of mass hysteria at the slightest provocation and students act as though they were in a street accident. Somebody gets high and then everybody else gets high around it. You have the same phenomenon when people are in somebody else's town at a football game. People who elsewhere are quite respectable act this way, because they are in a mass and not tied to a group. And what you are pleading for, for administrative reasons primarily, is perfectly obvious from a psychological point of view. But whether it is also more productive in terms of treating people, given the special pathology they have, is a question. And you can't always have both at the same time, because your group members are not all having the same sickness even though they are otherwise homogeneous and grouped.

Levinson   We have actively encouraged constructive competition among the units. And we talk about unit basketball teams developing, and trying to get each unit group feeling "We are the best unit in the institution." This is one way in which we consciously mobilize the group process you describe, around constructive goals.

Toch   When one says "therapeutic community" I suspect that the word "community" is as critical as the word "therapeutic." And you have laid out for us a potential which many people don't think exists. Because many of us are constantly faced with people saying you can't do anything in a prison, because it's such a large and intrinsically authoritarian place. Now you view prison as a conglomerative of subenvironments, and you undergird that natural organization. It is just like a city, where the life of the individual really takes place in the neighborhood, and it's crazy to indict the whole city when you're living in a little enclave and never go outside a six-block area. By formalizing this, all kinds of possibilities open up.

Birnbaum   We deal with an environment in the prison system, where the term "group," or the use of "group," is not always a positive concept. The traditional correctional approach, which still exists to a large degree, sees the group as being not so much a positive force as a negative force, and attaches a negative connotation to groups. So it has enormous implications for a department to begin to change its organizational view of the term "group."

Grant   Is the main thrust a one-to-one-type relationship, with the group getting in the way?

Birnbaum   I think the main thrust continues to be the control of groups by not allowing groups to develop a group integrity.

Grant   It's a liability that gets in the way of control.

Levinson   Of course, we do not let all the mafioso types live together in one place. This sorting goes on anyway, in institutions. I mean, every time a new man comes in, you have to find a bed for him. And we're saying, "Since you have to find a bed for him, let's do it in a systematic way." This means not only grouping, but neutralizing negative gang formation. We do not get all the Chicago inmates living together, all the Baltimore inmates living together, because frequently they can get a group going and you have predictable problems. So in one sense you are defusing the kind of group that you're talking about as you control where people live.

Toch   You are also making the staff part of the group, aren't you?

Levinson   Right. If nothing else, you've now got more eyes. There's better control now because there are people there who would never have been on those living quarters. They now have to be there, because that's where their offices are.

Jones   But the essence of what Fritz said is that the inmates who are isolated get a group identity. Through that group identity they begin to feel that they're real people. And I think that's one of the goals we're after.

Redl   As long as we understand that what we're talking about here is primarily helping the system function and helping the individual keep out of trouble.

Levinson   But it's also helping that therapeutic group. If the environment in which that therapeutic community is is a more safe and humane one, then whatever is going on in that unit is likely to have greater benefit.

DeLeon   I'm happy now. I think an important distinction is beginning to appear, and we're talking less about a rehabilitation model and more about an impact model. And we are saying that the core of the impact model is developing group strength, which borrows from a lot of good social psychological effort, and also is a good distinction. I would argue that drawing such distinctions dictates what kind of dependent variables you're going to look at. For example, the key variables that I see are management operations—you can show something about cost effectiveness. You can talk about morale of staff and clients. These are measures of "Are you having a positive impact on the institution?" A very different approach than "Have we applied a therapeutic rehabilitative model here, and what are the evaluative criteria of that therapeutic model?"

Toch   But you have no objection to gravy, right? I mean, Bob Levinson can say, "I'm happy on account of we haven't had a riot in two years, and the murder rate has dropped." And now, nobody is upset and he can do what therapy he wants to do. If after five years he can show that there's a reduction in his recidivism rate and people are functioning better, which may be his real goal, is that O.K.? If you have demonstrated improvement in the prison, it doesn't hurt if you also get change in people, does it?

Levinson   My bosses say that we're basically interested in three things: running safe institutions, running humane institutions, and providing programs so that inmates can have the opportunities, once they get out, of doing better than they might have otherwise. Now if you want to talk about the quality of those programs or the nature of those programs, fine and good. But you can't begin there. You first have to take care of the basics, the bottom level of Maslow's need hierarchy.

Chinlund   Orthodoxy issues, to me, have always been horrendously boring, because it seems that they try to fix accurately points which really defy fixing. And I'm ready to say here in this meeting that mine is not a therapeutic community, and say it flatly. Other people will want to masquerade as therapeutic communities, and, as a result, they are able to put their hands on money for some help. And I, because of my purity, am sitting here saying, "We are not a therapeutic community, we're an impact something-or-other," and we therefore X ourselves out of the opportunity to get help to extend change a bit further into the system. So I would welcome any set of definitions of a therapeutic community, even an ideal toward which a therapeutic community could move in its seeking. Moreover, the history of therapeutic communities has been a roller-coaster movement, so that you would not only have to have a definition of orthodoxy but a constant diagnosis to see whether a particular community is now in or out of that definition. On the other hand, maybe in saying we're not going to get into the definition game, we get too woolly and we don't really know what we're doing. But I think if we're operationally clear about where we're headed, and avoid moving under this banner or that banner, we can feel more comfortable and more honest.

14

PARTICIPATION, SELF-STUDY, ROLE-REHEARSAL AND THERAPY: WHERE ARE THE LIMITS?

Grant   I am very much interested in the change potential, whether you want to call it the treatment effect or not, of a person's participation in efforts to improve the human condition through the application of systematic study. I would argue that it is plausible that that kind of experience is a more powerful personal change vehicle than the psychotherapeutic couch. I don't want to get hung up on kinds of couches for kinds of people and kinds of experiences. I want to get across that I see that kind of participation as a very powerful experience for the person. Studying.

Now, last night someone asked me if I was a teacher. And I had had my second martini and it came out very easily, "No, I'm not a teacher, I'm a learner." What I meant is I would see myself as a scholar, and what I do is try to engage in learning and scholarship as a shared process with others. The kind of role that I'm trying to play and foster is to get people to share *their* knowledge and resources with the knowledge and resources of others to address a problem, to learn something about that problem, and to contribute to a broader set of knowledge by developing concepts that could conceivably have application to problems other than the immediate one addressed. Which for me is the heart of scholarship, and the heart of knowledge development. I don't see this as an arena which should be reserved for the high priests at Harvard.

Everyone needs to participate. I've come to this conclusion through working with Max Jones and his concept of living learning. I feel that there is tremendous power in taking some kind of crisis within a living group and studying it, working out some way to manage it. I ran a set of studies at Camp Elliott, where we had as a basic principle a thrust to maximize challenging uncomfortableness without inducing rigidifying panic. And we were in a crude way capitalizing on uncomfortableness stemming from problems that were very real, that people were part of, and which they were trying to work out and cope with. At the same time, we developed a set of offenders and a set of nonprofessionally trained enlisted men as researchers to work with us, and we carried that concept of researchers who came from the population being served and from lower-echelon staff, into the Department of Corrections.

I didn't see at that time anything like the potential of the proposition I tried to state for you earlier. I saw the potential of confined storekeepers helping with a research effort. They were locked up not because they couldn't work with numbers, but because they got caught working with them in a wrong way, but still were quite good at working with numbers. We found that nonacademically-trained but sharp enlisted men could not only look at sources of variance, and ways to handle it and ways to get it on the computer, but that they could do a fantastic job of working with even less formally trained and less skilled people, taking on tasks that they could do for just a day, or for a couple of weeks, and could build in checks so that you'd have the same coding going on by three different sets of people and another unit that would monitor the discrepancies.

The point being that I became very intrigued, enough so that I talked with NIHM, about how quickly you could get meaningful and effective participation in social studies with a wider range of the human race. We took that design to the California Department of Corrections, along with some of our navy people. And under the brilliant administrative leadership of a confined administrator of an international loan company that got caught making the wrong loans, we initiated this study of a research utilization thrust within our research efforts. We didn't want to just do studies and not have them get any place, and not have them be usable. We didn't want to limit our study ideas to what we were dreaming up with inmates and staff working with us off in the corner. We wanted to be able to get a more total involvement. So we thought of trying to recruit some offenders who could serve as research utilization specialists. We called them change agents in our formal proposal but the goal was to be able to change programs, to be able to change the system, as opposed to being a therapist who changes people. Now I wasn't yet aware of the possibility of linking those two. I was still thinking of how to get peer involvement with the inmate culture, with the prison officer culture, as a means for developing research ideas and as a means of disseminating research ideas.

Now, by this time, in addition to what Dennie Briggs was doing, there were about 15 therapeutic community equivalents around the Department of Corrections, such as camps running some kind of group activity. And we argued that people who were in these settings probably had more potential than the inmate starting from scratch, to be able to play a research utilization role. And I somehow saw these people becoming assistant training officers, assistant administrative analysts, assistant researchers around the department.

We went to the different centers where these programs were operating, and we took along offenders who were working in our research unit. We tried to generate a discussion about the role of the offender in improving the correctional system, and having impact elsewhere. We planted some seeds, and went back and had a second discussion with those who were still interested. There aren't too many shows going on in an institution, and so we drew pretty well. After our show, we gathered a list of inmates who were interested in volunteering to take part in four months of training during confinement, with the idea that upon parole they would have jobs at $6,000 a year. It wasn't much then or now, but it was a job back within the department.

We made it as clear as we could then, and we did all through the program, that they could work either at the $6,000 a year on parole, or at $25 a month reconfined. As far as I was concerned, if anything I'd rather have them for $25 a month. We nearly killed ourselves getting some understanding of what we were after and what we were doing. What we found was that we were spending a great deal of time we hoped would be spent developing projects, doing surveys—in fact, the first thing they did when we brought them to Vacaville, before we even showed them where their beds or the johns were, was to go out and interview six inmates and staff members about their reactions to our project. And with that we were in the business of learning through doing research, and concern with problems of interviewing.

We also had a lot of ranting and raving about anybody like Grant who's got the clout to do something nutty like this ought to be able to get me out at least three weeks early. They had concerns about the relationship between us and about relationships among themselves. We faced such issues in a daily living-learning session, from eight to nine at night, and the rest of the time you were supposed to stay on the damn job. We did have this very intense and very serious session in which we managed our real problems of living together, working together. We had our own living unit within the institution, where inmates had their own desk lamps, their own books, and their own typewriters, could stay up all night and many times did.

At work, we had these inmates while they were confined developing projects, inquiring into problems of the corrections system. Quite early, they were coming up with ingenious and creative ways to bring about modifications in corrections involving processes such as handling intakes and religious problems. They didn't talk about things, because we got them to think in terms of need assessments. They'd start to look at vague problem areas, and then we'd talk about objectives, and about how you would try to do something about those needs. You'd go out and do some talking with inmates and talking with staff, and you'd process ideas with a method we adopted from the Rand Corporation.

It consists of using five-by-eight file cards and grease pencils, and giving each group member three cards on which you ask them to print in five words or less, big enough so everybody can read it, what they see as issues in this kind of problem. And, then you stick them up on the wall. And you can pass cards out, and if no one crowds the spelling, you can put something in three to five words, and can paste things on the wall, so you're doing something, you're a participant. You're working with a group. Then somebody suggests, "Well, all of these ideas are not mutually exclusive, some of them go together more than others." So you start to organize a set of concerns. (We usually come up with seven.)

We also did some reading, and we introduced right away the role of knowledge in solving problems. Then we'd talk about the force field in which you're going to try to move to reach your objectives. And the inmates would say, "Steve, you sure as hell better case the joint." That was their term for plotting the force field. And we would clarify, as well as we could, the obstacles and the resources, and the dynamics involving them, because they aren't just a sum of those. We'd get laid out pretty well what we had to work through in implementing ideas.

I don't know that inmates are any better at this than other nonformally trained people, but "casing the joint" wasn't just a glib statement. They tend to have done a lot of figuring out of games on the street, or have run enough of them that they are quite comfortable with some kind of planning.

Then we moved to strategies. How do you get through the mine field? That breaks itself down into a set of tasks over time and people. We didn't stop here, and I think it's terribly important that we didn't stop here. You can take your strategy and you can spell out a set of expecteds over time. In other words, you not only specify that you are going to have a meeting with the superintendent, but you spell out what you expect to come out of that meeting with the superintendent. What are you going to get the correctional captain to do? What are you going to get some parents to do? And what's terribly simple but extremely important in the implications of this is that as soon as you talk expecteds you're close to the heart of the scientific method, where you set up a set of hypotheses, and then you check observations as to whether they come out or not. And you get people who've never taken a statistics course or an elementary sociology course, let alone a psychology course, and have them start talking about hypotheses—what they expect to happen. They do this in their own terms, and very real out of their having cased the joint.

We now look at outcomes from some program effort, which is what happens to the participants over time. You can have impacts on the system. You can talk about what changes your program will bring about in the way you operate a given institution, the way a policy changes within the department, changes within the attitudes of administrators, and so on. You can have a set of impacts on the system.

Now there's another kind of evaluation that's quality control, where you set up a set of observations about how many are showing up on time to meetings, how many are being released from a corrections program, how many are being returned. So you're having quality-control checks on the operation. That comes out like studying mining specimens, where you go in and you check periodically to see if the samples of ore are staying where they are. Or, if you're sending out Ford Motor cars, do a significant number of them run without blowing up?

But you also have a perfect right to call the effort to build the program itself a social phenomenon, and it's a tough social phenomenon, and warrants a body of knowledge about it, so that you have a science of program development, and we can talk about program development evaluation. And my group has finished five years working on a program development evaluation manual for 16 mental health centers around the country.

I'm very committed to moving this kind of approach to organizations and institutions through which personal and social change operates, to secondary schools, mental health centers, senior citizens' meal sites. I'm delighted to have the opportunity to come back where I started and talk about the possible implication of this for merging the participation of corrections staff and consumers with needs for correctional system improvement. I don't think that any institutions need to be defensive about the fact that they need to improve. Obviously the force field for corrections is changing, you have to be continually on the job of updating, moving, and bringing about change. And I'm suggesting one way to maximize the resources we have now to stay with the planning.

And this is where I said it's the equivalent of the couch, the fact that through participation in efforts to bring about structural change, in efforts to bring about change in the way mankind organizes itself and addresses its problems, we have a powerful modifier to the participant's own self-image, his ways of handling himself, his access to and appreciation of knowledge. Where we really became excited about that was with our 18 offenders, all of whom were at least two-time losers. And—granted it's a small group—we had a fantastically low recidivism rate. One of them went out to look up a man he thought was molesting his sister; he was too drunk to do much harm, but he tried to, and got locked up again for a while. But he's had a career since of 15 years working as an administration-of-justice planner for the county of Alameda. So without getting defensive about the plausible ineffectiveness of things we've got inmates doing now, including helping manage the institution—and we all know they're a very powerful force in managing our institutions—this gives us a possible way to get the force that we see as a liability turned into an asset.

Jones   Could I play back your phrase, because I think I want to check it. "The change potential of the person through his becoming a participant in improving the human race through systematic study." That's what you said.

Grant   I think that fixes it. What I wanted to get across for sure, Max, was that I was not belittling the crisis living-learning approach to a given family incident or a given group incident, and in fact we buy heavily into that in terms of keeping our game on the road, particularly early on, working with these populations. But we can move with more oganized, more systematic study of the problem, and then we not only learn emotional learning, but bring in formal knowledge to help with the development of problems. And Hans Toch and I have some beautiful stories about how police officers who thought of themselves as getting-old paratroopers, and never thought about doing anything for their department through the use of the scientific method, could come up with very creative approaches to problems, and start talking very sophisticatedly about analysis of variance.

Jones   You were allowing them to achieve a role that in their wildest dreams they would never thought possible.

Grant   I think that's certainly true. Not only wouldn't have thought possible, but wouldn't have been caught dead playing.

REHEARSING NEW ROLES

Briggs   Max Jones has described an evolutionary process people go through in social learning experiences, which includes both inmates and staff. In California we saw examples of the fact that the longer inmates stayed in our program, the more they wanted to move into new roles, from being a passive recipient into being an active collaborator, and beyond into having a real influence on the direction of the program, and on its day-to-day operations. I have also mentioned that when the social workers left, the correctional officers were able to make a break and take on new roles, which allowed the inmates to take on more responsibility than they ever had before. And this holds even for the people who left us.

Of our six psychiatric social workers, five left at one time. One left the correctional system and went to work in a smaller school for delinquents where he could have more autonomy. Another moved up in corrections into a high position as Deputy Director of Classification in a very short time. The others, interestingly enough, within two years came back into therapeutic community programs as administrators. Only one of the six went outside the correctional system. But for the correction officers it was different. There were six initially with us, and only one remained a correction officer. Of the other five, one became a sergeant, two became parole agents, and the others left the correctional system altogether. They saw it as not a place they really wanted to work—they saw no opportunities there, no future.

Max Jones has said that any kind of a unit that can't tolerate staff casualties really can't make any progress. You've got to be prepared to have staff casualties, and you must handle them, so that it becomes a learning process for the staff and a learning process for you. If you can't tolerate such crises, you can't evolve very much. But you can create a fluid structure where inmates as well as staff can take on new roles. As they are freed from stagnant and well-defined roles, they became interested in all sorts of things. The correctional officers became interested in research, and we had a research person with us full time. The officers learned research skills, and they became quite good. There were two inmates who did very nice studies, and the officers and the inmates collaborated on research. And they were fantastic as teachers. As we opened 12 new therapeutic community units, the inmates as well as the correction officers became involved in training. We took them to other institutions to train staff and orient them, and to train inmates and select them.

Chinlund   What "12 new therapeutic community units?"

Briggs   We had an opportunity, in lieu of building one new prison, to set up therapeutic community units in other prisons. I think every prison in the state had one unit, and each one was different. And we used our unit to train the staff for all the units, and to give them technical assistance.

Chinlund   Could you describe a little more what you did with the officers to help them get from where they were when you arrived, to where they were functioning as training technicians?

Briggs   We had to start with the staff the superintendent gave us and it was an absolute disaster. It took us a year to undo it. This was not a correctional staff, except for maybe two out of six officers who in any way were interested in the program. Besides, they had divided loyalties. They reported to the custodial captain, who was suspicious of our activities, and was constantly spying on us. One of the biggest crises in our community came one day when a man brought out in the community meeting that he was serving a sentence for second-degree murder, and that the captain had called him into his office shortly after we selected him, and said, "You'll be coming up for parole in a year or two. You'll be lucky if you're going to get a date before 7 years, more like 12 years." And what he had him doing was spying on the group and paying him in cigarettes through a lieutenant. This came out in the groups, and it was an extremely tricky problem to deal with, in a prison of 2,000.

CREATING CULTURE-CARRIERS

Chinlund   The evidence mounts having to do with the obstacles to having 12 officers who were ready to go forth and spread the gospel.

Briggs   We had to clean house and start all over with our *own* staff, our *own* inmates. We took a new housing unit, our own work project—not the one that was given us.

Chinlund   Can you say anything more about the training of the new group of officers?

Briggs   Well, it was a long process. Like I have described [Chapter 12], they learned by participating. In the first period, the officers wouldn't even sit in on the group meetings, because it wasn't the custodial thing to do. And when we had our own officers, they sat in the groups and learned to participate and to feed into the groups all of the information that was relevant. And they met every day just to work at thinking out their role, and how this role was different from what other officers did in the next housing unit. This was a long process of daily examining and reexamining. During this period, they had many crises with their peers, in the barber shop, the cafeteria, the officers' lounge. It took about six weeks before they would talk to me about these kinds of things.

Chinlund   If you had it to do over again, would there be anything that you would do differently, from the point of starting with your own people?

Briggs   Having an administrative-controlled unit was our biggest mistake. We found after two years that it was absolutely impossible to operate the unit unless you had line control. If you want to integrate discipline and treatment, if part of your goal is to resocialize or socialize people, you've got to have fresh observations from many different places where the inmate is, and the more second-hand it is, the less it means. So you've got to have disciplinary feedback. The mess hall is extremely important, their eating habits, the stealing of food, you can't get this through the captain and through other sources. You've got to have your own direct sources of data, if this material is to be integrated into your program. And if you're going to have a work project, you've got to have direct feedback from the people the inmates work with.

Chinlund   And you couldn't get that feedback?

Briggs   We had to do it through supervisors, who were trained totally in another discipline rather than in using this material for learning. We tried—we had training sessions for the laundry staff, and for the supervisor who operated the sweatshop for 22 years. You don't change people like this overnight. The supervisor attended the community meetings daily, but continued to operate his sweatshop as a sweatshop. We worked with him for two years and gave up.

After two years we got total line responsibility, a totally autonomous unit. I reported directly to the superintendent, and had disciplinary and custodial responsibility. And that was when we could get along with what we were doing. You have to be able to try things.

The most fascinating experiment developed when we had our counselor vacuum and the correctional officers became counselors after we got permission for them to take their uniforms off if they wanted to. The inmates suggested they be allowed to take over the custodial duties, and it sounded pretty wild to me. I wanted to take counsel with the custodial unit, but the superintendent said, "Go ahead with your plan and we'll give you a 30-day chance, do it and see what happens." The plan the inmates drew up was thorough, and they set up a training program that was many times better than the training program that the correctional staff received. They started with first aid, and got the nurse from the hospital to teach them a solid course in paramedical assistance. They said they were afraid the inmates might stumble at night, but it was more in case they got into fights. And they sought out the custodial officers in the prison that they respected for security expertise and got their ideas, and enlisted them as instructors for their training program. This was one of the things they did at night during their free time. They got rid of the television set to give them time to do it.

They called themselves "watch standers." To be on a four-hour shift, you had to have the community's sanction. This was considered a high level of responsibility. We worked out a scheme describing four stages of development a man went through, and when he was classified as ready to go on to the fourth stage, he was cleared to take on these kinds of responsibilities. We had many interesting examples that showed how the inmates took these assignments seriously. There was one man who had been quite a hoodlum and had a reputation on the yard as being pretty wild. And when the group thought he was in his fourth stage, and they were pushing him to take on responsibilities, he applied for the watch stander job and took the training. After a few nights he was taking a count when he passed a bed that had sort of a hump in it. And he did everything they taught him, and tapped it with a flashlight, and the hump didn't repond. He thought it was somebody who had escaped and had put a dummy in the bed, he panicked.

He ran and called the watch sergeant and reported that there'd been an escape. And within hours, this was two o'clock in the morning, the news was all over the place. And there was no escape—the man was just a sound sleeper. The amount of pressure the inmate took from the yard that morning at breakfast was incredible. There were 2,000 inmates and he was very well known. But that incident also was quite a turning point among our custodial staff in the prison.

Toch   Once you have made plowshares out of custodial swords, is it hard to beat them back again into conventional custodial roles?

Briggs   It tells us a lot about our system that we don't have many evolutionary roles for our staff.

Toch   You almost have to have new roles for them when you're through?

Briggs   I think so, sure. The people that I know that have gone through these things, they don't want to be administrators, they don't want to be wardens.

Toch   So you almost have to have other therapeutic communities for them to go to?

Briggs   Or other kinds of self-study units. These are the kind of experiences they get excited about, because they've got a taste of it.

Levinson   Can they seed other institutions in the system?

Briggs   A few but not many. They were thoroughly disgusted with corrections.

Devlin   When you were talking about the officers who were involved with you, I got the impression that there were a lot of percs in it for them. Percs in the sense that they almost became an elitist group.

Briggs   I would say the opposite. They were looked down upon. The first ones were assigned to us because the superintendent and the staff felt we could do a lot of good for them—put them in this project and soften them. For two or three it worked, but for most it didn't. When we could pick our officers we met with the inmates and said, "What kind of officers do you want?" The young inmates said they preferred having officers who were their own age, because they would be willing to be tolerant, and might also know something they didn't know. They didn't want older officers like their parents telling them everything. The other unit that was older people said they didn't want young officers, but wanted older officers who had experience and could show them how to do things.

Devlin   No fringe benefits to being a correctional officer within a therapeutic community?

Briggs   The fact that they could take their uniforms off was interesting, though they took a lot of riding by the other staff for doing this. We did a lot of things for them, like having university extension courses, and letting them go to meetings. Each made out a staff development plan, specifying where they wanted to go in the next five years, where they saw themselves in the next year, what kind of skills they were going to need to get there, and where they were going to get these skills. They wrote out a formal plan they all looked at. Part of their plan might be that they wanted to visit a state hospital one afternoon because they wanted to get some mental hygiene experience. If that was agreed upon they could have the afternoon off to do that. One correctional officer was interested in elementary schools, and he got a morning off so he could go spend it with a sixth grade to see what they were doing. They each could have a half a day for staff development.

Devlin   I can't understand how they could take all that razzing from the rest of the officers.

Briggs   They were all ambitious people who saw themselves not being correctional officers the rest of their lives. They saw this as an opportunity to grow and develop, without exception.

Over a two-year period, we were getting stronger and stronger, which made us more amenable to survival. For example, we had several inmates who refused to leave the prison when the parole authority gave them unexpected parole dates. They, in a group, said, "We're not ready to go out yet." And we had an awful session with the parole board. It just threw them into a tizzy when men asked them for six more weeks to stay in. We had men return after they got out and say, "Hey, we realize that we got out too soon, and we need another six weeks." There isn't any possible way that we could do anything about it at that time. I had some mothers call me—we had gotten some publicity on television, and they said, "Our kids want to come in there." We were starting to get that kind of support, which was very impressive to the superintendent and the authorities.

Elwin   Since I don't think you're going to find someone who knows corrections and also knows therapeutic communities, if you had your druthers, would you take a correction person and teach him therapeutic communities, or take a therapeutic communities person and teach him corrections? Which is the shorter route?

Briggs I'd opt for the first strategy—find the right correctional persons, and build an educational program to increase their effectiveness.

THE EXTENT OF CORRECTIONAL-OFFICER INVOLVEMENT IN THE COMMUNITY

Barker If I might interject, I didn't have the experience of working in therapeutic communities before, and I'm not a reader. But the allegation was made that I had a clear notion of where we were going and I just wouldn't tell them. The irony was that, apart from a general notion that I wanted more discussion about everything, particularly about people showing up with a black eye, I had no scheme in my mind. I'm still accused of having had the whole schmeer in my mind when I walked in.

Toch I think that generally with group process one of the problems one runs into is resisting the desire of a group for structure. And with all of one's feelings about not wanting to look like a schnook one maintains integrity in insisting that the group come up with its own solutions. And what one is contributing is the process, namely this refusal to yield to the desire for predefined content.

Briggs I think you need to go in with ideas as well formulated as you can, and share them with people in hopefully small core groups, so you can have a good interaction. Then you start ideas of, What can we do within this prison, with this ward or with this housing unit? What needs to be done? Let's have your ideas, and let's start planning a program. What are the obstacles, what's going to prevent us from carrying this out? Write these obstacles down on cards. And this can be the work of the unit for the first two weeks or the first month. And then you have to start doing some small studies. You find you hit the limits of your knowledge. Inmates have less knowledge than you think when it gets down to thinking things out. They have a hell of a lot of experience, but not much knowledge. And part of the teaching is to translate experience into knowledge. And you can introduce some simple reading, bring in a person from the outside who can give them more information. In this way, you keep building the program. This might take a month of building, revising, going back to basics. You forge this thing together. And you add two more inmates, you add one more correctional officer, bring them aboard, get their ideas.

Birnbaum   A lot of this process also has to be part of the training piece for the superintendent, the sergeant, and the staff. I think if it's not shared we will be creating resistance. And I suspect a lot of the questions that are being raised here ought to be thrown into that process. Perhaps by doing this, a lot of the problems one anticipates can be restructured even in the initial phases. And if it's not done, the external resistances we complain about will be replicated very quickly.

Toch   I think that's tremendous, because one can run into a stereotyping problem when one sees the external structure as a bunch of dinosaurs. If one does, it becomes self-fulfilling. At Patuxent the mental health staff went in and said those correctional officers are stupid and antitreatment, so we'll lecture them and patronize them and regard them as threats to be charged into and overcome. That creates the very kind of stupidity and lack of acceptance one predicts.

Wright   Maybe it is an implicit belief in stupidity, but it comes down to, if you're a correction officer all you can be concerned about is security.

Birnbaum   You've got to convince them that you don't think of them that way, because they think you do.

Barker   I think I've said that the guards in the programs at Penetang are not involved. They'd just as soon on any given date transfer to another section of the hospital and carry on grumbling. It would be treason to stay after three, one would be seen as a real fink. Occasionally a guard would get away with it if he wanted to, but mostly he wouldn't want to. And whether or not it's wise, I think that it has been possible for the inmates at Penetang to have a wide range of psychological freedom and choice of programs without the involvement of the attendants and without threatening the attendants, and without their getting absorbed in the inmates' lives and their own lives, in the way that is traditional in therapeutic communities. And that I think is potentially an option for someone moving into a system. Whether or not it's a good one is not for me to say.

Chinlund   With special respect to Elliott, I think he has said something declaratively, and then descriptively he has said the opposite. And I don't think it's a trick. I think he has said up front to his officers, "I will not subject you to humiliation of premature involvement with people you regard as screwballs and as dangerous who could make you look like a jerk. Therefore, the formal rule is no involvement. Meantime, by the way that the administration runs, it's clear that, to the extent that you want to and are willing to be involved and run those risks, you may." And I would presume that there's a lot of encouragement and support. "When you're ready, go ahead. I saw or heard that you were in a group and how did it go?" I don't see that as a contradiction.

Wright   Is that a balanced perception, that they are involved?

Barker   They are, but not nearly to the level of commitment that Dennie Briggs is talking about. Nor would they admit it to their peers. The original supervisor was subjected to the same harassment that Dennie described, and had to change where he drank in town, because of that pressure and harassment. But since then, staff transfer from other parts of the hospital into those units, and some would want to get out of them. There's no kind of screaming allegiance to the process. A man might say he doesn't mind working on those wards. There's never been a group of the sort Dennie Briggs described who discuss what went on in that ward meeting and try to understand the process. The staff can sit in on any meeting, and can in fact veto anything that's going on. They're wandering around, and they feel a sense of obligation to know what's happening. Not just at a security level, but they like the patients and listen to them, and they feel relaxed and in control, certainly from a security point of view. But there is not the flavor of the real therapeutic community.

Levinson   Is this because of the nature of the client?

Barker   I don't think so. I think it is that we're not really stuck on curing people. There's a real limitation, because you've got a guard who would say, "You're a rapist. You can go on blathering about being queer, but you look like a rapist to me." He might say those things in a group. Well, if you're really going to get into sensitive dynamics and the sort of psychotherapy that makes sense to psychotherapists, you can't have these guards coming around driving a sledge hammer through a person's private feelings. And that's a very real limitation, if you like, on the quality of psychotherapy that goes on. So if you want to cure people it seems to me that you've got to go whole hog and have involvement by the cleaner and everybody else who has contact with inmates.

THE PATIENT AS THERAPIST

Barker   At Penetang, we had a fair degree of involvement with the patients in different aspects of the programs. We had a continuous worry about iatrogenic suicide or homicide, and about our ability to assess suicide risk and potential homicide risks. And it was clear that the patients had the best capacity to predict dangerousness, although they couldn't necessarily be articulate about it. They never did have a suicide or homicide while I was there. The incidence of violence was very low, even when a chair was thrown or somebody got punched, because of the patients' skill in anticipating that kind of violence. The patients would recommend changes in medication for the psychotic patients, an increase or a decrease in dosage. They also would screen physical complaints before they were passed on to the attendant staff, to the nurse and to the doctor. If someone had a headache the patients would first decide whether it was psychosomatic, and have a group about that. There was always some uneasiness at higher levels about this, but the amateurs never did miss an appendix and problems of that order.

They were pretty good at doing progress reports, at assessing the mental status of each other. Not all of the patients were equally good, of course, but some of them had an enormous descriptive facility in not just doing a formal work-up that a psychiatrist is supposed to do, but commenting on where a person needed to change and where they had changed, and what kind of processes might be helpful in that change. At one time of severe staff shortage I discharged a patient who was very adept at doing mental status examinations, and hired him on my staff as a filing clerk. And he worked for six months seeing new admissions that I was responsible for, and doing the mental status examination and getting it on file—under my name, of course. He did very competent mental statuses, and that worked very well until he ran away with a number of people's belongings and credit cards.

The patients have always been fascinated by the fact that they in their daily activities are preoccupied with the same problem that wider society is with regard to sickness and sin, with regard to insanity as a defense, with the question of whether any particular deviant act is more a product of illness or perversity. And they had committee procedures that would deal with the one or the other, in a sanctions committee or a treatment committee, and in making a decision as to which body a particular problem area should go to.

On the admission ward for people coming into the hospital, we have run for probably ten years what amounts to a boot camp or a school, with a patient who is like a high school principal, and a staff of six teachers. And on this ward of 38, the trainees, as they're called, come in in a group of six or seven and are taught. There's purely didactic content. They study their rights under the Mental Health Act, and materials that we thought might be helpful in the kinds of programs we have in the hospital. How to disrupt group therapy, for example, in the sense that you can devalue the currency if everyone knows the procedures. How to manipulate well. And as we get really good manipulative patients coming in, they do revisions and additions to the manual of basic manipulations, and to our list of standard defense mechanisms as they understand them or think of them. We cover role functions in groups, and some of Bale's sociological and psychological descriptions of group interactions.

The privileges on that ward are geared to progress on examinations: it's because of the clear benchmarks that when a patient comes in he can derive a sense of progress. He's now passed one set of papers and is moving on to the next one, and his privileges are geared to that. He would start with almost nothing—not nothing at all, because they like things they can take away. He would have a mattress when he first comes in, but he would earn linen. He would start on paper dishes and would earn plastic dishes. But there's not a lot of complaint, although the patients are being assessed on that ward, and are there for 30 to 60 days. They are asked the day they're leaving to do an essay about their treatment on the ward. We've collected those essays for years, and they run about 95 percent, "This has been one of the more exciting experiences in my life." We always felt we had to store that information for the ombudsmen or for the people who come and say, "My God, what are you doing to these people?"

There is another program on that ward which developed about eight years ago. There is always the very difficult patient who consistently creates havoc or drains the potential of the group too much, and everybody needs a rest from him. We don't have the luxury of being able to discharge or transfer people. We're at the bottom of the barrel, and we can't pass anyone on elsewhere—the patients are married to us. So we have to devise strategies within the place to keep certain people from destroying whatever else is going on.

The patients developed what they called the MAP (motivation, attitude, and participation) program. And they took the most difficult people—usually placing six or eight in this group, which is run by two patients who are pretty adept at handling this kind of "dirty dozen." They would not be allowed the luxury of staying in their room. They would come out on double cuffs if they didn't want to come out voluntarily. They could shout and scream and yell, but they couldn't kick and hurt other people. And they would simply talk about why they were in that program, and why they got transferred off the ward they were on. And the surprising thing is that for long periods of time in that program there's exceedingly high morale. In the early years we had to keep purging the privileges—there were virtually none to start with—because we were always fearful somebody would slug somebody else to get the MAP program. They seemed to be having too cohesive or too good a time! Though on the surface of it they would seem to have nothing, that didn't seem to affect their attitudes.

We have role positions, as they call them, in the hospital. The teachers on the admission ward are paid as industrial therapy patients would be, a minimal wage, something like $20 a week. We have observers for the capsule and for the sunroom program—patients who would stay awake on shifts in a formal kind of way to provide food for people in the capsule and to intervene if there was violence, or to go into the sunroom and put someone on cuffs if there was a situation getting out of hand. And we also have two patients who operate the videotape equipment that's used on the various wards.

I'm inherently lazy, and have always been pleased, as is everyone who works with patients, at the enormous capabilities of inmates to manage and take over the responsibilities that you're supposed to have. Two or three months ago, one of the enormous preoccupations of the superintendent and the administration was the quality of progress reports on file. So I asked the supervisors of each of the four wards to send the heaviest guy on their wards down to discuss this problem—the most potent individual on each ward. One supervisor predicted that if we began to ask the patients on his ward what kind of progress reports should go on file, many of them would want to consult their lawyers before they committed themselves on the matter. That was a projection, I think, of a concern with the ombudsman and the annex-to-a-law-school kind of operation which is fashionable in mental hospitals.

I asked the group of four patients what they thought should go on file in the way of progress reports, telling them that they had a certain stake in the matter, that if the progress reports meant something to the boards of review that could release them, and the boards released the wrong people too consistently and the murder rate went up, they would suffer from it, because the release rate would be going down. I asked them whether they thought that the patients themselves should have direct input and how much, and should the psychiatrist and should the guards be putting notes on, and what should they be putting notes on about, and how in fact do you predict dangerousness and who to let out? I left that with them and gave them a deadline, and in two weeks they came back with an astounding document. They had had a series of meetings and discussions with the patients on each of the wards, had designed a questionnaire, and it had been completed voluntarily with about 98 percent response rate. They had analyzed and summarized the questionnaires, and their summary recorded the opinions of all the patients about who should be reporting and about other questions I'd asked them. Not being content with that, and not being able to come to a consensus, they each submitted a separate typewritten report of their own suspicions about where the raw data would be biased unfairly and wrongly. And they presented this to me. I was delighted, and had it xeroxed and circulated to the research staff and to others in the hospital. I was disappointed that I didn't get feedback from any of them. I don't think they're as impressed as I am with the capacities of patients to come to terms with those sorts of issues.

Levinson   The possibility might have threatened them!

Wright   Don't you have a very famous patient who wrote an excellent paper, which was published?

Barker   After he was discharged, the quality of writing in the place decreased. He had a way with words.

Wright   I'd be interested whether somebody as articulate as that, and obviously as bright as that, had influence in the hospital while he was there. I mean, did he dominate everything, or were there devices to neutralize him?

Barker   He had bad political judgment, as many schizophrenics do. And when he dumped everyone into the sunroom naked on a weekend, I had a hurried whispered conversation with him as to why he had to be denounced publicly, and I proceeded to denounce him. There were other strategies, though. It was always a problem to find ways of treating the heavies. Basically, I think, in exclusively patient-oriented and patient-run programs, it is one of the limitations that the powerful patient, even when you keep transferring him and balance the potent patients with less potent patients, tends to come out on the short end of the stick, with regard to whatever therapy is.

Toch   I want to thank you for what you have presented, because I think you epitomize the limits of what is possible.

Chinlund   I didn't notice any limit.

A CAUTIONARY POSTSCRIPT

Redl   Sometimes we got captured by slogans, and I think it's important with a new and hard-to-interpret project not to fall into the trap of using other people's slogans. For instance, it bothered me when Barker looked embarrassed and said he was a dictator, or was not democratic enough. The moment you use such terms you fall into other people's traps, because it is not at all dictatorial to use authority under certain conditions. And it is not part of democracy never to interfere. What if a student triumphantly says that school is never interesting, and what kind of a place is that? The form of intervention you pick out of your 21 or 32 possibilities is another story, but there's nothing wrong with the role of some authority in an intervention where that is needed, and that doesn't make you a dictator. And the moment we use words of this kind, we play into political issues, which of course get us into a difficult position, especially with those who just wait for the chance to criticize us and to get mad at us anyway.

It bothers me also that we live in an era of antiprofessionalism, and while it sometimes emerges semijokingly it bothers me, because there is nothing wrong with being professional. It is true that sometimes professionals don't know everything, or assume a role that goes beyond the one they should exercise. But we are not planning a revolution for the country, we are talking about jobs. And the knowledge of the professional has integrity and usefulness. The present idea that the less you know about something, the more you ought to do is dangerous, and I get this message every day, wherever I go. On the other hand, I know that sometimes people who are not trained in our profession may have special skills, or can be trained or helped to be better than some professionals. Because we know that some of our colleagues are dumb, or disinterested, or not very skillful. But the upgrading of nonprofessionals is not a substitute for the knowledge of the professional. And I would want to be sure that we cleanse ourselves of extreme antiprofessionalism.

Now the second part of that story is that some delinquent kids have skills which as professionals we work for a long time to acquire. These sons of bitches have diagnostic acumen to an enviable degree, way beyond what professionals may hope to acquire through training. I remember some delinquent kids I borrowed from a detention home or reformatory for an eight-week camp experience. Two of the group were especially interesting. One was a severe delinquent, and came from the same home as another delinquent who wasn't quite as severe in terms of his record, though he had also put in many terms in detention homes. The first young man was the type I now call the proud nonreader. He had a reading disturbance, despite the fact that I caught him once in my office going through my filing cabinet. Under "C" he found a bottle of cognac which I needed, though the campsite belonged to the state conservation department, which didn't approve. I arrived at my office unannounced, and he was there before me, had the cognac bottle and was just about to take a slug out of it. I said, "Hey, wait a minute, that ain't Coke, you know?" He said, "How would I know? Don't you know I'm a nonreader?"

Now, the reason why this kid was a nonreader was not because he was too dumb to learn how to read, but that he couldn't afford it. Where he lived he had to learn to read people's *behavior*, and especially the unconscious or preconscious signs in people. He described to me, for instance, a teacher he had had when he was still in grade school who was nice and friendly. And she always made a speech, wanting to be very democratic. Each time somebody was noisy she'd say, "Now children, don't you think we should be quiet now? Wouldn't it be nice if we all were quiet now? Raise your hand if you think we should be quiet now." And at that moment my boy knew she was getting dangerous, because three minutes later she would have a blow-up. And after a few minutes she invariably had a blow-up and got extremely mad and became dangerous. In that instance you didn't raise your hand, you didn't do anything, you just waited till the crisis was over. And he had to know this, he had to read the nonverbal communication potentials like somebody who had ten years of analysis and five years of training has to read the unconscious in his patients. He couldn't afford to read printed stuff, because he had to learn all that.

He also was good at composing groups. The way from Detroit to the camp was a four-hour bus ride. In these four hours he had already determined who should be in the tent in which he would be. And his selection was pretty good except I wasn't sure about the second young man I mentioned. But he thought he'd try it, and I let him try it because I didn't know who to put together, since group composition is one of our most difficult dilemmas, about which we know least.

After a few days, the young man came to me and said, "Fritz, get this boy out of our cabin before we beat him up for you." So I made my usual speech, "Everybody has the same right; what did he do, why can't you have him there?" He said, "Are you crazy asking such a question?" I said, "All right, so why don't you want him in there?" "Well, you know, he just doesn't fit." I didn't let him get away with this, and he said "Well, the guy steals." And at that moment I said the most tactless thing, namely, "Look who's talking." Because this young man had a record a mile long, and the other had a record only a yard long. He said, "But you don't understand, this guy's crazy, he's nuts." I said, "Well, don't give me a diagnosis, tell me what happened." "He's funny. There's the girl counselor, he likes her very much. She is away for the weekend with her boyfriend, he's jealous. Anyway, he goes to her cabin and goes through her trunk to swipe something. Everybody knows she's very disorganized. If he takes the cash she wouldn't miss it, if he takes cigarettes she wouldn't miss them. What does he do? He takes a little trinket which you put around your neck with something on it. And does he give it to me until camp is over to hide? (We have a hollow beam—he knows exactly where everything can be hidden.) No, he goes down to the water and buries it in the sand. Boy, that's nuts. I don't want anything to do with him, we can't have that in our group." Which means if I run a delinquent gang, I can't afford a neurotic in my group. It's as simple as that, and he's right. He knew that this kid's stealing was actually a young child's jealousy fit.

When you are two and a half, you might express jealousy by taking something away from the person you're jealous about. A more mature youth ought to be mean to his counselor when she comes back because she was away for the weekend with her boyfriend, or ought to be nasty to the boyfriend or destroy something. That's how one gets revenge. One also does *not* become attached to authority people that fast. If you are in a camp for delinquents, what kind of a tie is that? You can't have something like that, because next thing you'll squeal on somebody. That means this youngster's stealing was entirely different from any of the delinquent youngsters' stealing. This was psychoneurotic stealing out of an early childhood hangover fantasy, which was out of date in terms of developmental phase. The kid had a neurotic problem, and my friend was smart enough to catch this. That's why he didn't have time to read books. He had to look and watch people, and he was a bright kid, obviously.

But the point is, you must have comparable patients who have sufficiently comparable disturbances to help them be close to each other and to have an experience of being a group. They must be able to talk with each other to confess to each other what bothers them, to bring it into the open. Can you do that, if individuals are psychologically too far apart? Those two kids didn't fit together, they should never be in the same subgroup. Whatever I'd do in that subgroup would be wrong for one or for the other.

I think we have to face the fact if we do something as subtle as create a therapeutic community, in which patients are presumed to help each other, the question of the group composition becomes important. And the question of what else I have to do to make sure I have no uncovered psychopathology or undertake excessive risk taking, becomes a strategic issue. Ideally, we have to have a reasonably similar intake. At the very least, whether we do or don't have comparable patients in terms of their basic pathology, creates a different question about grouping and about staffing, and about which of the patients you can invite to take what roles. This kind of question must be addressed by persons with diagnostic, as well as group dynamics, skills. People who are not professionally trained in this sort of detail are not necessarily a replacement for the professional. You at least want to be sure that the professional you have available at intake is clinically still around and helps the others, to train them, to make them aware, so they can learn some of that. They don't automatically have it just because they are interested or sharp or very sensitive.

When we talk about therapeutic community process which highlights openness and verbalization of feelings, we must remember that for some people that is not necessarily comforting. It is not characteristic and it may be taboo. One does not want to talk about certain things. We found in traditional psychoanalysis that some kids cannot talk about how scared they were yesterday because to admit to this and talk about it is demeaning. After about eight years of age, if you live in a relatively tough area, you do not talk about those feelings.

If I asked a kid, "How did you feel?" and the kid was scared stiff, he couldn't say that. Because you are not supposed to be scared. If the kid got beaten up by another kid, and he still has a shiner, and we are trying to ask him, "How do you feel about it?" he'd in effect tell us, "Of course I feel it, but I wouldn't talk about it. I'm much too old for that." You pay it back after a while, you don't like it, but you don't feel good by talking about it. It isn't being done. Maybe after a long time you can talk about it under certain conditions, but certainly not in public, and certainly not with other kids around. And sometimes not even with your most trusted therapist whom you love and to whom you could admit any misdoing, but with whom you wouldn't discuss your feelings.

To talk about our feelings is a typical middle-class, upper-class caste and class kind of conditioned attitude. And most inmates come from different backgrounds. I have to take my punishment, we won't talk about it, there's nothing to talk about. One does it or one doesn't do it, I know it was wrong but it's nothing to talk about. This is a big problem even in group therapy. It is not real resistance, and people who learn of it always think it is. And that's what I want to make sure we remember, because when people don't play the game our way it doesn't mean they don't trust you. And it doesn't mean they are helped if after the first day they are encouraged to talk in front of everybody about some of their problems. It doesn't make them feel good and under those conditions they can't afford it. If you talk too much about you feelings, it means you are a sissy. The imaginary peer group would find it funny. You take it, or you give it, but there's nothing to talk about. Because the peer group, the nonpresent peer group, the group under the couch, is listening even while you are in a room with only one guy and nobody else. And with many adults this is still there. So much of what we think is resistance is healthy reluctance. What we think would be helpful may not be helpful to people who have to be proud that they live without complaining too much. For them, talking and having others listening in, may not provide relief, buy may be the opposite. At minimum, they may have to wait for a much longer time before they can do it. I felt I had to add this to the complexity because we frequently overlook it.

15

LOOKING AT PROGRAM COMPONENTS: A REVIEW OF TWO HYPOTHETICAL TECHNIQUES AND ONE CONTROVERSIAL ISSUE

Chinlund   I very selfishly would like to take advantage of the presence of this extraordinary group to get your comments, suggestions, ideas for change on two of the program pieces prospectively receiving attention in our program. One type of meeting, which seems of special importance, I have called a three-part group.

It is designed to respond to one of the greatest needs facing exinmates: a regularly scheduled setting in which problems can be constructively addressed and new positive choices can be confirmed.

The meetings will take place in settlement houses, churches, the office of the division of parole, and will be the continuation of similar meetings in which the inmates will participate in the prisons themselves, at all levels of security. The sessions will therefore be a foundation of continuity throughout the time of confinement and supervison. Participation in the program is voluntary, but the three-part groups will be required of all participants.

The first part of the session consists of a brief sharing, by each member, of some event, decision, or personal quality about which the member experiences good feelings. It may be major or minor, but it will be expected of all, including the leader. It may refer to work, home life, or peer relationships. It serves to improve self-esteem, develop consciousness about aspects of life that produce good feelings, start the meeting on a positive note, and counterbalance the cultural tendency to approve only grumbling, negative communication.

In my experience with this exercise, individuals from all walks of life find it difficult at first, but then come to recognize that it creates valuable and unforced changes in their lives.

The second part is usually the longest, consisting of the sharing of stressful situations—pain, anger, frustration, and sadness. The rest of the group is expected to listen carefully and to share similar or parallel experiences—not particularly to offer advice. The purposes are, first, to offer a setting in which strong negative emotion can be freely expressed without fear of negative consequences; second, to provide the support which comes from realizing that others have faced the same stress; and also to make it easier to hold in on-the-spot explosions (because of the expectation of being able to ventilate with the group). In contrast to part one, all members would not necessarily participate in part two.

In part three, the participants will share new plans and commitments. These will usually be expressions of ways in which the positive material in part one can be deepened and confirmed and/or the stressful material in part two can be corrected or minimized. The purposes of this part are to conclude on a positive note, confirm the strength of the participants, relieve stress, clarify the decision-making process (the fact that we need not simply be the victims of the circumstances of life), gain the power which comes from making a commitment to the group as well as to oneself, and realize the difference between saying you will *try* to do something (no commitment) and saying you will *do* something (commitment).

I welcome your reaction to this approach, drawn—as some of you have already recognized—from the philosophy and work of William Glasser (reality therapy) and Harvey Jackins (re-evaluation co-counseling).

The second major innovative type of meeting that we propose, and on which I would appreciate comments, is the family reintegration group. As you know, getting back into the family is one of the major challenges facing an inmate, one of his greatest concerns, one of the last things he will admit being anxious about, and a matter with which he gets little help.

There are many difficulties: the necessary separation involved in incarceration; lack of staff skills to offer guidance; the complexity and even violence represented by family problems; the bitter, long history of many of those problems; the confusion of symptoms ("we just need more money") with the underlying problems (lack of love, trust, self-respect, patience).

In the network program we propose, first, to establish inmate meetings to begin family–issue discussions, with special emphasis on stopping blame and starting to admit responsibility for our own part in the life of the family. Specific topics discussed will include family budget, use of leisure time, drinking, discipline of children, et cetera. Second, we'll establish family groups in the community with precisely the same approach. Each group would know that the other is meeting. Then, we'll establish combined groups, either in prison or in the community. There will still be a specific topic for each meeting. In all these meetings, there will be a continuing commitment to focus on *my* responsibility, and not to fall back into patterns of blaming.

The purpose of the meetings is the establishment of a new basis for the family, an experience of having talked out problems, of having created deeper trust through compromise and understanding.

The groups should be small, with a maximum of five couples in each. They will continue, hopefully, long after parole supervision is ended.

DISSECTION OF A TECHNIQUE: SELF-AFFIRMATION

Elwin　　The first sessions described by Steve start with an exercise requiring inmates to say something good about themselves. This self-affirmation process—how often would it take place?

Clark　　It would take place as part of the regular daily morning meeting.

Elwin　　I can see even the most egocentric person having difficulty getting by the first week.

Toch　　Is the purpose of this exercise to promote a more positive outlook about oneself, based on the assumption that one of the problems people face is that they hold themselves in excessive contempt?

Clark　　Yes, a looking at the positive kinds of things that you're doing.

Redl　　If this is the case, you have to worry about the other bastards who listen to my self-affirmation. They're going to bash my head in afterwards.

Barker　　Not if it's part of a three-part technique to balance out excessive crying in one's beer.

Devlin　　In the small-group process, traditionally when their asses hit the chair, there's been someone wanting to dump their feelings. And usually they want to alleviate their pain immediately. And what traditionally has happened is if you allow one of the group participants to begin crying in his beer, you may be sitting there for half an hour while he just wallows in his misery and self-pity. I see this as a technique to say, "Stop. Before we listen to your pain, tell us something good about yourself."

Toch　　How does that say, "Stop"? It says, "Pause."

Devlin　　A pause, yes.

Clark   I've experimented with this process with kids. I've also experimented with adult probation officers. It is more difficult to do with adult probation officers than it is with delinquent kids.

Toch   I would think so.

Clark   I guess one of the basic underlying assumptions we have about people who go to prison is that they don't have very good self-images. And we're looking at this technique as a possibility for confronting the negative self-image, and saying, "Look at something that's good about yourself," on a regular basis, in a prescribed kind of way.

Redl   "I can open any lock that anybody is not able to open—that's very good about me." Is that something you want?

Clark   Sure, that might be one thing.

Redl   Well, the staff will be very grateful because they always lose their car keys. "Without me they couldn't operate the outfit."

Toch   In the interim I'm becoming an offender who feels better about his antisocial activities.

Barker   I would think that other aspects of the program would have things to say about that, wouldn't they?

DeLeon   That's kind of essential and difficult. We have an isolated therapeutic technique, which is probably not even going to be applicable for all twelve people in a room.

It seems to me you need two things to make it productive. One is, what is the empirical rationale for doing it at all? And secondly, how does this technique integrate with the rest of the elements of a model? I'm nervous about the discussion of techniques out of context, without sufficient rationale.

Now, let's assume that the rationale was that the offender has a poor self-image. Well, there may be data to show that, and we could say it. Then comes the next question, is it an immediate therapeutic goal within the therapeutic model to lift the self-image? And if so, should we consider a set of elements which go on in a therapeutic community model which are designed to lift the self-image of the individual, the least of which, incidentally, is that he should proclaim it? In therapeutic community models which lean heavily on self-reliance, verticality, and the individual making contributions to a kind of communal productivity, self-image gradually elevates through social reinforcement.

Toch   Let me echo this, because I resonate to it. If I want to build a person's self-esteem, there are techniques such as giving him experiences of success, which build self-esteem in a parallel way to the way his sense of failure accumulated. The logic that my self-esteem is enhanced just because I say nice things about myself is the old fairytale of my looking into the mirror and asking, "Who is the most desirable individual in the world?" and getting the answer back, "Of course, you are." Is there any evidence that isolated verbal statements—saying things like, "I have very shiny bright eyes," or "Boy, do I have a sense of humor"—should be expected to have impact?

Barker   Evidence bothers me. You can evidence things to death. Our patients used this particular technique for about two years in what they called a positive mirror group. The task was to go round-robin and say what they liked about each individual and themselves. I don't think there's a more painful, difficult task you can assign. They always want to get out of it. It isn't a task which can be approached with the levity you're suggesting.

Toch   On the contrary, I'm saying that one reason I wouldn't approach it with levity is because it has a regressive flavor. It is undignified in certain ways.

Clark   Now wait a minute! Listen to what you're saying about affirming yourself. It's "regressive" and "undignified."

Toch   Yes. There is a stage where my daughter goes around saying nice things about herself now, at the age of five. She's quite open about it.

Clark   And what's wrong with that?

Toch   There's nothing wrong, because she's five, but there's something wrong with an adult acting like a five-year-old. I'm assuming we aren't talking about people five years old.

Barker   There's a cultural pathology that says you don't say nice things about yourself.

Toch   Well, that's one way of putting it.

Clark   Right. And I think there's evidence. Hayakawa has evidence in terms of language usage, and other people who've studied language constructs—John Cage has done studies of language usage. And if there's no evidence, why shouldn't we study it?

DeLeon   Let me comment on that. If you want us to discuss whether we should open a group with self-affirmation, I know that for 20 years groups have been doing that. I couldn't quarrel with that as a single group technique. If you want to go around the room and ask people to affirm themselves, there's really nothing to discuss on that level. It's a group technique, and it could be used properly in any group process.

I thought you were after the larger question, which is, in a therapeutic community model, how do you build self-esteem? And what do we know about building self-esteem in the criminal offender, or the dysfunctional or disaffiliated individual? I wouldn't want to get hung up on whether we should go around a room saying we're self-affirmed. I would focus on the larger question, what other elements in the therapeutic community model direct themselves to the important issue of self-esteem in the criminal offender? And maybe we can specify some of those elements and see whether they're usable or utilizable. One that I touched on, for example, to give you the flavor of it, is the entire regimen of the TC if it's focused around self-reliance, verticality, personal success in tasks, excellence, personal honesty—all these things that move towards the psychology of self-esteem.

Toch   Short-term tasks that give immediate experience of success are reliable.

Devlin   The years that I've been kicking around therapeutic communities, the only reward that I know we gave people was when they were doing well, give them a job change. A job change—that was it. You know, you got kicked upstairs and you got a better job. That's the way we rewarded people. You're talking about an institution now, and we can't give job changes. Everyone has their job, that the warden or whoever decides. How then does a person discover that they are doing something good?

DeLeon   I am in favor of any group technique which would introduce a balancing in the group. To me, that's group process. Whatever the form of negativity is, balance it with a positive, whether it's mirrors, asking people to keep logs of the positive and negative in themselves, report on the positive side of their activities for a day or a week. I'm not at all opposed to that as a group technique, I just don't see it as a point of discussion beyond sanctioning it and saying it's something to try in its various forms.

Barker   My opinion would be that it ought not be part of a 70-man meeting, and ought not to be once a day. Once a week is crowding it if you're going to live with the same people for a year or two years. My hunch would be that every couple of weeks maybe a group could run through it.

Clark   In terms of therapeutic communities I've seen, every day at a morning meeting somebody stands up and says what they did wrong the day before. And the process that goes on at morning meeting is that people get rid of the sins of yesterday. How come we're willing to build that into a regular process, and we're saying, "My God, I couldn't think of people saying something nice about themselves every day?" I mean, I have yet to see a therapeutic community meeting where somebody stands up and says something positive about themselves!

Elwin   I think it has a plus in the sense that institutions tend to have all the sticks in the world and no carrots. And one of the things about classical TCs is that you tend to bring in even more sticks—confrontation, playing with attitudinal development, image changing, the whole schmeer. One thing that I thought was interesting is that when Max Jones, in talking about confrontation, raised the issue of what's the balance, there was an implied response that there's tender loving care. But it's hard to read where tender loving care comes in.

Toch   Now why, if the issue is tender loving care, does it have to be conferred by the person upon himself or herself? Why wouldn't the form it takes more logically and naturally be positive feedback from others? Why wouldn't it be a matter of my saying nice things about you?

Elwin   But at what point do I buy it? I think, for a lot of our population, you can say nice things and it's like water off the back of a duck. They don't believe it themselves. There's a kind of feeling, "I'm inherently bad."

Toch   Couldn't you build in a requirement that I document it in some way, in terms of behavior of yours? I mean, that's the way it's done with the negative behavior. I don't just get up and say, "Boy, am I a louse." I say, "Yesterday I informed about Smith," or, "There's some underhanded lie I'm guilty of in order to get an extra piece of cake." Under those circumstances, I'm not just describing a quality in myself, I'm describing something I did which I feel is symptomatic of badness in order for the group to deal with it. Why can't that logic apply to positive feedback? If the problem is there aren't enough reinforcements, and the institution is too negatively skewed, we've got all kinds of technology to make people feel bad, but we don't have enough technology to make people feel good. Now shouldn't one be thinking about how can you convince a person, maybe against his better judgment, that he "ain't so bad after all?" And aren't there ways of dramatizing and demonstrating this to him, as opposed to simple assertions?

Elwin   Well, I think you now join George in asking, What are your whole basic thrusts for building self-esteem?

Toch   If you have groups, it would seem the most parsimonious technology would capitalize on group dynamics, which means it would be a damn shame for me to have to say things about myself if I've got this whole group who can do the job for me. And if that group, as in a therapeutic community, is embedded in a frame where it doesn't have to simply tell me how much they like me but can talk about my behavior in the shop, or how courteous I was in opening a door, or about the old lady I escorted across the street, they can tie what they're saying to activities in the therapeutic community. Which after all makes my behavior the ammunition of the group, or do I misunderstand therapeutic communities?

DeLeon   I think one reason the technology looks negative is that it historically grew out of the handling of the character disorder, who was a notoriously poor candidate for positive reinforcement. That's why psychotherapy failed with them, because it implied a kind of acceptance without earning, and the character disorder didn't benefit from that. There was a very good reason for what we would call negative or biting confrontation, at least in the old days. And it did rest in what we thought was the psychology of the client we were dealing with. Sometimes that psychology is not socially attractive, but it's psychologically sound.

Now I admit that populations, at least among drug abusers, are changing, and Max's populations were different than the ones we face in New York and other American urban areas. That's one of the reasons Max has collisions with the drug-abuse TC model. Now, in prison, I think we are primarily dealing with what we would roughly call the character-disorder population. If you want to talk about which way the balance should go, many of these people need a lot of honest, intense breaking down of the ordinary negative ways in which they've defended themselves. It's a deep and long psychology that underlies these confrontations. And I think we need to understand it.

On the positive side, I think that very carefully engineered events in the therapeutic community, reinforcements for behavior, need to be very wisely and shrewdly introduced. So that you make sure that you're not inadvertently reinforcing or strengthening something that they (a) don't believe, and (b) haven't earned. You don't say, "Should we just have people assert themselves or affirm themselves?" I need to hear what you know about this client and what would follow from the use of the technique. It's not a dangerous technique; it's benign. But if you want to talk sensibly, I think the issue has to be what's the whole approach towards building self-esteem and what are psychological rationales for the approach with this population.

Barker   I think there is a different dynamic in a person himself saying something positive about himself as compared to hearing it from other people. I would argue that both are valid and useful and frequently used. And we're short of useful ways of people rescuing themselves, so why not?

Toch   I'm now trying to introspect and ask myself what turns me off here besides the gimmicky and ritualistic flavor, and the issue of dignity and regression. The thought that comes to mind is that if I had the power to originate a therapeutic community, I'd do my damnedest to make the situation as natural and as organically linked as possible. And I can see that link with distress, since I assume that the people who express distress are people who happen to be going through some sort of crisis at that point. So it's a natural statement of their situation, and some sort of problem-solving approach to give the thing an outcome seems natural also. But unless I happen to get up this morning feeling that something I just did is tremendous, and I feel particularly good about myself, the same spontaneity doesn't undergird the affirmation exercise. And so essentially it's like much artificial ritual in self-styled therapeutic communities—such as walk around on all fours, and rub your back against somebody else's back—which strikes me as taking people out of natural life, and subjecting them to stuff which is very hard to bring back to life. If one of the goals is to get people to respond appropriately to reality, it seems a very indirect way to do it.

Redl   When it's a self-affirmation, I want to ask, "About what?" With kids, does he have to get up and say, "I'm very good at baseball?" That isn't relevant.

Clark   The question I used with kids is, "Tell me something good you did today."

Redl   "You don't give me a chance in this program. Where do we have a chance to do anything good?"

Clark   I would ask them again, "Tell me something good you did today. I'm not interested in what *my* faults are, I'm interested in what you did good today."

Redl   Good in *your* terms, you mean?

Clark   No.

Redl   Well, in *my* terms that isn't good, because the son-of-a-gun procedure said "shut up," so I shut up.

Clark   Did you think that was good?

Redl   No, I was too cowardly to say what I thought about you.

Clark   Then tell me something good you did today.

Redl   I had no chance to do anything good. I was sitting there in that place. . . .

Clark   Nothing at all?

Redl   No, how many chances do you get to do something good, except being obedient to the demands from above, in some programs?

Clark   Was there anything good about being obedient?

Redl   That depends on *to what*. Some guy who's very powerful says, "Sit down, you bastard, or I'll lock you up for a week." What's so good about complying—I was a coward, and that's not good.

Clark   Um-hmm. So there wasn't anything good you did today.

Redl   No.

Clark   What I'm saying is I had a lot of conversations like this with kids, where they would do this kind of thing. And eventually they got to the point where they started thinking about things they'd done that were good.

Redl   Good in whose terms?

Clark   Their terms.

Barker   You might say "Jesus, when I think of it, a month ago I'd have slugged that bastard in the face for telling me to sit down, and I didn't. I think that was good."

Redl   "I don't do it because I'm scared."

Barker   It might not be good, but he might say, "God, I think I'm improving."

Redl   I don't want him to be a liar.

Elwin   If I'm living on the same dorm with you, I may be able to game you for a week, I may be able to game you for two weeks. By the time you're going into the third week, you've heard all the classical self-affirmations I've given out and you're beginning to talk about, "Hey, in terms of what I've been seeing, I don't know when you've been doing all these things."

Toch But then you are adding a feedback component? You're saying that you would see the group as a corrective, in a sense affirming the self-affirmation or disaffirming it?

Elwin Yes, that's what I would see.

Barker In a group, before it has cohesion, before it has strength, patients have the capacity to be angry at each other and call each other "son of a bitch" and whatnot. At the later stage, people in the group feel strong enough to say nice things about each other—you don't get snippets of that until well into it.

Toch If you say they have developed the capability to say nice things about each other, wouldn't the appropriate exercise be to have them say nice things about each other?

Elwin I think that's part of a two-parter. If I'm gaming you, after a period of time you confront me on the classical gaming. By the same token, if I find that I am just not able to verbalize the positives, it may become the duty of other people sitting around the table to say, "Well, but didn't you yesterday?"—and I think that you can convert this into a positive force.

Toch It is conceivable that I listen to your self-affirmation in exchange for you listening to my self-affirmation. I mean, that's the ethic of the marketplace; it means that I suspend judgment because I want you to suspend judgment. So there isn't any listening, there is just acquiescence.

Clark If I know week after week after week that you're running a number, I'm not going to sit here and listen to you run your number again.

Schmidt It's going to take you a long time to catch on to my number.

Clark No, it's not.

Toch We're dealing with contrasting acts of faith, and I don't know how one can overcome this. You are not stipulating that there is a feedback element attached and I don't know how one can prove that immodest verbal statements have self-esteem-building, distress-counterbalancing qualities. My feeling is it is not necessarily true that self-affirmations need be confrontable, because that assumes thay are operationalizable. I can say things about myself that are positive and have to do with personal qualities that would be immune to any kind of corrective.

Barker   "I have hope now."

Toch   Yes, "I have hope now," or a new outlook on life.

Elwin   If I'm living with you 24 hours a day, I think that's confrontable.

Toch   Provided somebody makes an effort to confront it.

Elwin   I could live with self-affirmation if it is done in small groups on a somewhat regular basis—I blanch at every day—and if there is a feedback mechanism. I think with those kinds of caveats, it's worth playing with.

Devlin   I agree with that, and I say that not only do I want to hear you beat your chest, in a small group, every three weeks, I also say, "Don't be beating your chest unless you're going to kick yourself in the ass too." I think they go hand in hand, I wouldn't want to sit in a group where we just went around and everybody talked good about themselves. I would only want to hear you say something good about yourself when in the next sentence you're going to talk about your distress.

Then I get a better picture of where you're coming from. Because unless I can feel your badness, I can't feel your goodness. You can't say, "I have hope," as you said before, and then the next day say, "I stole a pair of socks."

Redl   Let's again say, "I'm a good baseball player." That has nothing to do with the issues I'm being treated for. It has nothing to do with the overall problem which I'm here for, what I'm supposed to work on.

Barker   Well, I couldn't see it as unrelated, if we're talking about the problem of self-esteem. It may not have occurred to a person he is a good ballplayer. He may never have really believed that he was, or understood that he was, or felt that he was.

Toch   Elliott, I have a concrete mind, and when you say to me, "I'm a good ballplayer," I say to myself, in terms of your behavior in the ballpark, there ought to be some criterion having to do with your performance. Either you ran that home run, or you didn't. Now if you put in a sterling performance in the ballpark, it seems to me perfectly appropriate to take credit for this. It's a horse of a different color if you flopped, and you say during this exercise, "You know, fellas, I'm a damn good ballplayer." I would think that in terms of such issues as the pegging of self-esteem onto appropriate conduct, which has to do with the real world and my place in it, one would distinguish those two. I'm not sure whether it's more healthy if I'm characterizing myself erroneously as being strong where I am weak, as opposed to being weak where I am strong.

One of the problems we had with police officers was that they saw themselves as powerful in situations in which they asserted their authority. Part of the exercise was to teach them that when they thought they had won, they had really permitted somebody to challenge them and goad them into playing the other guy's hand. Essentially where they thought of themselves with pride, they ought to have thought of themselves critically. And there might be a different criterion of self-worth, having to do with "I don't permit myself to get sucked in when somebody throws a gauntlet in my face." But that wasn't what would spontaneously occur to these people because it was an alien criterion of self-esteem.

Elwin   But if you ran a group of police officers, and you've got your group going with a fairly decent group leader, when the man says, "I did this bang-up job yesterday," someone ought to pick it up.

Toch   Yes, that's what happens when you have created a group culture such that they have learned new indices of self-esteem.

Elwin   And I guess one question here is, Is this self-affirmation process a viable one at the beginning of a group? Perhaps when you have some cohesion and everyone understands the ground rules, self-affirmation can be looked at critically or reinforced by the group, and have meaning. It may be a dangerous trick to play at the very start of a group.

Clark   I've used the process both before anybody knew anybody else, and after people have gotten to know each other. And it's equally distressing in either situation because people don't affirm themselves. As a habit, most people knock themselves. And it's interesting to me to see the lengths people will go to avoid doing any kind of self-affirmation.

DeLeon   In some morning meetings we have people get up and say very positive things about themselves, but the distinction is between "What have you done?"—which includes your own behavior—and "what I am." As a human being, you know, you're entitled to be affirmed.

Devlin   If someone misbehaves in our communities, we often say "O.K., until we tell you to stop, every morning you're to get up, and you're to put your name on the announcement board, and you have to get up in that morning meeting and give us a progress report." That's the words we use, "give us a progress report." We do this on a daily basis, and I can tell you that it is difficult for people to get up and articulate progress.

Redl   They may recognize that because they made a little progress here, they had other moments when they didn't do so well. And they don't want to brag when it's uncalled-for. Some of your most decent people may be embarrassed to make statements of self-affirmation.

DeLeon   John Devlin is saying that maybe a more pervasive element than building self-esteem is training in discrimination progress. How to take a person through yesterday and what they did—not who they were, but what they did—and train them to see that something has changed so they did it a little better or they did it a little worse. That involves very careful face-by-face monitoring, and is a very active and demanding training approach. If you use it in the affirmation model, you're really moving closer toward *what* behavior are we changing in these people, and what are they really learning, rather than what are they proclaiming.

Toch   But, doesn't that involve the devising of tasks which serve as signposts along which progress can be gauged? So that the person builds a sense of competence out of incremental improvements in his performance? Now, that points to a technology in which energy is directed at creating laboratory situations or activities that provide indices of self-esteem, not just the rehearsal of verbal formulas.

Redl   There are different levels on which people need self-affirmation. There are some people who really think they are no good, or they are ugly or stupid. In that case they need some reassurance, even though the content isn't quite what is relevant. For others, that's not the point. They know they are pretty and very smart. They need self-affirmation in terms of what they're supposed to change, in terms of their therapy. But there are different degrees and levels of self-affirmation. On the west coast, for very young children they had projects where, to show them that they are pretty, they made them look in the mirror. Now, if they make me look in the mirror before I buy a suit, that is not very flattering because I see what I really look like. I look terrible when I look in the mirror, and I'm entitled not to look in the goddamn mirror. Confrontation with the actual reality is not necessarily supportive to my self-image.

Devlin   I tell people, "You're not going to get pats on the back around here. If you're doing a good job, that's what you're supposed to do. But if you're not doing what you're supposed to do, you're going to get a kick in the ass." And we're constantly following through on this injunction.

Clark　Which is all of the things that learning theory says will not teach anybody.

Schmidt　At the same time, if you're preparing people to go into the big bad outside world, that's usually a kick-in-the-ass world. In the real world in which most of us live, people don't go around saying nice things about other people or themselves. It's the bad that comes home to roost, not the good.

Devlin　I'm still high on the fact that a week ago, someone gave me a rifle that was all pitted and rusty and I brought it back to life. It took me a couple of hours and I took the pits off. It's a week ago, and I'm still high on that.

Toch　Yeah, because somebody gave you a tied-down task with a built-in experience of success. See, the world is rough, but it's particularly rough for certain people because they are overly sensitive to the roughness. And if I have a propensity to resort to drug use whenever I run into serious stresses, and I come out of a program in which I've not built up my self-conception on the basis of performance but based on the experience of verbally rehearsing a favorable self-conception, I may be riding for a fall. I'm going to discover that my self-affirmation sounds hollow, in situations in which I'm getting feedback from my boss, my wife, the physical world, saying, "Not really!" If I hadn't been built up, that might not be half as bitter an experience as it is under these circumstances.

Barker　There's another factor, in that psychiatry and related disciplines have been totally preoccupied with pathology, and have an amazing lexicon for the nuances and subtleties of pathology and badness. I think that there's some tendency to try and change that, but we're devoid of an equal number of understandings of positive processes. We're victims of our history, and these are some of the half-assed and schmaltzy attempts to right that balance. That there can be more sophisticated ways I don't doubt. But there should be concern or preoccupation to correct that balance.

Redl　I have a gripe about the sequence of the exercise. If I am really distressed, I want you to be sympathetic enough to hear my complaints and my worries and my guilt. And if you really like me, offer sympathetic remarks. Then I'll be glad to admit that I'm also alright in some respects. But if I feel guilty about what I did yesterday, I first want you to deal with that. And then I'll feel better than if you first insist I say a few good things about me while I'm really worried about myself. And you're not even interested in the fact that I'm mature enough to recognize my weaknesses. I want you to be sympathetic about my weaknesses. Then I will believe you if you say, "But in spite of that, here are your strengths." Why should self-affirmation have to come first?

Barker   It's too mechanical a process that would override a natural response.

Redl   Yes, the sequence is too automatic. The three may be needed somewhere, but the sequence depends on many details, depends on at which time what is being discussed, what happened yesterday, what mood or frame of reference people bring to the situation.

FAMILY COUNSELING FOR INMATES AND THEIR SIGNIFICANT OTHERS

Devlin   Is the second suggestion we are considering that the inmates have a group just to talk about their relationships?

Clark   Yes, what do they do when they go back home, how do they relate to their wives, how do they relate to their families, what does it mean to be a father? A specific goal would be to focus on relationships.

Toch   We have at least one piece of evidence that shows the need for something like this, and it has to do with the furlough experience. One of the findings was that female inmates developed a functional blindness toward problems that exist out there. They lived in a make-believe situation for a week and went back to the institution, without having tested reality at all. This is an example of where this type of technology would be useful, because it would force inmates to face problems they anticipate, and families could learn to make them face problems when they come out. Then you might have real reality testing instead of a whole bunch of defenses. At present, when female inmates go out there, they don't assume child-care responsibilities, they don't even face them, nor face the fact that they may have abdicated them. They go out, sit by the fireside, go to the movies, and they don't talk meaningfully. And it's, among other things, a tragic waste.

Clark   In a study done by social workers out in the Midwest, they had children come in for special visits with their fathers on a weekly basis, and they did crafts or made things together. There was a wrap-up group afterwards for the fathers to talk about the experiences with their kids. And the reinvolvement process was described by inmates who participated in it as a meaningful experience, though some of them were too stressed by it to continue.

Redl   But this is when the fathers are captive, so they are not really in control of the kids. But when the father comes home he has a different involvement with his children. He also has an authority over what the kid does or does not do—it's not the same thing.

Clark   That was something that they structured in very carefully, that the father would be responsible for all discipline. The mothers didn't stay around. The father was there with the child.

Redl   While they are in this project. But it's a different problem when the kid has trouble in school.

Clark   Right. And there were even more drastic problems if a father hadn't seen his kid in five years, and suddenly here's this child. And the child doesn't like him, because he doesn't know who he is.

Toch   Could people be grouped in terms of length of separation from families? Could you have men together who were facing the issue of a very long sentence with a protracted separation, or men who maybe were younger and were temporarily separated?

Clark   My guess would be that they'll probably self-select into interest groups who would say, "I have five years till I get out, and I'd like to talk to other people who do that."

DeLeon   I think I see this as a reentry module, near-terminal phasing. I also think what's very critical in this is the number of sessions. Now, for example, problem identification could take some number of weeks. Seven inmates together, going back, let's say, to family life, do they have the discriminative powers to see what family problems they really have? And you don't want a group that's just ventilating family aches and pains. Now that we've identified some problems, this group is also here to help you set up some new behaviors. Well, that's an issue that's parametrically related to the number of sessions or the leadership quality. The third piece is matching the couples. Now you're into a high art form! Can you bring them in and have them sophisticated enough so they can use the group properly, to handle each other and learn something from a group? We've been stumbling along with that for years, when couples really benefit together in a group, and when they don't.

Elwin   The skill and knowledge of the person that leads that group gets awfully delicate. When I get carried away with myself I say I'm out of the ghetto, and I was born there. But when it gets to the point of interrelationships in terms of how even kids I know react to the opposite sex, I get thrown. Just in terms of their concept of the male-dominant role. And unless you've got someone in there that is able to deal with that, particularly if you're trying to teach new role models, that could be a very tricky experience. Particularly if you have a "teacher-therapist" in a room with 12 people, all of who have been reinforcing the same kind of negative male/female relationships.

Schmidt   One may need such groups most at release, but there are other occasions. Particularly for spouses, there is the first time they are cast into the single-parent role. And another time would be related to female inmates, in their feelings around being away from their kids.

DeLeon   I absolutely agree that you can do a number of things much earlier than the release phase. It could be relieving, and so on. I just thought that as a release or a reentry module, it was a very critical and ambitious one.

Toch   Maybe it can be integrated with some kind of parole follow-up. It would seem that if anything lends itself to a strategy that straddles the institution and the parole process, this is it. The issue of relief of pain is a complicated issue. For example, the literature suggests that the most prevalent adjustment mode of the female inmates is to decathect their family. Many female inmates involve themselves totally in the life of the institution, and try to stop being concerned with issues of separation from significant others, to mitigate the pain. Now, one of the corollaries of this procedure is it would revive some of that pain, which makes institutional adjustment more stressful. On the other hand, it makes it more reality-oriented and more valuable. There's no question but that being faced with a problem you want to forget can be rough.

Elwin   I think we sometimes lose track of the other half, particularly the female who's out parenting while the husband is in jail, as our sentence structure tends to be getting longer and longer. She has made an adjustment, whether you want to define it as good, bad, or indifferent. And the whole business of her having to change her interim adjustment is crucial. I don't know what the answer is, because I hear George DeLeon saying you need to have a significant number of sessions, and I don't know at what point she's ready to have that significant number of sessions. I don't know if she wants to start playing with that six months before he is scheduled to get out, when there's no certainty that he's going to get out in six months. And yet, if you wait till one month before he gets out, when you know he'll get out, you can't have the number of sessions George says you need.

Schmidt   If he doesn't have a date, I don't see how you could ask her to consider problems that are going to come up, which involve giving up roles such as primary disciplinarian. And if you get her ready to give up adjustments and then he gets denied parole, what have you done to whatever balance she has achieved?

DeLeon   I'm not sure it's as potentially disruptive as we anticipate, but it is real. I think your first round could be self-selecting and voluntaristic—use the motivation of spouses on the outside as an opening technique, rather than involving a mandate. And the safest way to go about it is you make the service available and you use education as the strongest exogenous motivation. In this way you minimize your concerns about, What if he doesn't get out? You use the highest-motivated group.

Elwin   One of the pluses in current trends is you're getting closer to being able to define what an inmate's release date is. Down the line you may be at a point where you've got an 80 percent shot at being able to read the date of release, which can be helpful in this kind of planning.

EVALUATION

DeLeon   In an introduction to a book in 1974 I may have said one true thing. What I said was that for a few years you don't really go after a phenomenon while it's unfolding. You don't research it. You look at it, observe it, stay away from it a little bit. Because you contaminate a process when it's not really ready. You must let it settle its procedure down, let its dynamics settle down. You don't become an intervener before the process starts.

Barker   To stultify creativity in the beginning stages and jeopardize a precarious operation, all you need is somebody trying to add a further variable by trying to control what's going on.

DeLeon   At first, the issues that need to have accountability are, Did we deliver what we promised in terms of procedures, staffing, and maybe one particular goal, let's say helping management: did we do that? I would cast the evaluation question in terms of, "This is a feasibility study, we're trying a lot of new things, and what we think we're doing it for is to improve management, and here is the way we intend to gather data to address that question."

About 70 percent of your research protocol gets to be addressed to assessing whether or not you delivered the goods and services you promised. Here's my staffing at the end of year one, here's the number of contacts we had, here's the number of groups that we had, here's the number of inmates that were involved. In other words, you simply show, as is proper to keep your accountability, that this is what we were trying to do in year one and here is what it looks like at the end of year one. It has nothing to do with whether the program is rehabilitative or whether profound things happen to inmates. I would even get off attitude studies in year one, and move them into year two. If I were a funder, I would say, "Those are smart people. So far the shop is operating as they said it would operate." You've got the least intervention on everybody around you, least of all your staff, whom you don't bother while they're trying to work on a lot of problems that they have to work out. So in year one, you're not in any classic evaluation situation. You're in what I call a good nuts-and-bolts evaluation phase, which tells you that the program is launched. Now, in year two you set up other goals. If you've still got a program at the end of year one, you can redefine the goals in year two. Do we now want to talk about inmate change, is that the real issue of year two? At which time we need another conversation, like, What's the model for studying inmate change?

Levinson   I think one has to be able to answer some place along the line in year one, Is it making any difference? One is going to have to answer the question to the system. And it seems to me, in answering the question one has to have some numbers.

DeLeon   We're in agreement on numbers.

Levinson   But what's going to make or break the program may be very irrelevant to what those numbers are. Somebody's going to come in, take a look, and say, "This looks like it's good," or "This doesn't look like it's good." There's a whole political issue that's going to go into how the decision is made. But one still is going to need numbers in order to back up one's position statement. To say, "Sorry, in year one you can't get any evaluative statement," doesn't suffice.

DeLeon   You may build in one pilot variable, one dependent variable, which may be a management variable. Here you're looking at the answer to the systems question. The survival question will be answered other than with numbers. Because the system's evaluation of a program will be based on what happens in that institution.

Levinson   Right.

Saunders   When a sponsor considers the budget of a pilot program, they want to know what has happened. What has made a difference between this program, what has happened between the time these people have been involved in the program and now? What significant changes have occurred?

Elwin   By and large, the game of having to satisfy your funding source has been always to try and inundate them with numbers. And I'm not sure we don't try to inundate them with numbers too early, and to our own detriment.

Wright   Always on the principle that they're stupid and don't know anything about something.

DeLeon   I made a specific appeal for first–year research which requires a creative act by your funder, which is if you want this enterprise to get off the ground, we want to have the nuts-and-bolts operations down pat. As a funder of this, what you really want to know is that the whole project, which is not a 12-month project, is getting properly launched, and that we have an accountability for that, a way of describing the launch of that project.
We make no claims about rehabilitation, no large promises about year one. Now, you might be getting inundated with evaluation models, which go into high-flying elation about the possibility of being extravagant types of research. You can get buried under that, and I'm just saying you have to be careful.

Toch   But there is a different conception of research, which has to do in part with what Doug Grant was saying, that people who are involved in something have a right to know, that curiosity is built into people, that the search for meaning is built into people. I think the people that are involved in an enterprise of this kind, the inmates and the guards, have a right to get as much help as possible with trying to understand what they're about, and to get as much technical assistance as possible with trying to understand the questions which are essential for them to answer in going about their business. I think understanding of that kind is the kind of technical competence which we can sometimes provide. Now I don't see us as sitting on truths that are mystical and nonshareable and nonteachable. I think it's not a matter of selling or monitoring, but that there are partnership possibilities here, if one gets the right combination. It's like marriage. It has to do with action research, or a research component of action.

Schmidt   If you follow along on Doug Grant's idea—that the program can collect its own data as part of the program—it gives you enough to justify the cost.

Levinson   That's very neat.

Toch   Yes, that's precisely the point. And there is another connotation of research which complicates your picture. It has to do with knowledge building, the business of doing things with all the awareness that one can put into the hopper, having to do with all available tools, written documents, diaries, people interviewing each other, people telling you what they think they're about. Knowledge building to me is not only objective knowledge building, but subjective. I think that a practitioner who's engaged in work gets a lot of meaning out of the exercise of being able to talk to somebody about what he's doing, because that opportunity is very rare. These are things that people think about, but life is a how-to-do process and keeps you from thinking.

Chinlund   I think that there are ways of building into a program questions of how are you doing, what do you think about the program, a disciplined list of questions that provide feedback. In fact, a researcher could say to the inmate and staff, "I'm going to pose a collective anonymous set of questions to the people running this program, so maybe you can be more frank with me than you would be with then." There are a lot of ways that this process can dovetail with a program from the beginning.

DeLeon   Phoenix was one of the places I learned about what are the restrictions in research, how much of a demand you can make on staff, how many forms you can really deliver, how much information you should be gathering separate from what's naturally flowing. I mean these are important internal questions. All I'm saying again is that for the bottom-line type of evaluation you can limit yourself to "What are the questions that we're going to be able to address in year one?" and answer them. We can decide what are the specific goals in year one. And then how are we going to account for whether we reach those goals or not?

Toch   Supposing you achieve unanticipated goals?

DeLeon   That's dividends, sure.

Toch   But you see, this hypothesis testing makes the process of discovery a bit more difficult. If one has set out to answer the question, "Did I achieve these specified goals?" instead of a more open-ended approach, which *in addition* tries to track the process and find out what actually went on. . . .

DeLeon   You don't track processes until there are processes to be tracked. It's like fighting a fire in year one. You're going to try and track the firefighters in year one. The best people who do that, as a matter of fact, are journalists and poets, not researchers.

Barker   I couldn't agree more. I heard you say that originally, that it's a creative process in the first year and it musn't be intruded upon. And an example is this conference, which is a kind of creative act. If you had somebody immediately breathing down your neck—"What are the objectives?"—it wouldn't have gotten off the ground, or you'd have been inhibited in the next stage of the creative process.

Toch   But that's exactly what did happen at this conference, and you weren't inhibited. The tape recorder was on continuously, and I'm going to audit those tapes. There is no difference between my subcategorizing the ideas that came out of this conference, rearranging them, sorting them, trying to make sense out of them, and "research." I don't think it thwarts creativity.

Barker   How about back at the moment when you thought, in some half-baked way, "Gee, maybe we could . . . ," and you phoned Steve Chinlund. I don't think you should have been subjected to critical analysis while the idea was forming in your mind. I think delivery of a program in its first year is a kind of sensing, "Where do we move here?" What's our next move—I've got this flak coming from there and I've got to react here?" It's an intuitive kind of artistic endeavor.

Toch   Wouldn't it fascinate you to get some feeling for what goes on in that artistic endeavor?

DeLeon   That's journalistic writing.

Toch   I can't draw any line between sensitive journalism and process research.

Eisenberg   I'm really appalled, because I remember hearing this when I was in graduate school. The whole split between the artists and the experimenters, and never the two can meet—the creative process being mystical, and one that can't be measured. Well, if you can't measure it, then you can't have my money as its sponsor. You have an obligation to take what you want to do and make it come alive to me in such a way so that I can understand it, and I can have faith in it. And I don't think it's dirty for me to say to you, "Did it have an effect?"

I'm hearing that funding sources are irresponsible when they want to know, "Did it work?" And that they're unreasonable because, when you tell them that you're busy being creative, you can't give them a complete picture, they don't want to give you further support.

Toch · Even in the absence of sponsors, we should want all the knowledge we can somehow get. If we are committed to social learning, this commitment has to extend to ourselves. To maximize learning—including through the tools of social science—is the only way we know to keep alive our programs, the process of community building, and ourselves.

APPENDIX

A CONSUMER PERSPECTIVE

INTRODUCTION

A recurrent theme in this book is the need to attend to the "larger" environment into which the therapeutic community must tactfully insinuate itself and within which it must establish and maintain itself. The most obvious—possibly even trite—point is that enthusiasm, effectiveness, and sterling behavior are not keys to survival, and that recent history is a graveyard of meritorious experiments that were unceremoniously discontinued. Wherever such reverses have occurred, conspiratorial views arise about reactionary elements in the organization who are bent on assassinating all reformers, and who are inevitably successful in doing so. This view is particularly seductive in corrections, where we are apt to stereotype administrators and custodial staff as dinosaurs.[1]

An alternative view is implied at various points in this book, and one of the ways to pose this view is to raise the question of precipitation of failures by the eventual victims of those failures. The hypothesis would be that an examination of lost battles is bound to bring strategic errors to the surface, such as failures to inform or involve representatives of the prison setting in one's activities or inadequate attention to the creation of support systems in the shape of influential allies. The need for autopsies is particularly acute for therapeutic communities, because our social learning model—which is as applicable to the TC staff as it is to TC clients—directs us toward personal contributions to developing crises. The model invites us to evolve new interpersonal strategies through an understanding of past mistakes. It demands that we see ourselves as others do, which is difficult to do if we discount the threats that we pose, or undersell the unprecedented nature of demands we make on our environments.

This appendix represents a palliative to cynicism because it presents the views of a prison administrator (the prototypical ogre of the reform literature) who has not only accommodated a TC but is an articulate proponent of the TC concept. The statement is also of interest because it describes the experiences that documented and cemented support for the prison TC.

This appendix bears on the issue of TC cross-fertilization. It not only refers to graduates of TCs who became key figures in subsequent experi-

---

This section is from hearings before the U.S. Senate Subcommittee on Penitentiaries and Corrections of the Committee on the Judiciary, 95th Cong., 2d sess., on S.3227, August 2–3, 1978. Printed for use of the Committee on the Judiciary. Washington, D.C.: U. S. Government Printing Office, 1978.

ments, but tracks such individuals from prison to community and back, illustrating the network possibilities implicit in the TC modality.

A paradoxical note is that key figures of the Fort Grant program have undergone dramatic relapses, without endangering the program's tenure. We infer that with sensitively garnered support, a crisis-studded TC can survive where "successful" TC's have failed.

A WARDEN'S EXPERIENCE: Testimony of Cliff Anderson, Director, Fort Grant Training Center, Fort Grant, Arizona

I was asked to come before the committee to give a warden's view of what a program of this nature means to an institution, some of the ramifications that are necessary to implement such a program, some of the trust factors that are necessary, and hopefully to answer any questions that might be outstanding in your mind concerning the operation of such a program.

I have prepared a written statement that I have submitted for the record.

Senator Hatfield. Without objection, that will be made part of the record.

[Mr. Anderson's prepared statement follows his testimony.]

Mr. Anderson. In early 1974 I was privileged to attend one of the workshops at the Marion Institution to take part in a week-long program in the Asklepieion community. During this time I had an opportunity to watch the men in this unit work. I had the opportunity to see three or four of the men who had been in there 2 to 3 years perform what I felt was a miraculous change in attitude and behavior in probably the most hardcore group in the Federal system.

As a result of what I had seen and the experience in this program, Mr. Moran[2] and I decided we would try an experimental program at Fort Grant. Fort Grant is a minimum custody male institution. The setting is totally different from the maximum security at Marion.

The lack of some of the problems that were experienced at the maximum security such as housing, movement of population, and restrictions, we felt would greatly enhance the program at the minimum security level. We also felt that the program could be adapted to any custody level.

We started with Monte MacKenzie, a former inmate in that program. Monte started the program with 13 inmates and increased this number to 35 within a month's time. He stayed with us for approximately 6 months to get the program operational. He then left our unit and moved on to Phoenix to develop what is currently the OK Community.

At that time Mr. Carlson[3] agreed to send another inmate, Bill Smith, from the Marion program to Fort Grant on a transfer basis. We were able to use his service for approximately a year before he was eligible for, and made parole. Following his parole, Bill was added to our staff in a paid capacity. He is currently on parole and working as a member of our regular staff.

We have had approximately 189 men go through the program in this 3-year period. Of those, we know of only eight men who have returned to the prison. Of all the inmates whom we have contacted or have seen in the program, we have had only one man to date, including the Marion program or any other therapeutic community setting, who has ever attempted to escape or escaped from an institution. I think that is a remarkable thing.

We have 650 inmates in our minimum custody setting. About 65 of these are currently in the therapeutic program.

The disciplinary process within the institution for the general population consumes approximately half of each working day. From the therapeutic community group we were able to reduce that contact by almost 75 percent and has proved to be a major factor in control.

Participation in programs following or during the therapeutic process, such as vocational training, education, and continuing education, was increased by 50 percent on a voluntary basis.

The primary component on each one of these units is confidentiality, which was alluded to a little earlier. This does not hamper the operation of any institution. It does not present any problem—or has not presented any problem—administratively for me or my staff.

There are a couple of exceptions on confidentiality. If there is a forthcoming violation of a major rule, law, or an act which would bring harm to another person within the institution, these are excluded. That information is supposed to come forth anyway.

Other than that, the community is designed to address and not to gloss over. The communities are actually double penalty in many cases over the ordinary disciplinary process or dealt with in a different manner, in addition to the regular penalty. This has removed some of the problems that we were facing and given us another tool for administrative control.

This concludes my presentation and now I will be glad to answer any questions.

Senator Hatfield. Senator DeConcini?

Senator DeConcini. Warden Anderson, thank you for your testimony. The 600 men who are in there are felons and—

Mr. Anderson. Yes, sir, these are a cross section of the prison population who were initially committed to the maximum security unit at Florence.

Senator DeConcini. They are not what you would call low risk or anything like that?

Mr. Anderson. No. We have a cross section—

Senator DeConcini. Of all different kinds of inmates who are there? Is that right?

Mr. Anderson. Yes.

Senator DeConcini. Do you have any cost information about what it costs per inmate to hold them in your institution versus the maximum security and then breaking that down into the therapeutic community?

Mr. Anderson. The cost of incarceration for each inmate of maximum security is roughly between $8,000 and $9,000 per year. We can hold a man for approximately $6,000 to $7,000 per man per year in the institution and still provide vocational training, education, and the therapeutic process.

Costwise for staffing, there is one staff member who operates the therapeutic community. That is Bill Smith whom we transferred in. This is the only staff member assigned. Costwise you are dividing that by 65.

If we are able to keep two inmates out a year, we pay the cost of the operation of the program.

Senator DeConcini. Is this just funded out of your normal appropriation?

Mr. Anderson. The normal State appropriation, our normal operating budget.

Senator DeConcini. Since Mr. Moran left, has there been any lessening in enthusiasm about the program?

Mr. Anderson. No. It is at the same level.

Senator DeConcini. It is still going well?

Mr. Anderson. Yes.

Senator DeConcini. How does one get into the program?

Mr. Anderson. Entry into the program is strictly voluntary and the exit is also voluntary. The inmate has to have the option of coming in or, when he feels the need, he also has to have the option to be able to say, "I don't think this fits me and I want to go out." We have many cases who exit the program, remain out for a month, and then decide they want to go back in. We have to make allowances for that entry-exit process in order to get the man sufficiently motivated.

There are many reasons why the man would want to go in. It might be pointed out that there are no provisions nor concessions made that this program in any way will affect the length of sentence or be given any weight by the parole board for parole release. It is strictly for their own benefit.

Senator DeConcini. Is there a process of getting in? Do they make application? Do they just come over and tell you they want to get in and then they are transferred? How does it work?

Mr. Anderson. Administratively this may sound a little strange but I have very little to do with the process of getting in. The inmate indicates an interest that he would like to go in. They must attend a preorientation series of classes to enter the program.

Senator DeConcini. How long is that?

Mr. Anderson. That is usually about a week long.

His counselor or caseworker will represent his desires to the classification committee and have him classified from job assignment into the program.

Senator Hatfield. This is a job assignment?

Mr. Anderson. It is a job assignment. It is a 24-hour living situation.

He may or may not have other duties assigned to him while in the program. Approximately 50 percent of the inmates devote 24 hours a day to the program. The other 50 percent, usually those who have been in for 6 or 8 months, are able to master some of the information and take a little less study, and are able to move into some vocational classes and some work assignments within the institution for a period of 4 or 5 hours a day.

Senator Hatfield. This program is an alternative, for instance, to kitchen duty?

Mr. Anderson. Yes. It is an alternative to education; it is an alternative to a general work assignment, and anything else.

Senator Hatfield. Is each inmate as he comes into the institution given the opportunity to know about this program? Are they recruited? How is that done?

Mr. Anderson. We have a regular orientation process for each group of inmates who come in from the maximum security prison. We present an overview of each of the programs. Hopefully, what we try to do is motivate them to go into something in which they are interested. We think we can get the most out of them if they will take an area of their own personal interest.

We try to explain what is available to them. Then they have a chance to check this out on the compound—to check to see what the rating is.

One of the biggest problems of the program is that as a man starts to do things for himself or as he assumes more and more responsibility, he also picks up labels from the other inmates. There is very heavy peer pressure not to enter programs that have direct impact on his performance within the institution. He becomes a snitch. He becomes an administration man.

Senator Hatfield. I spent years on the Sentence Review Division of our Supreme Court. I have more time in prison than most burglars, I think.

In any event, how do you resolve this conflict? In order for this program to operate, as you say, you have to have trust. On the other hand, the institution has its own rules. The institution runs for its own benefit, rather than that of anybody in it. That is not only true for prisons, but hospitals and everything else.

How do you overcome that conflict to make this program successful in your institution?

Mr. Anderson. Of course, I had a chance to take part myself in the community workshop and I think that is a very important factor. I am probably one of the few wardens who did go in and sit down and let those guys scream at me for a week.

Senator Hatfield. They put the judges in jail in Reno. That is part of the program there.

Mr. Anderson. That is a very effective part of the training process. It is difficult for an administrator of a prison to be able to allow the amount of autonomy that is necessary to one of these programs and unless he has become involved somewhat himself first to see what it is and to see what he is trusting.

The primary component for the whole operation is a clean environment. That responsibility is more than just a custody responsibility that is imposed upon the staff.

We are using an ex-inmate for the staff member. One of his primary responsibilities is to insure me that the environment is clean. That does not take the therapeutic community out away from the rules and regulations of the institution. They are subject to the same search procedures and the same types of rules as every other inmate.

They do go on to the regular compound for their meals and for their educational classes. They are not isolated into a removed unit.

Senator Hatfield. It does not resolve into a "con-boss" system? It seems to me that could be a possibility in that situation.

Mr. Anderson. If we had only clinical psychologists or college trained people, we could get into the "con-boss" routine. It is hard for a con to con a con very long. That is my feeling with the men I have had.

Eight of the graduates of the program are now working in the OK Community. It is very difficult for the guys to come out and run a con job on them. They have already been there. They can do it on me very easily or any other administrator. I expect to get beat once a day.

Senator DeConcini. Mr. Chairman, I have no further questions.

I visited the program there and certainly want to compliment Warden Anderson for participating himself and also for the tremendous support he has given it.

I do have one last question. Is it your belief that it would be advantageous to have legislation in the Federal area for such communities in order to give them more support and resources?

Mr. Anderson. It would be very, very important. It would be very, very helpful.

Also, to bring up a point that was addressed a little bit earlier, there is a need to have a structure as you have designed in the bill. There is a very definite purpose for that—to keep the type of people, plus the training directors that you need. These are not necessarily as selected by the American Psychological Association. Most of the directors of the program that you are looking [into] should be ex-inmates or people who have taken the time to become personally involved and know the trauma that is involved in this program.

Senator DeConcini. So you need the inmates really involved in the administration?

Mr. Anderson. You definitely need the inmates in the director's position.

Senator DeConcini. Once they have made that choice and put it together.

Mr. Anderson. That is right.

Senator DeConcini. I have no further questions. Thank you, Mr. Chairman.

Senator Hatfield. Mr. Tim Hart is our staff director. He has some questions.

Mr. Hart. Warden Anderson, based on your experience, what is the ideal size of a therapeutic community; that is, director and staff to inmate population?

Mr. Anderson. Approximately 30 to 1 is an operable unit. If you get beyond 30, you are straining your therapist. He almost has to work from 18 to 20 hours a day if you get beyond 30. Bill Smith has many times spent many more hours than that, but it is not satisfactory.

I would say that actually 25 would be the best number that you could get.

Mr. Hart. Does that include staff assistance in the sense that you have inmates as staff; that is, trainees?

Mr. Anderson. What we need to understand is that the program itself is a developmental process. They begin with the study of transactional analysis and develop into coordinators within the unit. The inmates themselves then take on responsible positions in the unit.

As they complete a course—roughly 18 months—they begin to assume some of the responsibilities from the program directors. In and of itself it should be a self-perpetuating program.

Mr. Hart. When you are talking about 30 to 1 or 25 to 1, you are talking about a program director and then residents or inmates at various stages of completion of the program?

Mr. Anderson. Yes.

Mr. Hart. Is there an approximate fraction—three levels?

Mr. Anderson. There are three inmates who will assist each director. That is what we use now. It seems to be a very workable formula.

Mr. Hart. At its initiation the program at Marion, a maximum security institution, was used as an alternative to segregation. Do you believe that is wise either in a maximum or minimum security setting?

Mr. Anderson. No, I do not. I do not believe that you can force anybody into treatment at all, nor do I believe you can have any impact on that inmate's behavior. It has to be a free choice, whatever his motivation for going into the unit. We do not at our institution offer it as an alternative for disciplinary action. It has to be of his own free choice. He may be wanting to look good at the parole board or have whatever other reason, but that is not the reason that we give for his going in there.

Senator Hatfield. Thank you very, very much.

[Mr. Anderson's prepared statement follows:]

Prepared Statement of Clifford W. Anderson

During late 1974 after realizing the void which existed in treatment of convicted felons within the Arizona Department of Corrections a joint effort was made by former Director John Moran and I to bring about an experimental program which appeared to be working very efficiently at the U.S. Penitentiary at Marion, Illinois.

The program appeared to be so effective that we began immediately to make arrangements for trained personnel to begin a duplicate model at Fort Grant minimum security facility.

The program began under the direction of Monte McKinsey a former inmate of the Marion program with 13 members from the general population. The program soon increased to 35 for several months when we were able to obtain the transfer of Bill Smith from Marion.

Monte turned over the directors role to Bill and moved on to Phoenix to establish the present O.K. Community.

Soon after Monte left the population increased to 77 inmates but by necessity was reduced to 55 due to a lack of trained staff to bring about effective control of "clean environment."

To date, 189 inmates have spent at least 6 months in the program prior to release. Of these, 8 are known to have returned to prison. This would amount to approximately 4.5%. If we assume an error of 100% or 16 recidivist we are still looking at a figure of less than 10%.

The figures presented are extremely crude due to vague and ineffective follow-up data collection methods, but at its worst there appears to be over a 50% reduction in those returning to prison as well as the reduction in the nature of the crime.

As a prison superintendent in the Arizona Department of Corrections I have had ample opportunity at this point to test the concept presented by Senator DeConcini for the past few years. My own experience coupled with the statistics gained from the same type program, I feel, lends considerable credence to the theory that the therapeutic community concept can be successfully adapted to any prison setting with high expectation for success in rehabilitation.

The original programs at Marion, Illinois Federal Penitentiary was developed in one of our finest maximum security facilities. The program developed at Fort Grant, Arizona was modeled very closely after the Marion unit with the major difference being the custody status of the prisoners involved and this is minimum.

The Fort Grant program required adherence to all institutional rules and regulations as in any other program with the result effect being a 75%

reduction in disciplinary action appearing before the institutional disciplinary committee.

A noticeable reduction in hostility level was experienced by the custody personnel in dealing with this segment of the inmate population.

To date only one inmate has been involved in an escape attempt, either at Marion or at Fort Grant due to the ability of the therapeutic process to address the problems, either real or imagined, which cause an inmate to arrive at the breaking point of escape.

Based upon my personal experiences as a Superintendent in the operation of a prison, my personal observation of behavioral change and the limited statistical data available, I would highly recommend this form of treatment to you, not as a panacea but rather as a meaningful tool for rehabilitation. This can only be effected by trained personnel who have experienced the trauma of having had the gates of prison slam behind them and who have demonstrated the perseverance necessary to bring about a self perpetuation of the program.

NOTES

1. Among pessimistic reappraisals of TC failures is Studt, E., Messinger, S. H., and Wilson, T. P. *C-Unit: Search for Community in Prison.* New York: Russell Sage Foundation, 1968. For a nihilistic statement about prison reform by an ex-reformer, see: Murton, T. S. *The Dilemma of Prison Reform.* New York: Holt, Rinehart and Winston, 1976.

2. John J. Moran was Director of the Arizona Department of Corrections, and he currently heads the Rhode Island corrections system.

3. Norman A. Carlson is Director of the U.S. Bureau of Prisons.

CONFERENCE PARTICIPANTS

Following is a list of participants in the Conference on Therapeutic Communities for Offenders, Institute of Man and Sciences, Renselaerville, N.Y., December 1978.

Elliott Barker

Jack Birnbaum, *Associate Commissioner NYS Department of Correctional Services*

Dennie Briggs

Stephen Chinlund

Cheryl Clark, *Network Project Director NYS Commission of Correction*

George DeLeon, *Director of Research Phoenix House Foundation, Inc.*

John Devlin, *Director, The Portage Foundation, Montreal, Canada*

Robert Eisenberg, *Director, State Facilities Bureau NYS Commission of Correction*

Edward Elwin, *Executive Director NYS Board of Parole*

J. Douglas Grant

Maxwell Jones

Robert Levinson

Fritz Redl

Mitchell Rosenthal, *President, Phoenix House Foundation, Inc.*

Marguerite Saunders, *Deputy Commissioner for Treatment and Rehabilitation Services, NYS Division of Substance Abuse Services*

Ann Schmidt, *Special Assistant, Law Enforcement Assistance Association*

Hans Toch

Jack Wright, M.D., *Assistant Commissioner, NYS Department of Mental Hygiene*

ABOUT THE EDITOR AND CONTRIBUTORS

HANS TOCH, Ph. D., is Professor of Psychology, School of Criminal Justice, State University of New York at Albany. His books include *Living in Prison, Psychology of Crime and Criminal Justice, Violent Men, Agents of Change* (with J. D. Grant and R. Galvin), *Peacekeeping, the Social Psychology of Social Movements*, and *Men in Crisis*, winner of the 1977 Hadley Cantril Memorial Award.

ELLIOTT BARKER, M.D., is founder and acting director of the Social Therapy Unit, Penetang, an innovative mental health center for violent offenders in Penetanguishene, Ontario. Dr. Barker's work has been widely emulated, and his international reputation partly derives from descriptive and theoretical work relating to the Penetang experiment.

DENNIE BRIGGS is Professor of Human Justice, Governor's State University of Illinois, and Project Coordinator at the Social Action Research Center, California. Mr. Briggs directed the therapeutic community at Chino prison. His books include *Dealing With Deviants* and *In Place of Prison*. Mr. Briggs has also been a practicing clinical psychologist.

STEPHEN CHINLUND is Chairman of the New York State Commission of Correction. He is a graduate of Harvard, Union Theological Seminary, and the Columbia School of Social Work. Mr. Chinlund is an ordained member of the clergy and an experienced correctional innovator. His past positions include those of Executive Director of Big Brothers, Inc., Superintendent of Taconac Correctional Facility, Director of Manhattan Rehabilitation Center, Co-founder of Reality House, and Assistant Director of Exodus House. Mr. Chinlund's writings have focused on issues of drug rehabilitation.

J. DOUGLAS GRANT is best known as Project Director of the New Careers Development Project and as co-originator of the Interpersonal Maturity Level Classification Scheme for offenders. Former Chief of Research for the California Department of Corrections, he is currently President of Social Action Research Center. His books include *Agents of Change* and *The Value of Youth*.

MAXWELL JONES, M.D., is the originator of the therapeutic community concept and a leader in the implementation of this concept in mental hospitals and other rehabilitation settings. He has written extensively in the area of social psychiatry and is a recipient of many honors, including the Isaac Ray Award of the American Psychiatric Association.

ROBERT B. LEVINSON, Ph. D., is Deputy Assistant Director, Correctional Programs Division, and Administrator, Inmate Program Services, at the Federal Bureau of Prisons. Dr. Levinson is outgoing president of the American Association of Correctional Psychologists and the recipient of two distinguished contribution awards. His scholarly papers deal with issues in clinical psychology, with prisons, and with applications of the former to the latter.

FRITZ REDL, PH. D., is an internationally famous psychoanalyst and educator known for landmark application of psychoanalysis to the reeducation of delinquents. He has pioneered the use of residential treatment facilities for delinquent youths. His books (including *Children Who Hate*) have become classics in their field. Dr. Redl is past president of the American Orthopsychiatric Association, and recipient of many honors and awards.

PETER SCHARF, PH. D., is Associate Professor in the Program of Social Ecology, University of California at Irvine. Professor Scharf's most recent books are *Democracy and Prisons* (with Joseph Hickey) and *Readings in Moral Education*. Professor Scharf is co-founder of the Just Community at Niantic Prison, and is known for other extensions of moral education to criminal justice settings.

ROBERT H. SCOTT is a professor at the School of Criminal Justice, Michigan State University. He is former Associate Director of Corrections in charge of the Youth Division, Michigan Department of Corrections, and has served on the Michigan Parole Board. Mr. Scott's innovative contributions have earned him the Silver Medallion from the National Conference of Christians and Jews for "outstanding service to the cause of brotherhood."